The Dark Side of the Moon

The Dark Side of the Moon

A New Edition

Zoë Zajdlerowa

Edited by

John Coutouvidis and Thomas Lane

HARVESTER WHEATSHEAF

New York • London • Toronto • Sydney • Tokyo

First published in 1946
This edition published in 1989 by
Harvester Wheatsheaf,
66 Wood Lane End , Hemel Hempstead,
Hertfordshire HP2 4RG
A division of
Simon & Schuster International Group

Typeset in 10/12pt Plantin
by Photoprint, Torquay, Devon

Printed and bound in Great Britain by
BPCC Wheatons Ltd, Exeter

British Library Cataloguing in Publication Data

Zajdlerowa, Zoë
    The dark side of the moon: a new edition
    1. Poland. Political events, 1939–1945
    I. Title   II. Coutouvidis, John   III. Lane, A. Thomas
    943.8'053

    ISBN–0–7108–1373–2

1 2 3 4 5 94 93 92 91 90 89

To the memory of Zoë Zajdlerowa,
and in honour of those whose sufferings
she brought into the light of history
from the dark side of the moon

Contents

Editors' Acknowledgements

Specialists in the history of modern Poland will be familiar with *The Dark Side of the Moon*. However, when it was first published in 1946 it attracted the attention of a general readership, having been reviewed in the weeklies by, among others, Kingsley Martin and Edward Crankshaw. One of our objectives in preparing this new edition is to make it available to a new generation of general readers at a time of intense Western interest in political developments in Eastern Europe and the Soviet Union.

Accompanying *perestroika* is a reconstruction of recent history. Those who read this book will see more clearly the striking significance of two news items in March 1989. In the first the Polish government spokesman, Jerzy Urban, accused the Soviet Union for the first time of having committed a massacre of more than 4,000 Polish officers at Katyń near Smolensk between 1939 and 1943. The second report announced the posthumous rehabilitation by the Polish government of five Polish émigré leaders who were stripped of their citizenship after the Second World War. One of the five is General Władysław Anders, commander of the Polish army in the Soviet Union in 1941–2, a bitter opponent of the Soviet-imposed government in Poland after the war, and a major figure in the events described below. Here, surely, is conclusive evidence of a deep-rooted historical revisionism taking place in the Communist Party in Poland which, if reciprocated by the Soviet Union, may lead to a reformation in relations between the states of Eastern Europe.

However, there are historical road-blocks in the way of reconstruction which cannot easily be pushed aside. To understand these obstructions a knowledge of what happened to the Poles and other Baltic peoples in 1939 and 1940 is indispensable. A reappraisal of the text of *The Dark Side of the Moon* will contribute to that understanding.

We have a second reason for wishing to reissue the work on this fiftieth anniversary of the invasion of Poland by Nazi Germany and the Soviet Union. Numerous conversations with Polish exiles in our separate localities have reinforced our belief in the credibility of *The Dark Side of the Moon*. It is a record of personal courage and human resilience, and a manual for survival under the harshest conditions. It stands alongside literature from the concentration camps, shedding light on the capacity of human beings to withstand and even overcome the most appalling circumstances. Those who survived are now, for the most part, elderly. They endured intense heartache, disappointment and, indeed, despair, but accepted their fate with stoicism and fortitude. Despite their resilience they are conscious of themselves as a people without a history, anonymous, unrecognized, buried under official and historical indifference. The republication of this book, with its new Introduction and Afterword, may represent a small reparation to them and their families for what they have lost.

In the preparation of this new edition we have incurred a number of debts. We wish to express our gratitude for information and insights to Robin Booth, Phoebe Winch, Mavis Pindard and Elizabeth Stevens. Neil Ascherson supplied new evidence about Zoë Zajdlerowa's war-time experiences which we received too late to incorporate in our Introduction. We have added the reference to Madame Zajdlerowa's autobiographical work to the Bibliography. For typing and retyping the manuscript in a succession of versions we depended on the skill and efficiency of Molly Kempton. Paul Taylor and Sophie Coutouvidis were indispensable in preparing the maps. We are most grateful to the staff of the Polish Institute and Sikorski Museum, the Polish Library, the Polish Underground Study Trust and the Public Record Office for help and advice. Finally, we wish to thank two successive editors at Harvester Wheatsheaf, Richard Purslow and Farrell Burnett, for spotting the value of the book and agreeing with us that the time was ripe for a new edition. Any errors or sins of omission or commission are, of course, solely our responsibility.

It is a pleasure to acknowledge financial assistance from our respective institutions. The Research Committee of the University of Bradford awarded a grant to facilitate research in British government records of the period and some of the costs of publication were defrayed by the Small Grants Fund at Staffordshire Polytechnic and the Department of European Studies at Bradford.

Our greatest debt is to the survivors who, in conversations, have confirmed the truth of the reconstruction of their experiences in *The Dark Side of the Moon*. Here is a brief but powerful endorsement by one survivor, Bogumiła Wacewicz, which deserves to be recorded:

> Just as time heals the wounds in a person's psyche, the passage of time blunts the mind and erases the experiences and facts that have been lived through. Yet it is sometimes possible to come across material which may help to brush aside the cobwebs of forgetfulness. *The Dark Side of the Moon* has this property; reading the book, every experience, now so distant, emerges alive and real.

The cause of this reaction, in my view, is the manner in which the book is drafted, facts being presented with penetrating clarity and accuracy, put together with correct and cogent assessment of the contemporary situation. Its general drift must astound every reader! Especially those who experienced this chapter of Poland's tragic history. This book is frightening in its realism! It also helps to restore the balance between the countless books recounting the martyrology of the victims of Nazi policies in Poland and the very few describing the Soviet occupation of Poland and its equally hellish consequences.

April 1989

List of Illustrations

Plates
(between pages 98 and 99)

Zoë Zajdlerowa.

'Looking through photographs of these children . . . is like looking through a register of human skeletons. . . .'

Soviet soldiers sporting watches.

'We lived in tents without floors. The tents stood on frozen mud.'

'The wretchedness of the prisoners' clothing is unimaginable. . . .'

'The patients lie about on the floor, sometimes covered by a piece of blanket, often not covered at all.'

A border post on the Nazi–Soviet frontier in Poland near Małkinia, September 1939.

Reunion outside Tehran in 1942.

Introduction

In January 1989 the Central Committee of the Communist Party of the USSR announced the mass rehabilitation of millions of victims of Stalin's purges. These unfortunates had been sentenced to death, corrective labour camps or internal exile in the 1930s and '40s. The announcement stated that the rehabilitation applied to Soviet citizens, but not to those guilty of treason, Nazi criminals, or 'participants in nationalistic bands'.[1] At the time of the announcement it was unclear whether the rehabilitation would apply to the more than one million former Polish citizens who were deported to the Soviet Union in 1940 and 1941. Inhabitants of the eastern provinces of the Polish state in 1939, they had witnessed the invasion of their country by the Red Army on 17 September 1939. A few weeks later, on 29 November, Soviet citizenship was bestowed upon them by law. It would appear that this compulsory citizenship might be the means of their rehabilitation fifty years later. West Europeans, who have been encouraged by the recent reform movement in the Soviet Union under Mr Gorbachov, may be optimistic about the rehabilitation of these Polish deportees. Sceptical Poles will be more cautious.

The story of the imprisonment and transportation of more than one million Poles and their subsequent consignment to penal camps and other places of exile in the Soviet Union was first told in English by the anonymous author of *The Dark Side of the Moon*. Despite many difficulties the book was completed in the winter of 1944, just over three years after the last of the mass deportations, and a little more than two years after the second evacuation of Polish citizens from Kazakhstan to Persia in August 1942. Memories were fresh then, and the author could call on numerous testimonies to help her reconstruct the course of events. We now know that the author was Zoë Zajdlerowa, the daughter of a Protestant clergyman in Ireland, who had married a Pole, Aleksander Zajdler, in the 1930s and had gone to live with him in Poland. In the 1930s she had published seven books, six of them novels under the pseudonym of Martin Hare. Her considerable talents as an evocative writer are evident in *The Dark Side of the Moon*, but she did not use these talents to over-dramatize

1

or exaggerate her accounts of Polish experiences. Their accuracy is confirmed by many subsequent descriptions of deportations and penal camps in the Soviet Union, from both Soviet and non-Soviet sources.[2] In fact, considering its terrifying subject matter, the book is remarkably sober and restrained.

Zoë Zajdlerowa had no first-hand experience of deportation or exile in the Soviet Union. It appears that she escaped from Soviet-occupied Poland to the still independent state of Lithuania and from there to England in late 1940. *En route* she was separated from her husband and was never to be re-united with him. Penniless and suffering from a head wound, she sought help from her literary agent Spencer Curtis Brown, who gave her a room in his house in London until she moved to her own flat in Chalk Farm. After working briefly in munitions with many other Poles she became a translator and then accepted a job as a reader at Curtis Brown.

Someone who knew her well after her arrival in London was Curtis Brown's daughter, Phoebe, who now, as Mrs Phoebe Winch, has been a most helpful informant on Madame Zajdlerowa's life during this period. She recalls her at this time being 'hugely Polish; one might say she had become Polish with a fervour and a zeal rather like a religious convert and spoke Polish perfectly'. She was intensely involved in the Polish community and her flat in Chalk Farm always seemed full of Poles. She was certainly great friends with Madame Sikorska, the wife of General Sikorski, the Prime Minister of the Polish government-in-exile.[3]

It is not clear how she got the idea for a book on the terrible experiences of Poles deported to the Soviet Union. It is likely that she met some of the deportees in England in 1942 or 1943 after the evacuation of about one hundred thousand of them via Persia. Some of the military personnel were sent to Great Britain by sea to reinforce the Polish armed forces there. After she finished working in munitions she did a lot of translating, for friends and perhaps professionally, and it is quite possible that some of the personal accounts in the book derive from this source.

However, many thousands of personal narratives and testimonies were made in the Soviet Union and in Persia by Poles who had escaped death in the camps and presumably welcomed the opportunity to create a record of their lives under Soviet rule. This information was well known in leading Polish circles in London and Sikorski referred to it in conversation with Churchill and Eden in March 1942 when he revealed that he had stopped publication of a 'red book' which described the 'unbelievable brutality' and 'barbarian methods' of the Bolshevik treatment of Poles in the Soviet Union.[4] It was stated in the first edition that Zoë Zajdlerowa had the confidence of General Sikorksi in compiling her book, and that he had given instructions that she be given access to official documents.[5] But there is no suggestion that the General inspired the idea, or that what she wrote was derived from the 'red book', even though both relied on similar evidence. Maybe Madame Zajdlerowa herself was so moved by what she heard and read, which was very much at variance with Western public opinion about the great Soviet ally at that time, that she determined to place a record before the public. As a professional writer with a good command of Polish she was well equipped for the task.

There is the further possibility that Spencer Curtis Brown, who had joined army intelligence and was seconded to the Polish military authorities in London, was aware of the documentation about Soviet treatment of Polish deportees and encouraged Zoë Zajdlerowa to write a book based on the Polish records. As a friend, as an army officer with strong connections in the Polish military, an enemy of Soviet totalitarianism and as Madame Zajdlerowa's former agent with first-hand knowledge of her literary gifts, he had an interest in the publication of a book illuminating the Soviet system of penal camps and internal exile. In the epilogue of the first edition, of which he was the author, Curtis Brown warned of the dangers of Soviet totalitarianism to individual freedom, 'of the constant subjection of every faculty to an alien and hostile doctrinal system, and the absolute cessation of any kind of private life'. Soviet domination of Eastern Europe at the end of the war, he argued, marked the end of an era, and perhaps portended the destruction of European culture.[6]

It was this possibility that interested and appalled T. S. Eliot. It is probable that Curtis Brown sent the manuscript of *The Dark Side of the Moon* to Eliot as a director of the publishing house, Faber and Faber. They issued the book in 1946. Eliot supplied its preface:[7]

The manuscript of this book came into my hands over a year ago. The book is the story of what happened to Poland, and of what happened to innumerable Poles, between 1939 and 1945. It is also a book about the U.S.S.R. It is incidentally a book about Europe – not the Europe with which we were familiar in the past, but the Europe in which we now have to live. The aim of the book is to provide a record and to state a case: as dispassionately and fairly as possible for a book, written by one of a people who have suffered so deeply as the Poles have suffered. I think that the author displays admirable moderation. The case is here stated: if there is a case for the other side, we have yet to hear it.

The contributor of a prefatory note to a book of this kind need not rehearse its contents. What is more important is to dispose of certain obstructions which may present themselves in the minds of some readers. There are those whose attention is engrossed by the immediate present, for whom each new iniquity obliterates the memory of its predecessor, and through whose minds a succession of sensations, apprehensions, and grievances has passed since the

events here related took place: to them this review will seem only a document
to be filed for the use, or for the curiosity, of future students of history. That
this record should be preserved and meditated upon by posterity is certainly
to be desired; and if it had been written only for that purpose it would still
have been worth the writing. To others, the book will be distasteful as a story
of suffering which is past, as an inventory of grief which cannot now be
appeased, and therefore might as well be forgotten. But even if concerned
with wrongs which cannot now be amended, the subject matter is not such as
we in this country have the right to avert our eyes from. It is not for the nation
which declared war upon Germany because of her violation of the Polish
frontier, and which subsequently was glad to avail itself of Polish soldiers and
airmen whose gallantry and sacrifice have served our cause and not their own
– it is not for us to forget Poland, or to decline to contemplate now, facts
which were given no prominence in the Press when they were news.[8] This
reason alone would justify the publication of this book in England. . . .

I have permitted myself these general observations, as a preparation for the
statement that this is not a political book. It is in part a record of "politics";
but the book as a whole is a document for the study of the methods of
destroying a culture, one pattern of life, and imposing another pattern. We do
not yet know to what extent such a transformation can be effected; we do not
know to what extent a people can be altered by the power of planned
ignorance.[9] The mutilation of a people by the destruction of its upper and
middle classes is serious enough: but that is an injury which a people can
inflict upon itself. Whether a culture can survive systematic destruction from
without, depends less upon its forces of active revolt, than upon the
stubbornness of the unconscious masses, the tenacity with which they cling to
habits and customs, their instinctive resistance to change.[10] A year ago, this
would have seemed to be a book only about Poland: it is now a book about one
instance of a general problem. And the problem in its most general form is not
merely the problem of the U.S.S.R.

For a European, the problem is whether Europe can survive. I do not
mean, of course, merely the physical survival or the material comfort of the
inhabitants, but the survival of the civilization of Western Europe.[11]

In agreeing to write a preface in this way Eliot set his seal on the book as
a dispassionate and moderate record of 'the methods of destroying a
culture . . . and imposing another pattern'; like Curtis Brown, Eliot
believed there was a question mark about the survival of European culture
in the light of the effective methods of suppression used by totalitarian
systems of both Right and Left.

But the heart of the book is not a disquisition on culture but a deeply
compassionate account of what happened to people subjected to almost
inconceivable hardship and deprivation. It was not just men, not even
perhaps mainly men, who suffered but women and children too, and some
of their stories are told in what follows. One witness, after intense physical

mistreatment and illness, commented that it is almost impossible to destroy the human body; on the contrary, most of the evidence presented by Zoë Zajdlerowa shows how easy it was, and how many hundreds of thousands of Polish deportees failed to survive the ordeal of prison, penal camp and exile, extremes of cold and heat, beatings and starvation, disease and epidemics, mental anguish and separation from loved ones.[12] Apparently Madame Zajdlerowa found the book difficult to write and the subject matter, as revealed to her in the written testimonies and in conversation, extremely harrowing, touching not only her humanity but her Polish patriotism, which is to be understood not as a crude and chauvinistic nationalism, but as a deep love for her adopted country and the people she had met there. Phoebe Winch believes that it was Curtis Brown who encouraged her to keep on; indeed, that the idea of the book may have been his in the first place. Even so, it was her physical weakness and emotional distress that delayed completion of the book, rather than a lack of belief in it on her part. One can infer that she saw the work as primarily an historical record of a major episode in modern Polish history, recounted by the participants who were, on the one hand, highly educated and literary people and, on the other, ordinary workers 'by hand or brain', unaccustomed to writing their own history, but perhaps glad of this opportunity to leave a record of the catastrophic and monstrous events which had afflicted them since September 1939.

We may also suppose that Zajdlerowa intended her book to be a memorial to the hundreds of thousands of Poles who met their end in Soviet penal establishments or who, after surviving those horrors, died of starvation or disease in their journeys to Polish areas of concentration in south-east Russia. She may also have had in mind those who were held in Russia after the evacuation of their countrymen and forced to take Soviet citizenship for the second time. Furthermore, during the composition of the book she did not know the whereabouts of her husband or even whether he was still alive. In this personal sense the book symbolized her continued fidelity to him by revealing to the world the pain inflicted on his country and people. We may assume that the anonymity of the book's author was preserved in order to protect her husband, if he were still alive, from reprisals by the authorities.

We cannot be certain about her motives, but we can be sure that she provided, and still provides, the basis for serious thinking about the Soviet Union. What the Polish deportees saw of Russia was, in the words of Arthur Koestler, 'as remote from the Western observer as the dark side of the moon from the star-gazer's telescope'.[13] Yet their accounts were not embroidered or exaggerated and their essential honesty was recognized by contemporary reviewers. Their truth was not the whole truth about the

Soviet Union, but it was a truth which had been unknown, or rejected as defamatory, by wide sections of Western opinion up to that time. In the light of it some serious re-assessment of the Soviet Union was demanded. One specific question seemed to require an answer: was there any difference between the Nazis and the Bolsheviks? In trying to formulate a dispassionate and honest answer to that question, people had to discard idealistic or diabolistic stereotypes, drawing conclusions from a careful analysis of the evidence. Many of those who had been accustomed to thinking of the Soviet Union as a brave new world found the task too difficult and preferred to denounce the Poles as fascist propagandists. But, as Kingsley Martin observed, 'there was no more reason why British Marxists should defend the NKVD than why members of the Church of England should justify the Spanish Inquisition'.[14]

To assess the charges of falsification, distortion or exaggeration we need to consider Zajdlerowa's method of selecting and presenting the evidence, which she obtained from 'very many hundreds of first-hand accounts' by Polish men, women and teenagers, of their experiences in the Soviet Union after arrest or deportation. She asks us to believe that those accounts are representative, that 'in the nature of things they set forth and describe the experience of those hundreds of thousands of others, their companions at every stage' and that out of the great mass of evidence which has been available, 'no single detail has been chosen to appear which is not of universal application'. She further gives her 'solemn engagement' that the whole of the evidence 'has been subjected to the most searching and scrupulous examination' and that 'not one word has been added and from it not one word (unless otherwise stated in the text) has been taken away'.[15] We are asked to rely, in fact, on the author's integrity and judgement. Furthermore, Zajdlerowa employed the device of recreating in her own words the essence of an experience which had been described in the numerous accounts which lay before her, perhaps only with variations in detail. Here she drew on her skills as a novelist, identifying with the experiences of others but using her own words to tell their collective story. It is clear that when she had available a well-written, vivid account of an episode, perhaps transport by ship on the Sea of Okhotsk, or the struggle for survival on a collective farm in a remote region of Kazakhstan, she would include it unchanged. But she was understandably tempted to dispense with more prosaic, halting or inarticulate accounts which seemed to her not to convey the drama or emotional intensity, the pain and deprivation, which the witnesses must have felt. In adopting this method she spoke to the reader's sympathies and imagination and she captured one important aspect of the truth. She did not burden her reader with a multitude of repetitive, plainly factual and badly-written accounts. But there are obvious dangers, as well as advantages, in this procedure. Individuals differ enormously in their responses to events, as we have discovered from our own interviews with survivors of the deportations. A prosaic account may not necessarily indicate an inability to express feelings adequately but rather that the emotional and imaginative response to what was happening was different from what Zajdlerowa supposed it to have been. Criticism of this approach, therefore, concentrates on Zajdlerowa's assumptions about the probable emotional response to events on the part of participants. It does not question that the events described took place or that her composite accounts of the events themselves are essentially accurate.

Criticism of Zajdlerowa's methods may have been more convincing when the book was first published. There was little evidence available in the West at that time about Soviet methods of transporting whole nationality groups, about prisons and interrogations, penal camps and places of exile. The numerous accounts of these phenomena appearing in the West since 1946 have abundantly confirmed the truth of Zajdlerowa's work. Those contemporary critics who affirmed that her methodology had transformed what could have been 'a dreary and sickening citation of repetitive horrors' into a work of art, could now add that it is a work of art whose essential veracity has been vindicated.[16]

Only a work of art could do justice to the terrible events which engulfed Poland in 1939. We in the West emphasize the brutally swift invasion of Poland by the Nazis on 1 September which triggered the British and French ultimata to Germany on 3 September and the ensuing state of war. We tend to ignore or pass over lightly the subsequent partition of Poland between Germany and the Soviet Union. This is partly the result of the Soviet Union and Great Britain uniting against Germany after the Nazi attack on the Soviet Union on 22 June 1941. It is also a consequence of the enormous and justified attention given to German treatment of Jews and Poles, first in the German area of occupation and then in the whole of Poland after the attack on Russia. The determination of post-war generations to reveal the full depths of Nazi brutality absorbed energy and diverted the investigative impulse away from the Soviet period of occupation which extended from September 1939 to June 1941. More than this, Western opinion was disposed to recognize the validity of Soviet claims to some, if not all, of Poland's eastern provinces.

This fourth partition of Poland, like its predecessors in the eighteenth century, extinguished the flame of independence in the Polish state. The First World War, which had resulted in the defeat of Germany and Austria–Hungary, and in revolution in Russia (the three powers which had absorbed Polish territory in the eighteenth century), opened the way for the declaration of Polish independence in November 1918. In the next three years Poland was able to define her boundaries by means of armed conflicts with her neighbours, the most important of these being the Polish–Soviet war of 1919–20, resulting in the defeat of the Red Army and concluding with the Treaty of Riga on 18 March 1921. The eastern frontier of the Polish state (see map 1) was set at between 100 and 150 miles west of the frontier of the Polish Commonwealth of 1772 before the first partition, but it still included part of Western Ukraine and of Western White Ruthenia (Byelorussia). These so-called borderlands (*Kresy*) fell to Poland as the result of war; they would not have been acquired if the

Map 1   Poland after the fourth partition, September 1939.

proposed Soviet–Polish armistice line (the 'Curzon line') of 10 June 1920 had been accepted by the Poles as the basis for their eastern frontier. However, the severe Soviet peace terms were rejected and the Poles fought on.

By 1921 the newly-independent Polish state had established itself behind agreed boundaries. This is not the place to consider the attempts of Poland in the inter-war years to strengthen her independent existence by means of economic development, diplomatic negotiation and military modernization. Suffice it to say that by 1939 Poland's weakness in relation to her Eastern and Western neighbours, the Soviet Union and the Third Reich, was palpable. It only required them to unite against her for her fate to be sealed and for 'this ugly offspring of the Versailles Treaty', in Molotov's words, to be liquidated.[17]

The notorious German–Soviet non-aggression pact concluded on 23 August 1939 between von Ribbentrop and Molotov contained a secret protocol providing for the delimitation of German and Soviet spheres of interest in Eastern Europe. When applied to Poland this agreement drew a line approximately equivalent to the Curzon line (see map 1) and pushed the Soviet boundary 100–150 miles further west. The pact envisaged the implementation of this boundary 'in the event of a territorial and political transformation of the territories belonging to the Polish State'.[18] The Poles did not have long to wait. The Nazis attacked on 1 September and by 3 September were requesting their Soviet allies to move their armed forces into the Soviet sphere of interest. The Russians were not yet ready, but acted on 17 September, by which time the German forces had pushed the retreating Poles up to and beyond the 'Ribbentrop–Molotov line'.[19] The unfortunate Poles believed that the Red Army was marching to their assistance but soon realized their mistake. In his broadcast on the invasion, Molotov justified Soviet action by reference to 'the insolvency and impotence' of the Polish state, which rendered null and void the Polish–Soviet non-aggression pact of 1932. Soviet security was also involved, along with the need to offer protection to the Ukrainian and White Russian inhabitants of the former Polish state ('our blood brothers') who had been abandoned to their fate as a result of the Polish collapse.[20]

The area of Poland occupied by the Soviet Union was, with some modifications, the area acquired by Poland in the Polish–Soviet war between June and October 1921. It had thirteen million inhabitants compared with twenty-two million inhabitants in the German sphere, but its physical area was slightly larger. Of these thirteen million, probably no more than 40 per cent were ethnic Poles, and a comparable number were Ukrainians. The remaining inhabitants were composed of roughly equal numbers of White Ruthenians (Byelorussians) and Jews (8 per cent each), with small numbers of Germans, Lithuanians, Czechs and Russians making up the remainder.[21] The fact that the *Kresy* were not 'indisputably Polish' provided the Soviet Union with the opportunity to make a plausible case for intervention. Poland was a multinational state, *Pravda* argued on 14 September 1939, and this war was a cause of the inner weakness. Polish government policy was characterized 'by the suppression and oppression of national minorities, particularly the Ukrainians and White Russians'. Polish domination was maintained 'by punitive expeditions, field tribunals, and White terror, fanning national discord'. It was, therefore, the 'sacred duty' of the Soviet Union to assist its brother Ukrainians and White Russians and to protect their lives and property when the Polish state disintegrated under the German attack. The Ukrainian and White Russian populations were depicted as welcoming the entry of Soviet troops into eastern Poland.[22]

Relations between the Ukrainian population and the Polish government were never good during the inter-war period. They reached a low point in 1930 when hundreds of buildings and estates owned by Poles were burned and general post offices robbed. During the Polish 'pacification' of 1930 entire villages where outbreaks of terrorism and disorder had occurred were punished.[23]

Thereafter matters improved. Events across the border in the Soviet Ukraine had their influence. Stalin's intensified collectivization campaign, leading to the removal of hundreds of thousands of 'kulaks' and their transportation to remote parts of the Soviet Union, was reported to Ukrainians in eastern Poland by fugitives who had braved the Soviet frontier guards equipped with machine-guns and searchlights. About 1932 it became known that all the inhabitants along the frontier had been replaced by people who did not speak Ukrainian. Furthermore, Ukrainian intellectuals in Poland knew of the execution of many of the leaders of Ukrainian social and political life by the Soviet authorities; unsurprisingly, Ukrainian communists with mild nationalist leanings were not spared.[24] So Ukrainians in Poland began to contrast the methods of the Polish government with those of the Soviets across the border, and started to appreciate more fully the civil rights which they held. This did not mean that they were satisfied with existing land distribution and ownership, and other advantages enjoyed by Polish settlers in the *Kresy*. Moreover, Ukrainian nationalists still aimed at an independent Ukrainian state. Those who supported the Soviet invasion as a means of promoting their economic and political objectives were soon to be disappointed.[25]

Poles who looked to Western Europe for support against the Soviet occupation were chagrined to find that there was understanding of the Soviet action. *The Times* of 22 September 1939 argued that '. . . once

Poland was defeated and overrun by the Germans, Russia would not let the White Russians and Ukrainian provinces fall into the hands of the Nazis, who would have formed them into separatist puppet states, a menace to Russia'. In the *Sunday Express* of the next day, Lloyd George published an article in which he attacked the 'class-ridden Polish government' and praised the Soviet government for liberating their kinsmen from the Polish yoke. In a broadcast on 1 October Churchill took a similar line, stressing considerations of Soviet security as a justification for the Russian invasion.[26] The British could not forget that the Poles had advanced beyond the armistice line recommended by Lord Curzon in 1920. It was widely believed that the Poles were now reaping what they had sown in the Treaty of Riga, and, as Sir Stafford Cripps remarked, it was natural for the Russians to enter Poland up to the Curzon line.[27]

The ethnic Poles in the population of Soviet-occupied Poland had most to fear from the Soviet authorities. It is from this group that most of the deportees were drawn and where the majority of arrests were made. Polish citizens could have had few illusions about Russian rule. It was within the lifetime of many that the Tsarist regime had wielded power in these regions, and Russian government stretching back to the eighteenth century was an abiding and painful memory. Moreover, Poles had some knowledge of the purges, deportations, labour camps and executions carried out under the regime of the new Red Tsar, Stalin. Nevertheless, the conditions of the occupation were a cruel blow, and could not have been fully anticipated.

The Soviet authorities moved with great speed and energy to incorporate the borderlands into the Soviet Union. They decided to seek legitimacy for Soviet rule through the process of elections to popular assemblies in the two regions of Western Ukraine and Western Byelorussia. In the various constituencies nominations were controlled and citizens were compelled to vote. The balloting process enabled the authorities to identify those voting against the official candidates. These people were subsequently arrested. When the two assemblies met they resolved that Western Ukraine and Western Byelorussia be admitted to the Soviet Union. The most recent study of these elections concludes that they were the 'first infusion of Soviet reality' into the daily lives of the inhabitants, 'their first experience of coercion-induced compliance' and 'a practical lesson in intimidation and collaboration, superb conditioning for both the subjects of the new order and the enforcers'. 'Fraud on a colossal scale' was the matter-of-fact comment by a member of the Polish government on this electoral process.[28]

By these dubious means the Soviet government claimed legitimacy for its occupation of the borderlands. It now had the green light for complete

'Sovietization' of the region and the elimination of all political, social and economic elements which might offer resistance to Soviet actions. The initial objective was to strike at the holders of private property by nationalizing industries, books, railroad rolling stock, large estates and commercial enterprises. Next, the area was to be made economically dependent on Moscow by the removal of reserves of raw materials and foodstuffs and all types of movable equipment. Zajdlerowa shows that the effect of these actions on the workforce in the territories was unemployment, lowered living standards and shortages. Shops were then nationalized and private homes came under the control of tenants' committees. At the beginning of 1940 collectivization was started in the villages.[29]

Some citizens felt the weight of the NKVD more directly and immediately. Under Soviet law individuals could be arrested on charges of counter-revolutionary activities injurious to the 'interests of the world proletariat', the 'revolutionary movement' or the 'basic achievements of the proletarian revolution'. By these definitions anyone who had held a position in the Polish government or the Polish army, who owned property, belonged to a political party or organization, or was in the slightest degree suspected of opposition to Soviet rule was a criminal and could be arrested.[30] A certain number of summary executions took place, particularly among civil servants and members of the legal profession. But numerous people were arrested: deputies to the Polish parliament, members of local governments, political activists whether Polish, Ukrainian or Jewish, of whatever party, magistrates, police officers, businessmen, army officers and trade unionists. Interrogated by the NKVD and denied every customary judicial procedure, they were sentenced to death or deportation. Many were elderly and long past the point of active work.

In the eyes of the Soviet government the inhabitants of these former Polish territories became Soviet citizens after the incorporation of the region into the Soviet Union. They were obliged to register with the authorities and to exchange Polish identity cards for Soviet ones. In certain areas Poles were constrained to sign declarations renouncing their Polish citizenship and repudiating any aspirations to Polish independence. Those who refused to comply with these requirements were usually deported. Registration facilitated the establishment of a rigorous system of surveillance and control by the police, assisted by a newly-created militia. It also made possible the conscription to the Red Army of young Polish men who were then posted to distant areas of the Soviet Union.[31]

The young were also the prime target of atheistic propaganda. The

Soviet authorities introduced a series of measures intended to eliminate all traces of religious conceptions and spiritual devotion, and to undermine the Roman Catholic Church as an alternative centre of loyalty. Numerous priests were executed and a number running into several thousands were deported. Certain churches and convents were closed and converted to cinemas or centres for atheistic propaganda. In most cases churches and synagogues had their property confiscated and were subject to heavy fiscal impositions which often resulted in their closure. It was calculated that about 4,000 churches and synagogues ceased to serve the needs of their congregations after the Soviet invasion. All seminaries were shut down and the teaching of religion in schools was forbidden, to be replaced by a very active atheistic propaganda striving in the crudest manner to disprove to the pupils the existence of God. Anti-religious posters were affixed to walls or paraded through the streets and agitators organized meetings at which religion and the priesthood were ridiculed.[32]

Children were also affected by the prohibition of the use of Polish as a language of instruction in almost all of the schools, and the removal of all Polish textbooks, to be replaced by Soviet ones when they became available. The teaching of the history and geography of Poland was forbidden. The aim was obviously to remove all sense of patriotism and to inculcate communist ideology. In these areas, as in the Soviet Union in general, children were encouraged to break their family ties and to denounce their parents to the authorities. Children of spirit who rejected this teaching and remained openly loyal to the religion of their parents were arrested and subjected to the same inquisition as the adults. Often they, too, were deported.[33] For a deeply religious people, the measures of the Soviet authorities were humiliating and demoralizing. The Polish president reported to the Pope in 1941 that 'eight million Catholics of both cults under Soviet occupation no longer have any contact with Rome'.[34] This sense of spiritual loss and deprivation was perhaps more bleak and disorienting than any other consequence of the draconian Soviet measures of this period. Eliot's fears for the survival of a culture under the impact of totalitarianism did not seem exaggerated in 1946. However, in our longer perspective, the remarkable resilience and recuperative power of the Polish Roman Catholic faith and, in his words, 'the stubbornness of the unconscious masses, the tenacity with which they cling to habits and customs' make us more optimistic about the capacity of the human spirit to resist oppression.[35]

That spirit was put to one of its severest tests in the experience of the mass deportations from Poland in February, April and June 1940 and in June 1941. Already many thousands of arrested citizens had been sentenced to deportation, and about 181,000 Polish prisoners-of-war, captured by the Red Army after the invasion of 17 September, had been transported to Soviet camps. The rank-and-file of the Polish army generally suffered the same fate as civilian deportees but some 9,000 officers received special treatment, being sent to three detention camps in the Soviet Union at Kozielsk, Starobielsk and Ostashkov. Later the corpses of some four-and-a-half thousand Polish officers from these camps were found buried in a mass grave in Katyń Forest, near Smolensk; all the evidence points to Soviet responsibility for their deaths.[36]

The mass deportations were not preceded by arrests and interrogations. Instead, hordes of people were awoken in the middle of the night, given a short time to pack some food and clothing, and then transported to the nearest trains where they were loaded into freight trucks for the journey into the Soviet Union. These deportations did not follow upon any specific charges and no indication was given of the length of the deportation. But when one considers the conditions under which the journey was made, the extreme harshness of the camps and the precedents of previous mass transportations inside the Soviet Union, nobody could reasonably doubt that 'the intention of the Soviet government was that these people should not survive'.[37] The deportees were taken mainly from the south-eastern region of the former Polish state, around Lwów, Tarnopol and Stanisławów, from areas bordering the Molotov–Ribbentrop line, and from the north-eastern district around Białystok. Sometimes the victims were picked up by accident, sometimes simply because they were ethnic Poles. Generally, though, the aim of the NKVD was to select for transportation groups considered 'socially dangerous'. These individuals had not necessarily aroused suspicion by anything they had done; what mattered was who they were and whether they might have an interest in withholding support for the new government.[38] Hence the deportees were not drawn simply from prominent persons in the higher social classes but from all social groups. Furthermore, each deportation had its own particular character.

The first, in February, took place during a very severe winter and, since it was unexpected, the deportees had not packed any belongings in anticipation. It was composed of quite large numbers of state officials, former Polish soldiers settled in the area after 1921, forestry workers and small farmers. The entire populations of a dozen villages were deported. All the members of a deportee's family was transported with him; the very young, the elderly or the sick were not spared. In April the second wave occurred. This included the families of those previously arrested or suspected of having gone abroad. It also took in smallholders, farm labourers from liquidated estates and victims of collectivization. There were few able-bodied men in the group, and many women, children and old people. This wave numbered approximately 320,000 people in comparison with the 120,000 of the first deportation.

The third wave, in June, was composed almost exclusively of refugees from Nazi-occupied western Poland, who had expressed a desire to return to their homes and now found themselves going in the opposite direction. They were joined by professional people, suspected of being counter-revolutionaries, and by small town merchants, mainly Jews, who were regarded as speculators. There were almost a quarter of a million people in this group. A year later, on the eve of the Russo–German war, a further 200,000 joined them, comprising all members of the above categories who had so far evaded deportation, plus witnesses of NKVD activity and collaborators with the Soviet authorities. A significant number of children living in orphanages or participating in summer camps were also included in the total. In addition to the four main deportations, smaller batches of up to several score persons were continually being transported to the interior of the Soviet Union. All in all, taking account of the deportation of prisoners and army personnel, some 1.2 to 1.4 million Poles were banished to the more distant parts of the Soviet Union. Half of them were women and children; half were of Polish nationality, perhaps 30 per cent were Jews and some 18–20 per cent Ukrainians and Byelorussians. Data from the Polish Red Cross in Tehran indicated that half the deportees may have been workers, tradesmen, farmers and members of the forestry service, while the rest were drawn from a miscellany of professional occupations including the law, academic life and the clergy.[39]

One of the great strengths of Zajdlerowa's book is her ability to portray the reaction of individuals to the numbing experience of the journeys from their homeland. Small children totally confused about why they had to leave their farm and animals; old people mortified by the humiliation of having to use an unscreened hole in the middle of the truck for their bodily functions; the constant noise of the military inspections of the cars; the filth and stink and lice; the perpetual and acute thirst and hunger; the deaths and the crude disposal of bodies; the mental agony and despair at the loss of fatherland, combined with anxiety about the survival of the family in this unknown future. One aspect of the journeys haunted her and remained inexplicable: the indifference and inhumanity of the NKVD guards in the face of extreme suffering. Yet she unconsciously suggests an answer to this problem in her comment on the lack of any interest in the freight cars or their contents by the local population when the trains stopped in stations: it was 'very difficult for people coming from outside the Union to take in that such things could be an everyday sight . . . that all this was not some otherwise unheard-of proceeding against themselves as foreigners, but that the whole system and the institutions to which they were being taken had . . . come into existence and continued to exist as a normal part of life for Soviet citizens'.

It was not easy for Poles to come to terms with the fact that what they were experiencing was part of Soviet normality. In the penal camps they soon appreciated that Russians also, and in far larger numbers, were the objects of Soviet 're-education'. The Poles were in fact entering a very well-established Soviet penal system denoted by the Russian acronym GULAG. The ostensible purpose of the camps was correction, the eradication, by a period of re-education, of ideas and values antithetical to Marxist-Leninism. They also served the purpose of removing from society harmful elements, those whose existence could imply even unspoken criticism of the régime, a process described by Solzhenitsyn as one of social prophylaxis.[40] This filled the sewers of the social organism with waves of class enemies, opponents of the proletariat and unreconstructed individuals. The waves then passed out into the tundra and taiga of the remoter parts of northern Russia and Siberia. The process of 'purging the Russian land of all kinds of harmful insects', in Lenin's words, began immediately after the October Revolution, intensifying and expanding in the next two decades until the NKVD, the main sewer attendants, presided over a mass production industry whose insatiable mass markets lay in the countless islands of the Gulag archipelago strung out across the continent. In his *History of our Sewage Disposal System*, Solzhenitsyn graphically illustrates how small rivulets of 'insects' swelled into mighty floods and turned a craft industry into a mass production process. Class enemies were joined by malingerers, priests by church choristers, railroad workers by telegraphers, socialist traitors by rebellious peasants. But this was only the beginning. There followed mass arrests of Orthodox believers, students and the technical intelligentsia, members of various nationality groups (the Yakuts, the Buryat-Mongols and the Kazakhs), leading party officials in the 1930s, the dispossessed kulaks (the largest wave so far) and other kinds of agricultural workers, teachers, academics and students, and the ample category of counter-revolutionaries. Every conceivable social group was swept up and in due course absorbed into the NKVD industry. This industry, too, had norms to be fulfilled, output targets to be met, camps to be filled with new slaves to take the place of those who had perished.[41] Deportees from eastern Poland entered the sewer pipes like every other enemy in the proletariat. 'It turned out that our brothers badly needed to be purged' noted Solzhenitsyn of the Poles, 'and from them, too, flowed waves of social prophylaxis . . . Thus the population was shaken up, forced into silence, and left without any possible leaders of resistance'.[42] The Poles could expect no especial interest in their plight from the Russian population; after all, they must have been guilty of something; and if not, their fate was no different from that of millions of Soviet citizens; in any case it was better not to look too closely or you might be swept off with them. Sometimes, as the prisoners marched from train to transit camp in some Russian provincial city, passers-by would seem to look at them with sympathy, but these people were usually the middle-aged or elderly 'who could remember another world'.[43]

Yet the other, pre-Soviet, world also sent its citizens into exile in Siberia and northern Russia. And among that not inconsiderable flow were Poles who had incurred the wrath of the Tsarist authorities. After the Polish rising in 1830–1 the captured rebels were condemned to penal servitude in Siberia. All 80,000 walked in irons the entire distance. Again, in 1863–4, the January rising produced its casualties, 'the tribunals and the official hangman preyed once more on a prostrate population' and 'Siberia welcomed its next massive influx of Polish deportees'.[44] These events were well remembered by large sections of the Polish population, and those who claimed to understand the Russian mentality, as the Poles did, could not have been taken completely unawares by the new deportations. It would be an interesting though melancholy exercise to discover how many of this latest consignment of deportees had forebears who had taken the same grim route into exile.

The mass deportations in freight trucks had not been preceded by trials and sentences. But many Poles had been arrested after the Russian occupation and, after periods in prison, vividly described by Zajdlerowa and her witnesses, were sentenced to penal camps. These were the 'politicals' who were usually convicted under the notorious and wide-ranging Article 58 of the Soviet Criminal Code of 1926. This article contained fourteen points and covered all forms of counter-revolution as defined by the code. There seemed to exist 'no conceivable form of human behaviour to which the label "counter-revolutionary" [could not] be attached at will by a court'.[45] The sentence for a person convicted under the code was almost invariably eight years in corrective labour camps, and this could be renewed after expiry. There was no judge or jury to hear and assess the evidence, render a verdict and pass sentence. Instead, the arrested person was subjected to interrogations, continually repeated if necessary, under prison conditions of extreme overcrowding, filth, deprivation, torture and psychological pressure. The main aim of this process was to obtain a confession from the prisoner. Sentence was decided, in private, by so-called troikas, or Special Boards (Russian acronym OSO) as they were later known. There was no appeal. Again the Poles were introduced to an already well-functioning system and took their places in the camps among numerous Russian offenders.

Two types of destination awaited Polish deportees. The corrective labour camps, referred to by Zajdlerowa as *lagier*, swallowed up most of the Polish POWs, politicals and mature males. Other categories might also be sent there. The remainder, perhaps largely family groups, women and children, and elderly people, were despatched to what have been described as 'areas of compulsory residence' or, to use Zajdlerowa's term, 'free exile'. This is not to be confused with the term 'voluntary exile' which applied to the wives and children choosing to take up residence with their deported husbands and fathers in nineteenth-century Russia.[46]

Most of the penal camps were situated in remote areas and experienced great extremes of climate. Their remoteness accounted for the extraordinarily long rail and boat journeys endured by the Poles. A glance at map 2 (pages 34–5) will indicate concentrations of camps of this type around the area of Archangelsk on the White Sea, the Komi Republic to the east and the island of Novaya Zemlya off the coast of northern Russia. Camps were dotted along the railway line from Vologda north of Moscow, eastwards to Kirov and on to the Urals. In Siberia there were numerous camps in the Kamchatka Peninsula, in territories running inland from Khabarovsk, Vladivostok, Sakhalin and Magadan and, in the most deadly region of all, along the Kolyma River flowing north into the Arctic Ocean. There were a few penal camps in central Russia or the Caucasus and none in the south. Although termed an archipelago by Solzhenitsyn, it was also, psychologically, a country or even a continent, inhabited by the millions of prisoners or zeks and their NKVD guards. The camps were grouped into zones extending over hundreds of kilometres, each camp enclosed by barbed wire, patrolled by armed guards and their dogs, and surveyed by sentries in look-out towers and storks' nests. In effect, this was an NKVD empire which, as Zajdlerowa describes, permitted considerable local self-government in the camps themselves. But it was this very delegation of powers to the non-political prisoners which made the camps the 'peculiar hell' which they were.[47]

Zajdlerowa hints at but does not fully explore or explain the sub-culture of the camps, in which the criminals, the so-called *pridurki*, reigned supreme over the politicals by violence and fraud. People who experienced the system for themselves found that their enemies were not only on the other side of the bars, as it were, but on the inside as well. Both Herling and Solzhenitsyn express their repugnance for these creatures and their helplessness in face of intimidation.[48] The criminals were professional thieves, murderers and bandits who received fewer years of hard labour for murder than the politicals under Article 58. The official attitude towards them was that they would reform, and their redeeming quality compared with the politicals was that they were not enemies of the people, but an integral part of the people and social allies of the Party. The NKVD generally turned a blind eye to the violence, theft, rape and murder which took place in the prison cars, barges, ships and camps. Some of the victims describe what happened to them in Zajdlerowa's pages at the hands of the thieves or apaches. But for a more vivid sense of the helplessness of the victims and the terrible unrestrained power of the oppressors, one has to turn elsewhere and consider their hold over young and fit army officers and NCOs like Solzhenitsyn himself. It is that and not what happened to a frail, blind Polish woman which is a real index of their hold over the politicals, through the connivance of the guards.[49]

The term 'free exile' suggests a more benign form of correction than that of the camps. This was partly true, but the reality of life in the remote outposts (or *posiolki*) was one of harshness, material deprivation, acute shortage of food and concern for the whereabouts and safety of relatives. The *posiolki* were usually far from railway lines or towns, the deportees lived in crude wooden barracks under the charge of an NKVD officer, and performed heavy outdoor work in extreme climatic conditions. They received payment for their work with which to buy food for themselves and their dependents. Payment was often insufficient for their needs and survival depended on a capacity to barter their limited possessions for food and other necessities. As we see in one of the most personal accounts in the book, some deportees were sent to collective or state farms in Kazakhstan where the battle for survival was as intense as in the camps.

There is evidence that many Polish deportees lived in hope of release, which distinguished them from their Russian camp brethren who had no such expectations. If death did not overtake them before the end of their sentence, they saw enough examples of sentences being extended for a further eight years to doubt that they would ever return to their homes. Many Poles, by contrast, lived in hope of survival and liberation; others correctly calculated that a Nazi attack on the Soviet Union could transform their prospects and lead to their release. Their faith was vindicated, as least in part, by the turn of events.

On 22 June 1941 Hitler launched his attack on the Soviet Union, sweeping through the eastern provinces of Poland in two weeks and making inroads into Soviet territory. By August 1941 the survival of the Soviet Union lay in the balance. The Ukraine was almost entirely in German hands, Leningrad was surrounded and Moscow threatened. Stalin needed all the help he could get, and the Americans and the British quickly came to his aid and made common cause against the Nazi enemy. Shortly after the German attack President Roosevelt announced the release of Soviet dollar reserves to enable the Soviet government to purchase American arms and then sent his representative, Harry Hopkins, to Moscow. There, Western aid was promised to Stalin and the knot binding the Americans, British and Russians was firmly tied. Despite mutual fears of a separate peace there was to be no going back.[50]

For the Poles the decision whether to ally with the Soviet Union was more difficult. Soviet actions in breaking treaties, invading Polish territory and taking punitive measures against millions of Polish citizens could not be forgotten. Nevertheless, the Polish Council of Ministers had recently determined that Poland's main enemy was Germany, and in a conversation with Sir Stafford Cripps a few days before the German aggression against the Soviet Union, General Sikorski, the Polish prime minister, expressed the belief that co-operation between Poland and Russia would be possible provided that the Russians changed their policy on Poland's frontiers. Sikorski envisaged the formation of a Polish army out of Polish POWs in Russian penal camps to fight alongside the Red Army. Clearly here was an opportunity to use Russia's difficulties to Poland's advantage.[51]

The Soviets were not prepared to meet all Poland's demands; indeed the negotiations, which were conducted under British mediation, were quite difficult. Some members of the Polish government were uncomfortable with the outcome. In particular, the use of the term 'amnesty' in respect of Polish deportees in Soviet camps caused considerable indignation in Polish circles. In the end the prospect of taking part in the war against the Nazis on the Russian front, of freeing Polish POWs and internees from Soviet camps, and restoring Polish–Soviet relations on the basis of the inter-war treaties between the two countries proved too enticing to be rejected. In the forefront of Sikorski's mind was the fate of his fellow countrymen and women in Russian penal camps and other places of exile. In a later conversation Sikorski recalled his feelings: 'You know, when I had to sign that treaty and I was struggling with myself whether to delay any more, I heard, as it were, the whisper of thousands of voices . . . hurry, O please save us'.[52] Critics of the treaty among Poles in the United Kingdom believed that not enough concessions had been extracted from the Russians, especially as regards the restoration of the pre-war boundary between Poland and the Soviet Union. Moreover, they were sceptical about Soviet good faith, fearing that concessions on the establishment of the Polish Army and the freeing of internees would be revoked when war turned in the Russians' favour. The Russians had already dragged their feet on both these issues and perhaps their true position could be discerned from their original negotiating stance. But those who had suffered most from Soviet action, the deportees, were naturally over-whelmed by the news of the Polish–Soviet treaty. It saved their lives and gave them an opportunity to serve their beloved country against the enemy occupying Polish soil. In Poland itself the underground press appears to have approved the treaty on the grounds that the first priority was to defeat Nazi Germany, and that Sikorski, dependent as he was on the hospitality and support of the British government, had no choice but to accede to British wishes for a *rapprochement* between Poland and the Soviet Union.[53]

All in all the treaty was probably the best deal that could have been obtained in the circumstances. But in reality the Soviet Union had less need of Polish manpower to fight the war than of British and American war *matériel*.'We are not concerned with your five, ten or fifteen divisions', the Russians told the leader of the Polish military mission in early August 1941, 'we have hundreds of our own. If we start to arm your divisions an equal number of ours would have to go unarmed'.[54] Part of the price for Western supplies was some concessions to the Poles. These included the Soviet declaration that the German–Soviet pact of 1939 was regarded as non-existent, that diplomatic relations between the Soviet Union and Poland would be resumed and an autonomous Polish army would be established on Soviet soil to fight under the general direction of the Soviet High Command. These points were incorporated in the Polish–Soviet treaty of 30 July 1941, which added the following protocol:

> As soon as diplomatic relations are re-established the Government of the Union of Soviet Socialist Republics will grant amnesty to all Polish citizens who are at present deprived of their freedom on the territory of the U.S.S.R. either as prisoners of war or on other adequate grounds.[55]

The test of the success of this treaty would lie in the manner of its implementation. Would it bring concrete advantages to the Polish slave labour in Russian camps? The Poles could be divided into two broad groups: the prisoners of war, who would presumably constitute the bulk of the newly-constituted Polish army, and the civilian deportees, including many women and children, who would in the main have to find employment in order to support themselves, or perhaps could rely on relief supplies from abroad.

As regards the army, the treaty left the detailed arrangements for the establishment of an effective fighting force for discussion between the two sides. Some 181,000 Polish soldiers and 9,000 officers had been taken prisoner by the Red Army in 1939. A proportion of these had died as a result of the extreme physical conditions imposed on them in the camps; most required a period of rest, recuperation and adequate food before they would be fit for active service. There were other males of military age among the civilian deportees who could be available for service. The Poles also asked for the release of some 100,000 of their countrymen recruited for the Red Army in Poland in 1941, and for their transfer to the Polish army. It is therefore possible that there was a pool of several hundred thousand men available for enlistment.[56]

Their organization was discussed at meetings between Soviet and Polish military officers in August 1941, eventuating in the Polish–Soviet military agreement of 14 August, with additional protocols, some of which were not ratified by the Soviet government. The terms of the agreement were vague and ambiguous and provided ample scope for differing interpretations. It was agreed, for example, that Polish units would be moved to the front only when 'fully ready for action' and that they would operate in groups not smaller than divisions (the Russians later interpreted this as meaning that single divisions could be sent to the front). Furthermore, arms and equipment would be provided 'as far as possible' by the Soviet government and by the Polish government from Allied sources. In practice, this meant that Polish re-armament would depend on a willingness to make some supplies available to the Poles at the expense of the Red Army. Sikorski saw the faults in this agreement and required his emissary to obtain amendments, notably that the Polish units would be used as a whole for operational purposes under Polish command. He was later informed that the Soviets had accepted this Polish proviso. The Polish command was determined that Polish units should be fully supplied and trained before they went into action against the German army. Even more important for Polish morale was that the army should fight as a distinct unit of several divisions rather than be dispersed among the Red Army divisions in individual units.[57]

Of crucial importance for the Poles in the camps was the size of the Polish army. The Poles argued that the agreement of 14 August placed no upper limit on the size of the army. Indeed in the first protocol the Soviet authorities proclaimed that all Polish citizens should report to the Polish army and all Polish citizens who wished to serve with the Polish army be released from the Red Army. The Poles interpreted this to mean that the numbers to be enlisted would be at the minimum 100,000. The Soviet side, however, listed the number of members of the former Polish army as about 21,000, or approximately two divisions. General Anders, for the Poles, accepted this figure as a point of departure but never envisaged that this number would constitute more than a small fraction of Polish citizens fit for active service.[58]

From the outset, then, there were potentially serious problems to be overcome based on different assumptions and intentions. The Soviets had to pay a price for Allied war *matériel* but were determined that it should be as low as possible in respect to the Polish army, the civilian deportees and post-war Soviet–Polish relations. The Poles obviously would interpret the agreement in the most favourable sense to themselves, out of self-interest and compassion for their fellow-nationals held in Soviet camps. But in the contest for the ear of the Western Allies they had few cards to play and their accusations of Soviet bad faith often foundered on genuine Russian claims that the Soviet government was experiencing enormous difficulties in face of the massive inroads of the Nazis into their territory. The Allies could not altogether disregard such considerations when faced with Polish protests about non-implementation of the Soviet–Polish agreements.

In the autumn of 1941 the Soviet side refused to expand the size of the Polish army beyond two divisions, claiming a shortage of supplies. Even then, only one of the divisions was adequately equipped, and it was short of artillery and anti-tank equipment. Sikorski complained to Churchill that a Polish army of four to six divisions could be formed only if the Allies stepped up their supplies. The negotiations between Harriman and Beaverbrook[59] and their Soviet opposite numbers in September and October were a grave disappointment to the Poles since none of the abundant war supplies promised to Stalin were specifically earmarked for the Polish Army. Sikorski later claimed that in the course of the first year after the signing of the Polish–Soviet military agreement not a single shipment of British arms reached the Polish forces in Russia.[60]

There were direct consequences for Polish deportees of this inability or refusal to arm additional Polish units. Thousands of Poles from all over the Soviet Union trekked down to the headquarters of the Polish army in the vicinity of Saratov and Orenburg in the lower Volga region (see map 2, pages 34–5), but were unable to join the army owing to the absence of equipment or shortage of space in the camps. They were forced to take jobs or to join Soviet labour battalions; the Soviets expected the Polish government to provide for them or to transport them to other territories in the Soviet Union to prevent overcrowding and civil disturbance in the Volga region. Moreover, it was observed in October 1941 that transports of former Polish POWs were being redirected from Polish military training camps to cotton plantations and irrigation and construction projects in Uzbekistan where, it was said, the Soviet authorities intended to settle 100,000 Poles.[61] Since the numbers in the training camps had now risen to 46,000 the Soviets threatened to provide food for 30,000 only. General Anders refused to send to Uzbekistan the surplus 16,000, but many others were compelled to go there, where the mortality was very high. In other cases Soviet local authorities were failing to release all Polish military personnel from the camps. General Anders, the Polish commanding officer, protested at this intolerable detention of his 'fellow soldiers' in prisons and labour camps. While he agreed that men not fit for active service should go to Uzbekistan, it would be disastrous for morale if he were to send effectives to this type of work, and damaging to the common fight against Hitler.[62] Anders and the Polish government envisaged an army of some six or seven divisions, fully trained and equipped and fighting as a unit, perhaps having responsibility for some distinct sector of the front. The Soviet authorities still claimed shortage of equipment for failing to supply more than two divisions (only one of these adequately) and were showing signs of impatience at Polish refusal to commit one division to the front. After the high hopes of July and August, Polish troops and other deportees who genuinely wished to join the fight against Hitler, though only on the right conditions, were increasingly frustrated and dismayed by the obstacles placed in their way and by the knowledge that so many of their fellow Poles had yet to be released from the camps, and many others were consigned to privation and disease in Uzbekistan.

It was at this point that General Sikorski, whose visit to Poles in Kuibyshev is described in the text, decided to visit Stalin to try to make the Polish–Soviet agreement work. Again, he was motivated by concern for Poles who had not yet been released and by a desire to break the *impasse* over the Polish army. Sikorski saw the army as a fighting machine, but he also saw its presence in the Soviet Union as a reassuring symbol for the mass of Polish exiles and as a kind of guarantee of Polish pride, identity and morale in Russia. Without it there would be a return to the sense of complete powerlessness and alienation in an unfamiliar and hostile land.[63] The army, however, was not the only object of his attention on this visit. He was also determined to ensure that the conditions of existence for those released from camps, including women, children (many of them without parents), the elderly and the infirm, should improve through the implementation of existing agreements.

Sikorski based his case on the additional protocol to the Polish–Soviet agreement and Soviet assurances about implementation since August 1941. Under the amnesty all Polish citizens deprived of their freedom in the USSR would be released. But arrangements had to be made for their welfare after release. Were they to be cared for by the Russians or by representatives of the Polish government? If they were to come under the care of the Polish agencies, how were they to be reached given the vast distances involved? How were these agencies to be financed? Who would man them? What services should they provide? Answers formulated to these questions would have to take into account the extreme physical weakness of many of the deportees, the diseases and sickness which were rife among them, their hunger and lack of suitable clothing, the need for education for the children who had been deprived of it for too long, the necessity to reassure those separated from loved ones and the deep hunger for pastoral care and spiritual solace from the priesthood.

The man responsible for trying to establish a satisfactory standard of care for the liberated civilians was Józef Retinger,[64] a close associate of Sikorski, now appointed chargé d'affaires until Professor Kot's appointment as Ambassador was confirmed. Retinger hoped to establish co-operation between the Soviet local authorities and the embassy and its representatives, in their common interest. His first aim was to identify men of trust in the localities where Poles were concentrated and to liaise with these appointees to compile lists of Poles in the area and to establish their most pressing needs. He further asked for the release from prisons and penal camps of all Polish citizens and for their transfer to temporary assembly stations where they would be sorted out and sent to the army or to work in industry or on the land. Those unfit for work, especially women and children, the old and invalid, would be directed to localities with a benign climate, in principle in regions where there would be Polish military camps. He asked the Soviet authorities to provide the appropriate living accommodation and food supplies and other necessities for these people. As much help as possible would be provided by agencies of the Polish government and Polish welfare organizations. In order to identify the most urgent problems and needs he requested the establishment of mixed commissions composed of one Soviet and one embassy representative to tour the regions inhabited by Polish citizens.[65]

In practice, Retinger found at first that the Soviet authorities were slow to release prisoners because of the need to ration labour in the camps to meet the output norms. However, on 28 August 1941 the Soviet government informed him that orders had been given to release Polish citizens, to provide them with free transportation and subsistence for any journey, and to permit them to seek work in an area of their choice, or, if they preferred, to remain in their present locality. They further confirmed the appointment of 'men of trust' and agreed to mixed commissions.[66]

Kot arrived in Moscow on 4 September 1941. Among his chief responsibilities as ambassador was the organization of a system of social assistance for all persons who had held Polish citizenship before the Soviet invasion of Poland on 17 September 1939. The protection and assistance of Polish citizens was to be concentrated in the consular department of the embassy so that welfare agents on the spot would have diplomatic immunity. The embassy's tasks were to establish how many people were to be released, to prepare lists of names, to sound out the Soviet government for a loan to finance the welfare system, to try to have Polish people settled in more temperate regions and to inform the Polish government of the kinds of assistance needed.[67]

The Polish embassy was soon swamped by work. By mid-September over 1,000 letters and telegrams, many of which could not even be opened for lack of staff, arrived daily. Kot failed to get permission to set up consular posts throughout the Soviet Union, largely because the consular service was equated with espionage. Hence there was no effective direct contact at this time between the deportees and their embassy.[68]

It has been estimated that in the two months following amnesty 300,000 Poles were released. They told much the same story: each had been released individually and many more Poles were held in captivity because the local authorities needed their labour. Usually the healthiest prisoners were detained since they were more productive. It has been calculated that between 15 and 20 per cent of the deportees had perished, owing to the harsh conditions of their captivity, before December 1941.[69]

By mid-October Kot was writing to Vyshinsky requesting that all Polish citizens should be released in accordance with the agreement. He asserted that many thousands had not yet been informed of the amnesty, and those who had been released had not received the free travel and subsistence promised earlier by the Soviet government, nor offers of employment in accordance with their qualifications. Consequently large numbers of emancipated Polish citizens, as Zajdlerowa reports, were wandering about aimlessly, camping out at railway stations or localities chosen for their residence and scavenging in rubbish dumps. No progress had been made in establishing welfare and relief agencies for Poles without means of subsistence. Vyshinsky could only mutter that problems were complicated and difficult.[70] Shortly afterwards, he announced the suspension of mass movement from north to south, presumably to reduce the numbers trying to reach the vicinity of the Polish army, and refused the Polish request for a bigger loan to help in dealing with the dependent among those released. On questions of employment Polish citizens were to be placed on exactly the same basis as Russians. Finally, Vyshinsky admitted the possibility that the embassy might delegate temporary agents to visit certain areas in order to issue passports and to bring assistance to Polish citizens.[71]

As in the case of the army, there were many unresolved problems for Sikorski to discuss with Stalin and Molotov in early December 1941. Until a satisfactory solution was achieved Polish deportees would continue to linger in camps, to exist in acute hardship and deprivation after their release, to suffer from a myriad of diseases and illnesses and to be prevented from joining the Polish army. The Polish aim was still to participate in the war on the Soviet side and to assist in the liberation of Poland from Nazi rule. They wanted good relations with the Soviet government but were becoming pessimistic about that possibility in the face of apparent Soviet obstruction. There were genuine difficulties on the Soviet side and these might have been more fully acknowledged by the Poles if the Soviets had shown them a modicum of good will. But the Russians were sensitive to Polish pretensions to superiority over them, one expression of this being Stalin's outburst at his meeting with Sikorski, and the Poles in turn were resentful about Russian behaviour in 1939 and unwilling to concede that Russian intentions were honourable. The auguries for the talks were not good, but Stalin was under pressure from the United States and Great Britain to make concessons and, in the end, some positive results for the Poles were achieved. Space does not permit a detailed discussion of the fascinating exchanges between Stalin and the Polish negotiators. What the Polish deportees would want to know was how far their still desperate plight would be eased by the agreements.[72]

First, Stalin conceded an increase in the size of the Polish army to six or seven divisions and permitted about 27,000 men to leave the Soviet Union to reinforce Polish units in the United Kingdom and the Middle East. This would mean, according to Polish calculations, that about 96,000 men would constitute the Polish army in Russia. Second, in order to provide adequate space for training and a better climate for the physical recovery of the recruits, the army would be based further south in the Tashkent, Alma-Ata and southern Kazakhstan areas. Third, the supply problems would be met by substantial shipments of arms and equipment from the United States and the United Kingdom and, in the light of Sikorski's assurance on this point, the Soviet side agreed to provide food for the additional recruits. Sikorski and Anders re-stated their intentions that the Polish troops should fight side by side with the Red Army as soon as they were properly supplied and trained, with the proviso that they enter the front as a single unit and not be dispersed among the Soviet divisions.[73] In each of these agreements there were Polish gains. If implemented, they provided the opportunity for most of those who wished to join the Polish army, with the prospect of participating in the war and fighting their way back to Poland in alliance with the Red Army.

But, of course, Sikorski had in mind not only the army but the mass of civilians who were ineligible for military service and whose lot had barely improved since the Polish–Soviet agreement of 31 July 1941. Again, the discussions seemed to yield substantial gains in the form of assurances from the Soviet side that all internees would be released from camps immediately and encouraged to settle in the same areas as the Polish troops. Moreover, appointed Polish delegates would be permitted to enter Polish communities to discover their real needs. The provision of an adequate welfare network would be partly financed by a substantial loan to the Polish government from the Soviet Union. This major contribution to the well-being of the Polish community went into effect on 23 December when the regulations governing their activities were approved. The delegates faced a gigantic task of relieving suffering and hunger, providing clothing and shelter, compiling a register of Polish people in their vicinity and issuing Polish passports (thus replacing the Soviet citizenship imposed upon them in 1939), directing Poles to suitable employment and organizing cultural activities for adults, education for youth and health care for the very substantial numbers whose physical condition had deteriorated in the camps.[74]

The Sikorski–Stalin agreement in respect of the Polish army was not upheld. First of all the evacuation was delayed, the Poles suspecting that this was connected with their continued resistance to Soviet requests to send at least one of their divisions to the front. Then conscription was curtailed, limiting the numbers enlisting in the Polish army. Even so, the army had grown rapidly between December 1941 and February/March 1942, when its strength was approaching 70,000 men. The Russians had been true to their word in permitting it to concentrate in the Tashkent–Alma-Ata area. In March, however, they reneged on their undertaking to supply food for up to 96,000 men, blaming a food shortage which they attributed to the late delivery of American wheat. Stalin announced to Anders that since the Polish army was not participating in the fighting it was not entitled to full rations and from the end of March the Soviets would supply food for no more than 44,000 men. Anders received permission to evacuate the rest to save them from starvation.[75]

It seems probable that the Soviet government tried to force the Poles to fight, firstly by delaying evacuation and then by threatening food supplies. No one wished to fight more keenly than the Poles but they had genuine reservations about the conditions, and could not express openly some of their apprehensions.[76] Furthermore, the Allies were increasingly enthusiastic about the evacuation of some Polish troops in view of the deterioration of the position of British troops in North Africa after Rommel's offensive in early 1942. This seemed to many Poles to offer the possibility of fighting *after* being properly armed and trained rather than before, and would also serve to get them out of the grip of the Soviets whom they distrusted. Consequently, in late March 1942, some 31,000 military personnel (including the original figure of 27,000 agreed in the Stalin–Sikorski talks) left the Soviet Union for Persia where they were received by British troops. They were accompanied by some 12,000 members of the soldiers' families. It was understood by the Polish authorities that recruitment of Poles to the army in Russia would continue and that further evacuations would follow, permitting the strengthening of the Allied cause outside Russia and perhaps hastening the opening of a second front, which was one of the Soviet Union's highest priorities. Nevertheless, it was Sikorski's intention to leave 44,000 troops in Russia to fight in due course on Russia's western front.[77]

This course of action failed to meet with Soviet approval. Recruiting was discontinued on the grounds that there were rations for only 44,000 men. Instead, a number of Polish citizens were being recruited into the Red Army and labour battalions. Sikorski wanted to keep the army in existence in the Soviet Union but Anders and the British wished to evacuate it and make it available as reinforcements in the Middle East and North Africa. After negotiations between the British and the Russians pressure was brought on the Poles for a second evacuation which was eventually agreed, with the proviso that a Polish recruiting mission should be maintained in the Soviet Union and that up to 20,000 civilians should be evacuated with the troops. In August 1942 the second and final evacuation took place, consisting of some 44,000 troops and 25,000 civilians. In sum around 75,000 troops and 37,000 members of families left the Soviet Union up to two-and-a-half years after being deported there from Poland. But this 112,000 was a tiny fraction of the total number of deportees. What had happened to the rest and what was to be their future?[78]

After the agreement between Stalin and Sikorski immediate progress was made in the appointment and disposition of Polish delegates and in the establishment of Polish relief and educational centres whose familiar and reassuring atmosphere is so well evoked in Zajdlerowa's text. In January 1942 an instruction was issued by the Soviet government to local authorities to co-operate with the delegates of the Polish embassy in their activities. Special rations were to be supplied to hostels, nurseries and other Polish institutions of a similar character, and food was also to be provided for Polish citizens who were unfit for work but could not be placed in an institution. Poles who were employed in Soviet enterprises were to receive ration cards and to be treated in the same way as Soviet citizens.[79]

This was indicative of the co-operative attitude in the first quarter in 1942. An effective relief system was created during this time. The Polish embassy was at the centre of a network of contacts and nineteen delegates were appointed to republics and *oblasts* where Poles were concentrated. Soon 387 'men of trust' had been appointed. In addition to supplying clothes, food and medicines, these agents founded a total of 807 institutions, including eighty-two orphanages for 5,364 children, 175 kindergartens, 111 schools and educational centres, ten hospitals and convalescent homes, seventy-one hostels and homes for the disabled, one crèche and one laboratory, 191 feeding centres, 117 medical and first-aid posts, and forty-seven workshops. Supplies of food, medicines and clothing were being shipped to Russia from Egypt and the United States in ever-increasing quantities. In April and May 1942 more than 1,500 tons of supplies were shipped through Archangel and in June an even larger amount. Supplies were also entering through Vladivostok and Ashkhabad (see map 2, pages 34–5) helping to alleviate the undernourishment and spread of epidemics among the deportees, especially children. Shipments were checked by local delegates and forwarded by rail to various destinations.[80]

In the spring the first signs of Soviet interference in this system of relief began to appear. A special law was passed to forbid Soviet citizens to establish contacts with foreign legations and missions, and this was followed by NKVD restrictions on the relief and passport-issuing activities of the Polish embassy. The really damaging action began in July 1942. First of all the diplomatic privileges of some of the embassy delegates were withdrawn and other delegates were arrested and their offices closed down. The official records were seized and the embassy's accounts in the State Bank were blocked. Telegraphic communications between the embassy and its delegations were interfered with. Consequently the distribution of food and clothing to tens of thousands of Polish citizens ceased, supplies at the ports and in local storage were left unprotected and were pilfered in consequence, and orphanages and old people's homes were deprived of suitable care. Orphanages, surgeries and hospitals began to be closed by the Soviet authorities and their functions taken over by Russian equivalents. Over 100 'men of trust' were arrested.[81] The Soviets contended that these Polish agencies had been engaged in espionage, an accusation vigorously rejected by the Polish Embassy. The system was breaking down rapidly and it was easy for the Russians to say that they had no obligation to continue the distribution of relief.[82] The *coup de grâce* was delivered in January 1943, when the Soviet government announced that citizenship of the USSR was to be enforced on all Polish citizens on the territory of the Soviet Union. This was the fourth time the citizenship card had been played by the Soviets on Poles from the eastern Polish provinces. The first had been in December 1939, the second after the Polish–Soviet agreement in July 1941 when the deportees regained their former citizenship, and the third in November 1941 when Polish citizens of Ukrainian, Byelorussian, and Jewish ethnicity were prevented from joining the Polish army as not being ethnic Poles. This latest decision meant that the relief system had to be wound up, since the Polish embassy had no jurisdiction or responsibility for Soviet citizens.[83] Furthermore, it rendered impossible the evacuation of Polish orphans and the families of Polish soldiers serving abroad, for which the Poles had been lobbying for several months with some international support. The continuing protests of the Polish embassy to the Soviet government about the taking over of Polish-owned relief institutions and the forcible imposition of Soviet citizenship on Polish people were terminated by the breaking-off of diplomatic relations between the Soviet and Polish governments on 25 April 1943 as a result of the discovery of the mass grave of Polish officers at Katyń by the German occupying forces in Byelorussia.

This marked the end of the chapter which had begun on 31 July 1941, characterized by intense activity on the part of the Polish authorities, by hopes and expectations on the part of the deportees and by continuous frustration and disappointment on the part of everyone. The Poles had now come to terms with the reality that in Soviet law they were citizens of the USSR and that no more relief would reach them from outside. There could be no hope of early release for the very large number of Polish deportees still held in camps. They would be cut off from their government in London and from their fellow countrymen in Poland itself. They would be condemned to lives of isolation and renewed despair after a period of high hopes and restored identities.

In December 1943 the Polish Social Information Bureau in London sent a report to Clement Attlee, the British Deputy Prime Minister, on the Soviet deportation of Poles. The report was intended to be factual and objective; the circulation was to be limited to a few specially selected persons; its aim to disseminate, confidentially, information on the fate of Polish citizens under Soviet rule in order to avoid misunderstandings and 'to refute certain false statements'.[84] We can feel confident that the estimates in this document were made with care and circumspection. No one knew for sure how many Poles remained alive in the Soviet Union, how many of the original deportees had died, how many were still in camps and places of exile. The compilers of this document came to the following conclusions based on the evidence at their disposal. After 31 July 1941 less than half, i.e. about half a million, of the Poles deported to the Soviet Union had been located by the Polish embassy and its delegates. The remainder had been denied release from the camps or remained in the far north and could neither leave nor contact the Polish authorities. Perhaps 200,000 had died since entering Russia, and some 100,000 had been evacuated. Of those remaining in the Soviet Union who had 'retained their freedom', perhaps some 270,000, there were approximately 96,000 women, 76,000 children (perhaps the majority orphans), 30,000 old persons unfit for work and about 30,000 members of families of Polish soldiers, sailors and airmen serving in the Middle East and the United

Kingdom. In May 1943 the Soviet government announced that a Polish division was being formed as part of the Red Army, absorbing perhaps 20,000 Polish soldiers.[85]

All these figures are tentative, but we must remember that the Polish embassy compiled lists of names from the registrations undertaken by their delegates in some twenty localities in the Soviet Union. There were also numerous first-hand reports from Poles about how many of their compatriots still remained in the camps. These figures cannot be lightly dismissed; indeed the mortality figures may be regarded as conservative.[86] Those remaining in the Soviet Union were to be joined by another wave of deportees from Poland, perhaps 100,000 in number, after the Red Army entered Polish territory for the second time in 1944–5. Later, repatriation began; about 270,000 in 1945–8, some 300,000 in 1955–6 and approximately 30,000 in 1959. If re-education had not completed its work, the process could be continued inside the People's Republic of Poland near the area where it had started during the first Soviet occupation in 1939–41. The wheel had come full circle for that minority of deportees who had survived their savage ordeal in the Soviet Union. For the remainder there was to be no return.[87]

The first edition of *The Dark Side of the Moon* comprised chapters of historical and geographical description and chapters composed largely of personal testimonies, or reconstruction of the collective experiences by Madame Zajdlerowa. In preparing this new edition we have taken the view that the stories of the deportees told in their own words, or on their behalf by Zajdlerowa, constitute the distinctive and irreplaceable element in the work. We have therefore retained virtually all the material from the chapters of personal accounts and direct description, omitting only some short sections of historical background which impede the flow of the narrative. However, we have re-organized the testimonies on a thematic basis. Zajdlerowa's chapters, it is true, are partly thematic: 'The Trains', 'Prisons', and 'Penal Camps' are examples. But she includes a long chapter of personal narratives which cover the entire range of experiences. We have now located these narratives in the appropriate thematic chapter. On occasion this has meant juxtaposing material from the original thematic chapter with new material from the personal narratives section. In order to ensure continuity and understanding we have inserted a few short linking passages in italics. These are few in number and, we hope, unintrusive.

Our second aim has been to help the readers make sense of these personal accounts by presenting the historical context in which this human tragedy occurred. The original edition attempted to do this, but in the last four decades much scholarly work has been completed and a new edition must take account of recent research. Moreover, the historical chapters, besides being dated, are often confusing and unsystematic analyses, with no references to the sources used, often polemical in tone and repetitious in content. Sometimes personal narratives are introduced in the middle of an historical account. Where this happens we have removed them to the appropriate thematic chapter. We have tried as far as possible to separate the testimony from the historical background. Consequently the original chapters entitled 'The Pact', 'The Army', 'The Civilians', and 'Certain Inalienable Rights' will not be found in this edition, nor will the two chapters on 'The Background'. Instead we have attempted, in this Introduction and in the Afterword, to explain to the modern reader the historical reasons for the events which will now unfold. 'History from the bottom up', of which this book is an example, makes assumptions, raises questions and demands explanations. As a work of art it stands on its own feet. As a work of history it does not. We have tried to anticipate the supplementary information the reader will require and have included this in our introduction. We hope that this will, in a small way, enhance the value of the book.

We have included photographs which speak for themselves and also a bibliography for the assistance of readers who wish to pursue this topic at greater depth. Maps, which were absent from the first edition, are produced here. If our own experience is a guide, consultation of them will be indispensable. They are, however, meant only as supplements to the description of the geography of the dark side of the moon presented in the original edition and particularly in its Introduction[88] from which the following passage is extracted:

Here, where what is unimaginable elsewhere may be the stuff of everyday – a far cry from Soviet Europe, and farther still from our own knowledge of it and of such centres of Soviet civilization as Moscow or Kiev – lies almost entirely the background to this book.

Starting round about the mouth and middle reaches of the Volga . . . and extending southward, south-eastward, and north-eastward across the Urals, the Soviet East contains a part of the Caucasus (itself a small continent, probably the oldest in the world), the whole of Central Asia (formerly Turkistan), the whole of Northern Asia, and the Soviet Russian Far East. To the south-west, the frontiers of this Soviet dominion are the frontiers of Persia and Afghanistan, to the south and south-east, those of Mongolia and Manchukuo. In the far north-east, they extend beyond the Arctic Circle. In the east, to the Pacific Ocean . . . throughout million after million of square miles, and far southward again, through immensities of primeval forests, the great Siberian rivers, the Lena, the Ob, the Yenisei, and a dozen others, alone provide the means of transport and communication. Yet these great rivers,

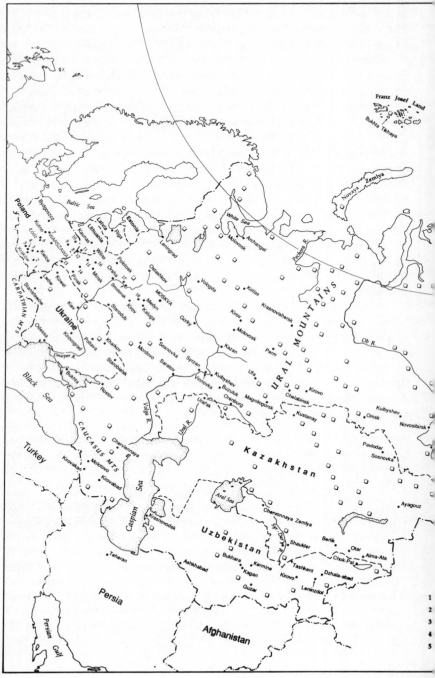

Map 2   The USSR

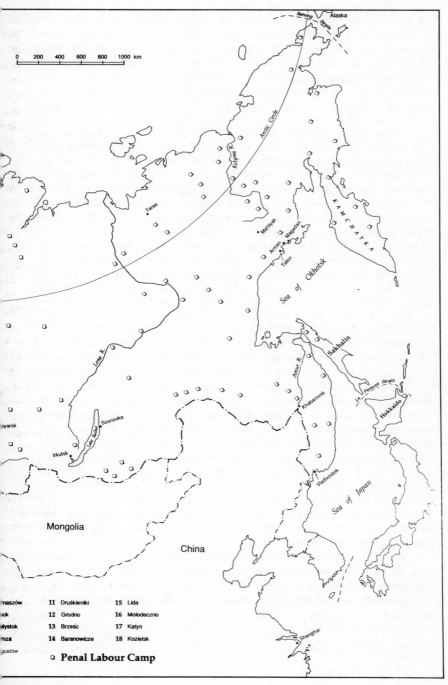

		11	Druśkieniki	15	Lida
		12	Grodno	16	Mołodeczno
		13	Brześć	17	Katyn
		14	Baranowicze	18	Kozielsk

◻ **Penal Labour Camp**

orld of camps and exile.

the mightiest waterways of the world, the basin of each of which is at least
as large as the whole of western Europe, remain frozen throughout almost
the whole of their length for the greater part of the year. In spring, released
during a few brief weeks from their strait-jacket of ice, their waters race along
in torrents; yet none of this flood water can be drained off underground. . . .
Southward again of this area is Central Asia, whose landlocked shores and
expanses of boundless steppe were once the bottom of the sea; the most
continental area of the whole earth; the 'land of thirst'.

All these are abysses of space: chasms into which millions of lives may be
cast without awakening any more echo than the rolling of a stone into a gulf.
Here cities, once the capitals of fabulous empires, are silted up with ancient,
unaerated sand. Extinct volcanoes rise like towers out of expanses of
otherwise totally unbroken plain. Tempests rage from October to March,
hurricanes carry snow, cyclones and anti-cyclones devour all that the
cultivator has laboured to achieve. Recurring famines ravage lands between
which lie other, so-called 'black', lands of fantastic fertility. Here are regions
in which for sixty days it is unbroken night; and others in which, day in, day
out, summer and winter alike, there is an average of over twenty degrees of
frost. Here, north of the Aral Sea, in Central Asia, temperatures are registered
which, in January, are lower than in Moscow or Leningrad, and in summer
higher than anywhere else in the world, except only in the Sahara, Arabia, and
on the Equator. In the infinite, horizontal expanses of steppe, unbroken
vertically by a single tree or shrub, mirages of cities hang above the corn.
Locusts move in formations, like the formations of armies when they invade.
Mosquitoes darken the daylight, winds cut like knives, and the sun, over
oceans of dust and sand, blisters and strikes yet does not warm. The sky, at
night, instead of vaulting the earth, bears down upon, and seems almost to
touch it. Huge stars, blindingly white and bright, hang so low as for us to
seem magnified out of recognition. Here – primeval as their own dark forests,
taiga and tundra, burning suns, eternal steppes, sky and snow, snow and
sky – the inhabitants of this immense world – Evenks, Tungus, Manchus,
Ostiaks, Samoyedes, Yakuts, tribes of the Amur basin and Palaeo-Asiatics
who inhabited the Far East before anybody else at all, Kazaks, Kirghizi,
Kara-Kalpaks, Turkmans, Uzbeks, lone fur-clad fishers of the Arctic,
nomads of the infinite plains, Buriats on Lake Baikal, yellow-skinned
Mongols off the edge of China, Pacific men from the north of Manchukuo and
scores and scores of others – of their own free will have altered nothing of their
habits throughout a thousand years.

For ourselves, the small settled people of Europe – orchardmen, farmers,
city workers, members of the learned professions, butchers, bakers, trade
unionists, back benchers, taxi-drivers, oil-and-colour merchants, miners,
civil servants, and the rest, lovers of our own back gardens, frequenters by
preference all our lives of a single public-house – these oceans of dust and
sand, grasses higher than a horse and his rider, forests never penetrated by
daylight, oceanic slopes, lake floors and Polar drifts, are paralysing in the
imagination.

It is within these unimaginable expanses, against these wastes of snow and sky, beneath the blind roofs of these primeval forests, along these ice-bound waters and across these oceans of sand and steppe – and not against any background or upon any stage which may even conceivably be compared with what we know – that the events now to be recorded have taken place.

Editors' Notes

1. *The Times*, 7 January 1989.
2. See, for example, Gustav Herling (1951) *A World Apart*, reprinted 1987, Oxford: Oxford University Press. Alexander I. Solzhenitsyn (1973/74) *The Gulag Archipelago*, Parts I and II, New York: Harper and Row.
3. The following prefatory note appeared in the first edition of *The Dark Side of the Moon* (1946) London: Faber and Faber:

> This book was begun during the lifetime of my husband, General Władysław Sikorski, and a comparatively short time before his tragic death. But for his confidence in the author and his instructions that she should be given access to official material and documents it could not have been written. The actual writing of the book entailed an enormous amount of collecting, sifting, and checking of material and evidence and my husband was no longer alive when, in the winter of 1944, *The Dark Side of the Moon* was finally completed. The manuscript thus never came into his hands, but it is certain that he knew the author for a woman of scrupulous integrity and fairness and that he had complete confidence that the material entrusted to her would be used always with a single purpose in view – the purpose of presenting truth as an essential preliminary to understanding and therefore to peace.

4. General Sikorski Historical Institute (renamed the Polish Institute and Sikorski Museum) (1961) *Documents on Polish–Soviet Relations 1939–1945*, vol. I, 1939–43, London: Heinemann, pp. 296–9 (henceforth referred to as *Documents on Polish–Soviet Relations*); Winston Churchill and Anthony Eden were respectively prime minister and foreign secretary in the wartime British government.

   With regard to a 'red book' it is perhaps relevant to note that Sikorski's position as prime minister and commander-in-chief was under threat after the signing of the Polish–Soviet pact of July 1941. See J. Coutouvidis and J. Reynolds (1986) *Poland 1939–47*, Leicester: Leicester University Press. Criticism of the Soviets would, in 1941–2, have reflected badly on Sikorski who had based his future on supporting his British allies (see note 8, below). Such criticism, accumulating as material for a 'red book', came mainly from August Zaleski who in August 1941 had resigned as Polish foreign minister and who supported the publication of a book which eventually came out as *Stalin and the Poles, An Indictment of the Soviet Leaders* (1949, London: Hollis and Carter) and from Generals Sosnkowski and Anders who also disagreed with Sikorski and whose subordinates also published a 'red book', as explained in note 5 below.

5. General Władysław Sikorski, as head of the Polish government-in-exile and as commander-in-chief of Polish military forces (see J. Coutouvidis (1976) 'The formation of the Polish government-in-exile and its relations with Great Britain, 1939–41', PhD Thesis, University of Keele) would, formally, have had access to a number of official sources of information concerning Polish citizens under Soviet domination after 17 September 1939. Our examination of the archives held by the Polish Institute and Sikorski Museum, PISM (the file headings given below are in translation), suggests that the files of the Prime Minister's office (PRM –/–) contained information which would have given Zajdlerowa the main outlines of the book she was to assemble. See PRM 4/2/471, 'Situation in Poland under Soviet occupation' and PRM 4/1, 'Information received from the Ministry for Internal Affairs of elections (under Soviet aegis) in Poland'.

The files of the Ministry for Internal Affairs (A.9/–) contained detailed accounts of relevant material. Indeed the first accounts of the transportation of Poles to Siberia, copied on file in English, occur in A.9/III/2c/2. These letters are similar in style and content to Zajdlerowa's evocation of life for Poles in the Soviet East on page 141 of the first edition; see also pages 136–7, below.

> We are now far away [almost 2200 miles] in distant Siberia . . . beyond the Ural mountains. It is still and beautiful here, the climat [*sic*] European, nothing but steps [*sic*] wherever you gaze, and not a tree nor a shrub to meet the eye. The bird family is represented here by . . . lapwings, bustards, and . . . pigeons . . . the houses are made of clay . . . There is a complete lack of fire-wood . . . and cow-dung and grass from the steppes are used for heating . . . We left at 9 o'clock in the evening [of 13 March 1940] . . . accompanied by the sounds of dreadful wailing. . . . The journey to the Soviet frontier took three days. Here we were transferred to Russian broad-gauge railway vans. We were not given stove [*sic*] nor were we any longer provided with hot food. Thus we journeyed for fourteen weary days and nights without a break until we arrived at our destination . . . There are about 2,402 deportees here. On our way we encountered many transports proceeding from different parts, from Zabie . . . Białystok, Przemysl, Lvov [*sic*], Sambor, Stryj, Wołynie etc. We are employed on hard labour and as the result many of us have fallen ill. . . . Innocent people are suffering. . . .

This report is dated 25 May 1940. An earlier letter of 15 May 1940 also suggests that communication was possible between Poles at home and their relatives in exile:

> Please inform everybody that we are alive – and that is all. After 22 days of a devilish journey we were landed in the Kirgisian stepps [*sic*], deep in Asia, amid wide open spaces stretching for hundreds of miles, not a tree in sight . . . We now living [*sic*] in the steppes in clay-built huts, which are very damp. We sleep on the floor and are exposed to terrible hardship. . . . My husband has lost weight to an alarming degree and can hardly stand on his feet; I do not know how I shall manage. He has to be washed and dressed and is not able to do anything for himself. . . . Whatever we get I stuff into my husband, so that he may regain

his strength, only there is nothing to be got in this wilderness. How are things with you? Would it perhaps be possible for you to send us some fats, tea and flour. Parcels are allowed up to 8 kilogram(s). . . . Parcels should be addressed in Russian. Lots of love and greetings – pray for us. . . . I doubt if my letters reach you, as you don't mention them in your telegram. Anyway we were mad with joy when we received your telegram. I implore you therefore, if nothing can be done about a food parcel send me at least some linen, light clothes and sandals; my feet are swollen and I have no shoes. My thoughts are with you continually. Do write us and do pray for us. Love to all other friends. Who else has been deported?

This information, it would appear from a copy of a report headed Washington, DC, 31 October 1940, reached the West five months after it was composed (see A.9/III/2c/2). Sikorski most certainly had access to it as it is copied in PRM/23/1940, 'The Soviet Occupation', i.v. 1940 – Copies of letters from Poles deported to Siberia . . .'. Also available to the Polish premier were the 'Reports of the Embassy in the USSR'. See especially PRM 42/5/1941, 'The Situation of Poles in the USSR', Kot (see above page 26) to the Polish foreign ministry (MSZ) 8.8.41–29.10.41 (131 pages in 52 files). These are also to be found in the A7 – files of the Polish embassy in the USSR; see especially A7/307/5–32. PISM has Ambassador Kot's files from 1.9.41–13.7.42 and Ambassador Romer's (Kot's successor) from 12.10.42–6.5.43. The balance of this material, archives of the Polish embassy in the USSR, 1941–4, resides at the Hoover Institution Archives (HI), Stanford, California, USA. These archives also contain the (General) Władysław Anders Collection, 1939–46. HI material is described in detail, relevant to our edition of *The Dark Side of the Moon*, by Irena Grudzińska-Gross and Jan Tomasz Gross (1981) *War Through Children's Eyes. The Soviet Occupation of Poland and the Deportations, 1939–41*, Stanford: Hoover Institution Press; and in Jan T. Gross (1988) *Revolution from Abroad. The Soviet Conquest of Poland's Western Ukraine and Western Belorussia*, Princeton: Princeton University Press, which is also referred to in note 28, page 42 as well as in note 3, page 179).

From the summer of 1941 after the Polish–Soviet treaty and the organization of a Polish army in the Soviet Union under the command of General Anders (see page 153) and especially after its evacuation to the Middle East in 1942 (see pages 169–70) Sikorski could have supplemented the information received from his ambassadors with that received through military channels. See especially the information on files (Kol 138/–) assembled by Col. Winsenty Bąkiewicz, the head of intelligence of Anders's 2nd Army Corps who maintained contact with Sosnkowski's underground network. Of interest here are Kol. 138/168, 256, 'Recollections of Russia by Poles' and Kol. 138/288, 'Reports of deportations to the USSR', which number 1,700 entries. These files are a likely source for Zajdlerowa; as a group, within which each document 'might have been replaced by almost any other', they most certainly gave an 'identity of content' and a striking 'identity of form' which she noted on page 116 of the first edition of *The Dark Side of the Moon* (see also page 6, above).

Also of interest is Kol. 138/255, 'Kazimierz Zamorski'. In the file entry the name which follows Zamorski, Sylvester Mora, is crossed out. This is Zamorski's pseudonym which appears alongside Piotr Zwiernak as authors of *Sprawiedliwość Sowiecka* (*Soviet Justice*) published in Polish in Italy in 1945. This book in earlier stages of its production could easily have been the 'red book' (see note 4 above) that Sikorski had suppressed in 1942. It may, in earlier drafts, have provided Zajdlerowa with the outline and some content for her book. (In selecting photographs for our edition it was interesting to notice that the Archives of the Polish Underground Study Trust – APUST – contained photographs that appeared in Zamorski's book. See also APUST file 7.6.1, 'Report on the deportation of Poles to the USSR', and their *Armia Krajowa w Dokumentach*, vols 1 and 2, London: n.p. 1970, 1973.) However, having identified similarities in content, style and organization, we would not claim to have established a direct relationship between the sources mentioned in this note and the contents of Zajdlerowa's book; such was not our primary objective. What we may suggest is that Sikorski, having alienated Sosnkowski, Anders and Załeski, himself felt the need for a 'red book'; at the turn of 1942–3 he realized that it was the Red Army and not the Western Allies who were to 'liberate' Poland. Also the break in diplomatic relations had occurred in the meantime and therefore there was less to be lost. Zajdlerowa/Curtis Brown/T. S. Eliot, well placed and well connected in wartime London, obliged the Polish leader, who died in an aeroplane crash on 4 July 1943 (see note 3 above) with *The Dark Side of the Moon* (see also note 63 below).

6. *The Dark Side of the Moon*, first edition, pp. 229–30.

7. The circumstances under which T. S. Eliot, whom Curtis Brown would have known as a publisher, came to write the preface are, in part, explained in a letter of 1 March 1985 written by Mavis E. Pindard, Permissions Manager at Faber and Faber: 'The fact that T. S. Eliot wrote a preface, must I think, be because he was particularly impressed when the manuscript arrived here. Obviously as one of the directors of the firm it would be a natural thing for him to do.'

The preface is one of Eliot's uncollected pieces of prose. It was translated into Polish in 1946 by T. Ichnowskiej, in *Przegląd Polski* (London, I. 2 August 1946), pp. 3–6. In 1985 Mrs Valerie Eliot gave permission for the preface to be reproduced in its entirety in an edition of one hundred copies only of *Text and Context, Journal of Interdisciplinary Studies*, published by the Department of Humanities, Staffordshire Polytechnic (see vol. 1, no. 1, autumn 1986, pp. 31–45).

8. The formal basis for Anglo–Polish co-operation was the Treaty of Alliance between the two states, 25th of August, 1939. For a discussion of Anglo–Polish relations see J. Coutouvidis and J. Reynolds (1986) *Poland 1939–1947*, Leicester: Leicester University Press. The history of the Polish military forces in exile is best found in General Sikorski Historical Institute (1959) *Polskie Siły Zbrojne w Drugiej Wojnie Swiatowej*, vol. II, part I, London: GSHI. It may be said, in agreement with T. S. Eliot, that Polish valour as displayed, for

example, during the Battle of Britain, was ill-rewarded by the British government in its dealings with the Polish government over the 'Polish Question'. In the context of Anglo–Soviet relations, strict censorship was applied by British authorities over Polish material which could offend the Soviet Union. For example, the Polish Ministry of Foreign Affairs was prohibited, in 1941, from publishing an account of Poland under occupation 'because it failed to distinguish between Nazi and Soviet actions in Poland'. See minutes on *L'Occupation Allemande et Sovietique de la Pologne*, Public Record Office (henceforth PRO), FO, 371/26724/C4932 and 371/26727/ C10269, and see note 31 below.

9. The meaning of this sentence, in particular of the phrase 'power of planned ignorance', may, perhaps, appear more clearly in the light of the following statements: 'the initial phase of the Soviets' rule in the eastern areas was marked by the spoliation of their reserves of raw materials, commodities, foodstuffs and even factory machinery and equipment. But it was not a case of common pillage. . . . The economic management of the Soviets has led to the economic disorganization of the Polish eastern areas and the pauperization of the population . . . .' (see PRO, FO 371/26727/C4343).

10. In 1948, two years after the publication of his preface to *The Dark Side of the Moon*, Eliot published his *Notes towards the Definition of Culture* (1948, London: Faber and Faber; also 1949, New York: Harcourt, Brace). The book's second chapter, entitled 'The Class and the Elite', explains Eliot's understanding of the cultural relationship of strata within society. 'The Class and the Elite' first appeared as an article in the *New English Review*, vol. XI, no. 6, October 1945, pp. 495–509. Judging by the date of the reference in the footnote on p. 508 of this article (7 July 1945) it seems reasonable to suggest that it was written by Eliot whilst he had access to the manuscript of *The Dark Side of the Moon*.

11. For T. S. Eliot's thoughts on the future of European civilization see the Appendix entitled 'The Unity of European Culture' in his *Notes towards the Definition of Culture* and in *The Idea of a Christian Society* (1939, London: Faber and Faber).

12. See below, page 90.

13. Arthur Koestler (1945) *The Yogi and the Commissar*, reprinted London: Jonathan Cape, 1964, p. 146.

14. *The New Statesman and Nation*, 29 June 1946.

15. *The Dark Side of the Moon*, first edition, p. 57.

16. Edward Crankshaw, *The Spectator*, 5 July 1946.

17. *Documents on Polish–Soviet Relations*, p. 65.

18. *Ibid*, p. 40.

19. *Ibid*, pp. 43–6.

20. *Ibid*, pp. 66–8 and see *The Polish White Book* (1933–9), *Official Documents Concerning Polish–German and Polish–Soviet Relations*, London: Hutchinson for the Polish government (henceforth referred to as *Polish White Book*).

21. PRO, CAB 118/69, 1941–5, 'Document from the Polish Social Information Bureau', December 1943; CAB 119/132. 128070. 5 May 1944, p. 14; see also

L. Kirkien (1945) *Russia, Poland and the Curzon Line*, London: Caldra House, p. 47.

22. *The Times*, 15 September 1939; *Polish White Book*, p. 120.

23. Ann Sue Cardwell (1944) *Poland and Russia: the Last Quarter Century*, New York: Sheed and Ward, pp. 162–3.

24. *Ibid*, pp. 162–3; Adam Zołtowski (1950) *Border of Europe: A Study of the Polish Eastern Provinces*, London: Hollis and Carter, p. 313; R. Umiastowski, *Russia and the Polish Republic, 1918–1941*, London: Aquafondata, n.d., pp. 72–3.

25. *Documents on Polish–Soviet Relations*, pp. 67–8.

26. W. S. Churchill (1948) *The Gathering Storm*, London: Cassell, pp. 351–2. The Prime Minister, Neville Chamberlain, expressed agreement with this view.

27. E. Estorick (1945) *Stafford Cripps: A Biography*, London: Heinemann, pp. 247–8. See also Bernard Pares' article in the *Manchester Guardian*, 31 May 1941.

28. Jan T. Gross (1987) 'The first Soviet sponsored elections in Eastern Europe', *Eastern European Politics and Societies*, I, no. 1, Winter; see also his (1988) *Revolution from Abroad, The Soviet Conquest of Poland's Western Ukraine and Western Belorussia*, Princeton: Princeton University Press, Ch. 2, 'Elections', pp. 71–113, and see *Documents on Polish–Soviet Relations*, p. 123. We have also consulted PISM, PRM 4/1: 'Ministry of Internal Affairs report on the election in Poland (under Soviet occupation)' (see references in note 5 above).

29. See below, pages 52–3; Umiastowski, *op. cit.*, pp. 241–2; PRO, FO 371/26723, C4343, 15 April 1941.

30. *Hearings before the Select Committee to Conduct an Investigation of the Facts, Evidence and Circumstances of the Katyn Forest Massacre* (82 Cong. 1 and 2 Sess. House Select Committee, 1951–2), pp. 1639–40.

31. PRO, FO 371/26724/C4932, 3 May 1941, '*L'Occupation Allemande et Sovietique de la Pologne*' p. 41. This 47-page galley proof of a publication by the Polish Ministry for Foreign Affairs (headed by August Zaleski; see note 4 above) caused much alarm (as explained in note 8 above) in Foreign Office circles. See especially minutes by Roger Allen, 24 May 1941 and Frank Roberts, 14 May 1941.

32. *Ibid*. pp. 43–4.

33. *Ibid*, pp. 43–4. Umiastowski, *op. cit.*, p. 266. See also his reference to the memo '*L'Occupation Allemande et Sovietique de la Pologne*' on p. 276.

34. Letter, from the Polish President (W. Raczkiewicz) to the Pope, 6 April 1941, copied in PRO, FO 371/26723, C1827, 23 April 1941.

35. See extracts from Eliot's preface to *The Dark Side of the Moon* pages 3–4 above. T. S. Eliot may have overlooked the possible radicalization of the (Polish) masses as a consequence of the war. It is an aspect to which Professor Lewis Namier drew attention in his report to the Foreign Office quoted in J. Coutouvidis (1984) 'Lewis Namier and the Polish government-in-exile, 1939–40', *The Slavonic and East European Review*, vol. 62, no. 3, July, p. 423. See also the chapter on 'Poland' by J. Coutouvidis, A. Garlicki and

J. Reynolds (1990) in S. Slater and J. Stevenson (eds) *Working Class and Politics in Europe and America, 1929–1945*, London: Longman.

36. See J. K. Zawodny (1971) *Death in the Forest: The Story of the Katyn Forest Massacre*, London: Macmillan.

37. Report no. PC3. From Lt. Col. L. R. Hulls, Hqrs. Polish Army, Yangi Youl, USSR, to H.E. The (British) Ambassador, Kuibyshev, 28 July 1942 in FO 371/31088, XC/A 011475. See also his earlier report of 18 June 1942, *Ibid*, quoted on pages 172–3 of the Afterword. Hulls was the British liaison officer with Anders' army. His appointment is discussed in PISM, PRM 1941, PRM 42/4 1941 'General Anders' Letters'. Hulls took a pro-Anders and anti-Stalin line and was critical of Sikorski in the sense discussed in note 4 and 5 above. FO minutes on Hulls' reports read: 'Col. Hulls had come up in a conversation between Eden and Sikorski in Nov. (1941) (C11309) and Sikorski thought Hulls had a bad influence on Anders. . . . These reports show that Col. Hulls has lost his sense of proportion and that his appointment should not be renewed despite Gen. Anders' request.' F. K. Roberts advised, 'Col. Hulls may have not unwillingly taken on the colour of his environment . . . we cannot blame him . . . his statements are unfortunately factual and should go on record . . . on the other hand he reveals a very critical attitude towards the Polish Government, of whom he of necessity knows little . . . suggest when time comes he is replaced and explained as normal administrative procedure'. *Ibid*. F. K. Roberts was head of the Central Department at the Foreign Office during the war.

38. PRO, FO 371/26724/C4932, 3 May 1941; PRO, CAB 118/69. December 1943.

39. PRO, CAB 118/69, December 1943; *Documents on Polish Soviet Relations*, pp. 168, 573.

40. Solzhenitsyn, *op. cit.*, I, p. 42.

41. *Ibid*, pp. 24–92.

42. *Ibid*, p. 77.

43. See below (main text) page 74; see also PRO, CAB 120/670 C496/19/55, 15 January 1942.

44. Norman Davies (1984) *Heart of Europe: A Short History of Poland*, reprinted Oxford: Oxford University Press, 1986, pp. 167–8.

45. Solzhenitsyn, *op. cit.*, pp. 60–8; Robert Conquest (1968) *The Great Terror*, London: Macmillan, pp. 557–61.

46. For further information see PRO, CAB 118/69, December 1943; George Kennan (1958) *Siberia and the Exile System* (a reprinted and abridged edition of the two volumes originally published in London: Osgood, McIlraine, 1891), Chicago: University of Chicago Press, p. 26.

47. Solzhenitsyn, *op. cit.*, pp. 543–9.

48. *Ibid*, pp. 501–7, Herling, *A World Apart*, pp. 20–31.

49. Solzhenitsyn, *op. cit.*, pp. 505–6; see also below (main text) page 81.

50. See Herbert Feis (1967) *Churchill, Roosevelt, Stalin: The War They Waged and the Peace They Sought*, Princeton: Princeton University Press, pp. 10–13 and United States (1959) *Foreign Relations of the United States, Diplomatic Papers*, Washington, I, pp. 768–9.

51. *Documents on Polish–Soviet Relations*, p. 107. Sir Stafford Cripps was British Ambassador in Moscow at the time of this conversation.

52. See M. Kukiel (1961) 'Polityka Polska wobec Układów Brytyjsko-Sowieckich w.r. 1941–1942' ('Polish Policy in the Face of British–Soviet Relations in 1941–1942'), *Bellona* (London), No. 3/4, pp. 163–82 and repeated to one of the editors in an interview with General Kukiel in October 1967.

53. PRO, CAB 120/670 C496/19/55, 15 January 1942. It should be noted that, on the same day that the Polish–Soviet agreement was signed, the Foreign Office in London issued an assurance that the British government did not recognize any territorial changes effected in Poland since August 1939.

54. R. Umiastowski (1946) *Poland, Russia and Great Britain 1941–1945*, London: Aquafondata, p. 29.

55. *Documents on Polish–Soviet Relations*, pp. 132–144; it was Cripps who persuaded Stalin to agree to the general liberation of the Poles detained in the Soviet Union. See also PISM, PRM 41/3, 8 August 1941.

56. *Red Star*, 17 September 1940; *Documents on Polish–Soviet Relations*, pp. 107, 115, 158, 462.

57. *Documents on Polish–Soviet Relations*, pp. 147–52, 156, 165–6.

58. *Ibid*, pp. 147–9, 207–8, 222–3.

59. Averell Harriman was President Roosevelt's personal representative; Lord Beaverbrook was the Minister of Supply in the British government.

60. *Documents on Polish–Soviet Relations*, pp. 123–4, 167–70. 215–6; PRO, CAB 120/670, 17 September 1941, 28 January 1942, 3 August 1942.

61. *Ibid*, pp. 187–9, 223–4.

62. *Ibid*, pp. 176–8, 202.

63. *Ibid*, pp. 347, 377.

64. As explained in J. Coutouvidis (1976) 'The formation of the Polish government-in-exile and its relations with Great Britain, 1939–41' PhD Thesis, University of Keele, Sikorski, ignoring the Ministry for Foreign Affairs and the Ministry of Information, established his own propaganda organization in London. Ambassador Raczynski, the Polish Ambassador in London, was told by Sikorski that '. . . Retinger would conduct Polish propaganda in Britain.' This had angered the Ambassador (see Count Edward Raczynski (1962) *In Allied London: The Wartime Diaries of the Polish Ambassador*, London: Weidenfeld and Nicolson, p. 45), and his doubts with regard to Retinger's authority are echoed in a letter to him from Hugh Dalton (Minister for Economic Warfare, 1940–2, in Churchill's Cabinet) 'I am not really sure how far Retinger is really authorised . . .' See Letter, Dalton to Raczynski, 10 October 1939. PRM1/3 PISM. A Foreign Office minute elaborates the concern felt in British official circles about Retinger's role(s)' . . . On personal points it is quite clear that Retinger has, for good or for ill, enormous influence with the Prime Minister [Sikorski]. The latter laughs at him, it is true, and calls him '*le cousin du diable*', but he is clearly regarded, both by Sikorski and by his family, as a sort of household pet and everything of importance is discussed with him . . .'. Minute by H. M. Jebb, 1 January 1941, PRO FO 371/26722, C188. Jebb also wrote, 'Retinger plays the role of

an "*eminence grise*" to G. S.' *Ibid.* See J. Pomian (ed.) (1972) *Joseph Retinger, Memoirs of an Eminence Grise*, Sussex: University of Sussex Press, pp. 83–145. It is interesting to speculate to what extent Retinger was involved in the production of *The Dark Side of the Moon*. See note 5, pages 38–40 with particular reference to his probable role as go-between of Curtis Brown and Polish government circles (see also note 3, page 37).

65. *Documents on Polish–Soviet Relations* pp. 153–5.
66. *Ibid*, p. 157.
67. *Ibid*, pp. 158–60.
68. See Stanisław Kot (1963) *Conversations with the Kremlin and Dispatches from Russia*, Oxford: Oxford University Press, pp. 37–52.
69. Bronisław Kusnierz (1949) *Stalin and the Poles: An Indictment of the Soviet Leaders*, London: Hollis and Carter, p. 80 (see note 4 above).
70. *Documents on Polish–Soviet Relations*, pp. 176–80.
71. *Ibid*, p. 221; PRO, CAB 21/968, 4 November 1941.
72. A full record of the conversation is to be found in *Documents on Polish–Soviet Relations*, pp. 234–42. In response to Sikorski's request that Polish troops in the Soviet Union be sent for training to Persia, where conditions were better, Stalin burst out, 'That means that we are savages and that we cannot improve anything . . . that a Russian can only oppress a Pole, but is unable to do anything good for him.'
73. *Ibid*, pp. 236–55; PRO, CAB 120/670, 6 December.
74. *Documents on Polish–Soviet Relations*, pp. 233–4, 257–8.
75. *Ibid*, pp. 294–5, 301–9, 448–50.
76. The Polish government was apprehensive about sending ill-trained and inadequately-equipped troops to the front line. Frequent and insistent requests that they do so must have aroused suspicions that the Soviet military command was indifferent to the fate of the Polish army.
77. *Documents on Polish–Soviet Relations*, pp. 319–21, 342–3, 597–8.
78. *Ibid*, pp. 351–2; see also W. Pobóg-Malinowski (1969) *Najnowsza Historia Polityczna Polski (Modern Political History of Poland)*, London: Gryf, III, pp. 240–1 and PRO, CAB 120/670, 2 July 1942.
79. *Documents on Polish–Soviet Relations*, p. 282.
80. *Ibid*, pp. 413–4. Also PISM, A. 11, 49/Sow/7, 'Memorandum from the Polish Ministry of Foreign Affairs to Ambassador Biddle', 10 July 1942.
81. See PISM, A 11, 49/Sow/27, 'Report on Chargé d'Affaires Sokolnicki to the Ministry of Foreign Affairs', 13 September 1942.
82. *Documents on Polish–Soviet Relations*, pp. 417–21, 478–80.
83. *Ibid*, pp. 478, 515. Molotov emphasized that the Polish embassy would have 'very little to say in the matter of institutions whose staff and inmates are for the most part Soviet citizens'.
84. PRO, CAB 118/69, December 1943.
85. Ibid, PRO, CAB 122/927, 11 May 1943, 27 May 1943, 23 June 1943.
86. Compare, for example, the higher mortality figures in Kazimierz Plater-Zyberk (1982) *In Defence of Poles in the USSR*, London: Polish Ex-Combatants' Association, p. 5.

87. Some few thousand members of the Polish First and Second Army Corps who had fought in the West returned to Poland after the war. The great majority refused to go, largely for political reasons.

88. See *The Dark Side of the Moon*, first edition, pp. 11–14.

ONE

The Occupation

O f this Soviet entry and subsequent occupation, two layers of consciousness, related yet distinct, separate yet inseparable, inhabit my mind. There is a layer made up of what it felt like at the time. This layer is all emotion; loss, shock; initiation only into a grief whose sum and term could hardly be estimated at the time. Then there is the layer which is all looking back, and distinguishing, in what seemed merely experiment and chaos during that time, an inflexible order, and the spearhead of an enduring plan.

In recording those months, I do not believe that any purpose will be served by artificially separating the two layers, since they are co-existent; and since both have been a part of the experience of all those persons with whom this record is concerned. In the present chapter, then, in setting down the sequence of events, I shall set down, too, as much as I can of the emotions and sensations through which we lived while the events were taking shape.

For this I must begin at midnight on September the 16–17th, when, with my companions, in a small house on the edge of the Pripet Marshes, I listened to the broadcast from Moscow which announced that Soviet divisions, with armour and air cover, had crossed our eastern frontier.

From this night onwards the Moscow radio broadcast almost uninter-ruptedly that 'the internal bankruptcy of the Polish State had been revealed', that 'the Polish State and its Government have ceased to exist', that 'Warsaw no longer exists as the capital of Poland', and that 'therefore the Agreement concluded between the Soviet Union and Poland had ceased to operate'. It is noteworthy that the first German siege of Warsaw was at this time still going on, and that on September the 19th the capital was still bearing itself in such a way as to receive the broadcast message from 'the people of Britain to the city of Warsaw' which declared: 'All the world is admiring your courage', and that Poland had become 'the standard-bearer of liberty in Europe'.

The stupefaction in Poland was so great that many units were surrounded and taken prisoner before they could fight back. Others fought desperately on, but there was not now the slightest hope for our

47

shattered forces, caught between the two heaviest and most powerful armies in the world. Of the civilian population, very many – the majority – as we know, believed in the first hours that the Russians had come as friends, that they were to fight the Germans and join up with the Polish divisions re-forming in the marshes.

From this time onward, we found ourselves in a night of doubt and confusion. Great mists of grief and horror oppressed our minds. The stream of refugees which had flowed east now began to flow back again towards the west. The millstones moved relentlessly together, and hundreds of thousands of people were caught between them, enduring every kind of progressive wretchedness and horror. As well as the tens of thousands of refugees on the roads, tens of thousands of soldiers and marines now began retreating westward again, standing here and there to fight and retreat again: more often, to lie where they had fought or to be taken as prisoners to the Soviet Union. These men were desperately weary, famished, and short of everything; shortest of all of sleep. Many of them had been marching fifty or sixty kilometres a day. Rumour of course came with them. They knew even less than ourselves. Many of them kept right on believing that when the Russian and German armies met they would fight each other. Half of the men were too exhausted to talk at all. The worst thing was the condition of their feet. Too exhausted to be roused, they were incapable even of surveying their own bivouac fires; the chill of the autumn nights, following on the fantastically hot and cloudless days, barely reached them in this deathlike sleep. Only the very sick rested anywhere for more than a few hours. Polish and Soviet patrols were stumbling over each other here and there; some of them had talked together. More than once, a Red soldier had produced tobacco from his own pockets and given it to the tobacco-starved Poles. Many of them had said that they did not know what to make of this war. They had been told they were to march straight through against the Germans. They had had no idea that their leaders were sending them in to secure their share of a new partition of Poland. Later, I was to hear this story over and over again. I do not know if what they said was true. The perfect autumn weather added to the horror of all that was taking place.

Of the household in the eastern marshes in which I found myself at the time, I think that I may usefully give a description, since the house itself, the life lived there and the mistress of the house, are all of them almost perfect types of such houses, the life lived in them, and the people who lived it. In the text the house is called K. and its owner N.

'. . . K. was the same, and yet not the same, as I remembered it. N. still went about the gardens, the bakeries and the byres in her patched skirt and thick stockings, with her scissors and keys hanging from her belt and a little basket on her arm. Her stockings had been darned so often that, as a last resource, they had now been mended over the heels with squares of cloth.

'When she was not doing this, she was doing the estate accounts or turning a garment or sorting winter beans or doing any one of a dozen other things. From seven o'clock in the morning until the whole household had gone to bed at night, she never spent an idle half-hour.

'She was eighty-three, and her first recollections were of a childhood in Siberia, between a father in chains and a mother who had followed him into exile. The Great House had been destroyed three times in her lifetime: when her father had been made a convict; by the Germans during the last European war; by the Bolsheviks in 1920.[1] Each time what was rebuilt was plainer and poorer than it had been the time before. When I knew it, it was still called the Great House, but it could hardly have been compared with an English farmhouse. Only N. in her worn clothes, with her stained and work-hardened hands, made it splendid. It was the Great House because she lived in it, and because she had built it, when she was already more than sixty, with those very hands. . . .'

N. was passionately attached to this house which she had built. Above the foundations, which were of stone, it was of rough wooden logs, covered with plaster, and it was whitewashed inside and out. Like most Polish houses of its kind, it faced east. There was only one storey, and one living-room. This living-room was entered at each end from three or four shallow steps leading out of a short veranda. Leading out of this room again was a second, much smaller, room, in which N. slept, a short passage ending in a kitchen and indoor larder, and two more very small rooms, leading into each other. Out of the living-room a short flight of stairs, really a ladder, led to a sort of upper room in which N. was accustomed to keep water-melons and white flour, and which was also her grandson's bedroom when he was at K. This grandson was the heir.[2] Each room had a stove built into one corner, reaching from the floor to the ceiling and also plastered and whitewashed. In the living-room there were a very large table and chairs, a very old wireless set and a few books; in the others, a chair, a bed, and a jug and basin on an enamel stand. In summer, there were mosquito nets on all the windows. It is not, after all, quite true to say that this particular house, as it stood, could be taken as a type of all other manor houses in Eastern Poland. In essentials it was the same, and in spirit; but its extreme simplicity, even poverty, was rather an exception, even where all was simplicity and where there was no wealth, as we understand it here. N., at sixty, had not been able to do more. To do so much, she had lived for years with a peasant family in the village, and herself worked on the site every day. A really typical manor house of the kind would also have been low and plain, one-storied, and facing east; but it would have had many more rooms, with a lot of offices and passages built on to the main part, and a great overhanging shingled roof; and a large porch would have divided the building in two, with the veranda leading into the porch from both sides. Inside, there would have been more comfort, and the accumulation of generations of cultured, if hard, living: for not all families were as unfortunate as the family at K., and not all had lost everything twice within one generation. At K. there was not so much as one silver fork or spoon. In the town house in Pinsk (the market town for Polesie, with possibly 50,000 inhabitants and also mainly built of wood) a few family miniatures had been preserved, and a few little worn leather boxes containing old Polish coins or medals commemorating the risings of 1830 and '63, in trust for the heir. The only pictures on the whitewashed walls were a polychrome of Piłsudski in 1922,[3] and a cheap black-and-white print of Emilia Plater in 1831.[4]

This house and the farm, of some 100–150 acres, were now taken over by Soviet order and put under the nominal control of a village committee. N. was not yet expelled. All waited for the N.K.V.D. authorities themselves to appear.[5] While we were waiting,

'. . . inventories of what was now said to be the peasants' property were begun daily and never finished. It is not that the peasants cannot read and write. It is that they have no heads on their shoulders for what is not their business. . . . What they understand is the seasons, the rivers, the forest and the soil. In this kind of knowledge there is nobody who can teach them anything. But within three days the flour was sour. The windows of the store-rooms were left open. The salt was spilled and wasted. The maize was left to spoil. Out of sheer anger at the sight of it, we went out and worked in it ourselves. I stripped the maize-cobs ten hours a day. Weeks afterwards I still had the welts left on my hands. For the rest of my life I never want to see maize or dried haricot beans again! The winter beans were left on the verandas to freeze in the now nightly frosts. . . . The beetroot and the cabbage lay out on the surface of the ground and froze too. The Holland cows stood in the stalls all day. The people from three villages ran with bottles and jugs to milk them. . . . None of the herd was ever milked clean. For days they bellowed with pain and then went dry. The few hogs that remained were better off, for the swineherd went doggedly about his business as he had always done. The gun-dogs starved at the end of their chains. Two died in the sun. The fowl escaped into the trees. The over-ripe melons and tomatoes, already past the time when they should have been gathered, turned to mush. The kitchen and the offices were full of feasters twenty-four hours a day. . . . Ever since I knew anything about Eastern Europe, I had known that Poland is Europe's frontier there. Any shrinking of Poland is an advance of Asia. I saw it now with my own eyes. The Polish dyke had been levelled. The tide from Asia was up to our necks within a week. . . .[6]

'N. changed nothing in her normal routine except that she sat longer over the estate-books, since the agent was no longer there . . . for hours and hours she sat each day at this book-keeping. Her back never bent. She put the pen aside only when the arthritis in her fingers brought on a particularly violent cramp. When the cramp passed she would go on again. At nightfall she complained of having no lamp to continue by . . . the book-keeping was in arrears. It was an obsession with her to finish it. . . . The peasants had seldom taken their wages. What they preferred was to accumulate a sum over years, only taking out of it such trifles as tobacco, an occasional length of cloth or hide for the moccasins they make themselves, until they wanted it for getting married, buying a horse or building a new cabin. . . . Everything taken from the land went back into the land. The forest paid the crushing taxes and gave her the fire she sat by; nothing more.'

In the processes of expropriation and of switching over to Soviet economy, which now began, the first step was the so-called nationalization of commerce. In practice, this worked out at the seizure of practically all goods still left in the country, which were then sent to the Soviet Union. Of the 8,500 shops in Lwów alone, 6,500 were stripped and closed under this pretext. Factory after factory had its whole plant ripped out and carried off, and the personnel, with their families, were ordered to be ready to leave with the plant. In many such factories the workers locked themselves in and were forced away from their barricades only at the point of Soviet bayonets. Furniture and equipment of all kinds was taken out of houses and offices; including the doors, frames and sashes of windows and planks torn up from the floors. Apparatus from laboratories and clinics, roots and crops from the farms, timber from the forests, grain, sugar, tobacco, coal, hides, pig-iron, cement, drugs and textiles – all these were carried off from the most backward areas of Eastern Poland for the enrichment of the Soviet Union. In exchange for all that was being taken out, the new administration brought into Poland during the first months some matches, some very inferior salt, some worse soap and a few herrings. Because of a total lack of raw materials, at least 67,000 small workshops employing very many very highly skilled men had to put up their shutters for ever.

Next, the złoty, whose pre-war value had been twelve roubles, was first reduced to the value of one rouble and then withdrawn altogether from circulation. The population, already almost totally out of employment, had now to face the further catastrophe of every penny of its savings being rendered valueless overnight. The standard of living fell at runaway speed and to a point far below anything which would have been believed to be possible only a few months before. The monthly earnings of a highly skilled artisan in full employment fell, as a result of this substitution of the rouble for the złoty, to at most 100–150 roubles, whereas prices soared to a level which was truly astronomic. In February of 1940, the price of two and a half pounds of potatoes was five to six roubles, of the same amount of meat thirty to fifty roubles, of lard and butter, seventy roubles. In certain districts a hundredweight of rye cost 700 roubles, two and a half pounds of sugar, sixty to seventy-five roubles, and the same amount of tea 700 roubles. A pair of second-hand shoes could easily be sold for 500 roubles.

In January 1940 the League of the Godless arrived, with a government grant of three million roubles with which to start its programme. This programme included the closing of churches, the prohibition of the saying of rites by priests of all denominations and the inclusion of atheist propaganda in all radio programmes. Law courts were instructed that the practice of religion was a valid cause for divorce. Many clergy were deported. Special Commissioners were appointed for the propagation of atheism throughout schools. The whole story of the schools, of the ordeal of school-children generally and of the immense fortitude and determination those children displayed, in their resistance to the new teaching, must be told elsewhere. I have no space here to do more than record the fact.[7]

In country districts, the ruin of the farming class, including peasants and small holders, was no less complete. Soviet propaganda during the first few weeks had talked of an immediate, and wholesale, redistribution of land. In Eastern Europe, where the soil in the main is poor and very much of it both unreclaimed and irreclaimable, land hunger is an emotion which probably goes deeper and lasts longer than any other. There is no emotion of which an Eastern European peasant is capable which is not at some time incomparably weaker than this. In certain very backward areas these offers had been eagerly heard. But the promised redistribution of land in Eastern Poland turned out, as it had turned out years before in the Soviet Union, to be a chimera. Indeed, the peasants were themselves shortly being urged to pool their own holdings and to start farming on collective lines. To a peasant who would no more move off his own land, or part with any corner of it, of his own free will, than he would part with his own life, this was compulsion not to be borne. The sale of livestock, too, was now rigidly controlled. No sale of livestock or produce was legal without the consent of a committee, and the committee itself could do nothing without the consent of a body still higher up. The necessary and natural exchange of goods between countryside and town ceased altogether to operate. The peasants' own movable property was also menaced. Those sheepskin jackets, even, which the climate make [sic] an absolute necessity and which in themselves represent a substantial share of a peasant family's movable goods, were requisitioned in many districts and dispatched to the Union. The population of these districts, accustomed to a standard of living already more than frugal, were astounded and startled by the unfamiliarity of the newcomers with practically everything that they themselves considered necessities of life. Not only was the whole fabric of economic and public life, as we knew it, being brought down in ruins. At every step we were also being brought into contact with reactions utterly unfamiliar to us, and quite passing our comprehension. The invaders – and not only the rank and file but highly placed officers even of the N.K.V.D., the most privileged caste in the whole Union – were seized with astonishment and admiration at the sight of the simplest articles offered for sale in the most primitive store. In the towns they would rush into all the shops in a street and come out again after having bought up literally everything in sight; not because they were in need or even often understood the use of what they had bought, but from sheer exuberance, and from astonishment at the shopkeepers' freedom to sell, and the customer's to buy, any article either chose – a phenomenon never present in their experience until now.[8]

This behaviour, in persons coming from the Soviet Union, although it surprised us, was not, looking back on it, surprising. In the Union, rigidly controlled State-owned shops, when they had any goods to sell at all, had always sold not what the customer required but only what the State cared to furnish. The peace-time freedom of people in other countries to buy what they wanted, when they wanted it, seemed to them first plainly incredible and then a reversal of everything they had been taught.

Fundamental, and quite insuperable, was the totality of difference between their conceptions and ours of those standards a human being sets himself in his private and particularly in his physical life. Conceived of as little more than cattle, housed as cattle, monstrously herded together in hovels worse than byres, eighty to ninety per cent of the Tsar's subjects had never known, and had barely even aspired to the standards of human beings. Tsardom at an end, their fingers had been taught to handle intricate machinery and their tongues to repeat a new lesson, but for the great majority the physical conditions under which they lived had hardly changed at all. The new régime, intent on its vision of the future, occupied in the present less with bodies than with minds, had not yet embarked on transforming the personal habits left over from centuries of serfdom.

This abyss of difference between the standards of Soviet citizens and the standards of the poorest or most primitive Polish home became fully apparent with the arrival in Poland of wives and families from the Union. The state to which these families could reduce a normal lodging within a few hours of taking possession, the accumulating filth in which they were satisfied to live, their total lack of discipline in respect of physiological functions, the crowded promiscuity of all the arrangments they made, the complete absence we observed in them of any instinct towards any other order of things – all this, we felt and felt with truth, had brought Asia into our homes.

During all this time, civil administration of the Occupied area, as in the Soviet Union, had been in the hands of the N.K.V.D., who at once assumed the same power over Polish citizens as they exert over citizens of their own State. The German armies had been accompanied by the Gestapo. The Soviet armies, in their turn, came accompanied by political commissars. These commissars, again identically with the Gestapo, came ready furnished with lists of persons to be arrested within the first few hours.

On lists of persons to be immediately arrested had appeared in the first place all representatives of political parties of whatever shade of opinion, including the leaders of all Polish, White Russian, Ukrainian and Jewish Socialist organizations and of Socialist trade unions, and after these all such persons as town councillors, members of trade union executives, members of working-class committees, organizers of working-class, peasant and other youth institutions, civil servants, government and local government officials, members of the police forces, forestry workers, engineers, skilled workers of all kinds, members of the learned professions, barristers, procurators and all other servants of the law.[9]

The experience of a person who fitted one of these categories is briefly described.

The author, a well-known leader in all working-men's movements, a functionary of the Central Union of Miners and member of the Executive Council of the Polish Socialist Party, was arrested under circumstances which he has described on the 27th of September 1939.

'On the 27th of September 1939 I received an order from the political authorities of the Soviet administraton in . . . to call a meeting of all the workers' organizations in . . . and to dissolve these organizations in view of the new legal and political situation. At this meeting, the N.K.V.D. representatives present handed me the text of a resolution to be submitted to the delegates of the workers' organization and to be passed by them. By this resolution, the workers were to express satisfaction at the incorporation of our eastern provinces in the U.S.S.R. I refused to submit the resolution. Immediately after the meeting, I was arrested, and confined in the gaol at Drohobycz. In the course of the investigation which followed, I was accused of betraying the interest of the workers, of action inimical to Stalin, of support of Trotsky and other Soviet "traitors", etc. I was sentenced on the 15th of December 1939 by a military tribunal and condemned to ten years' hard labour in *lagier*.[10] Until the 10th of January 1940 I was kept in the Drohobycz prison, and then transferred to another prison in Lwów, and later, from Lwów to Odessa.'

All this, however, was still too little. A secret registration was simultaneously being prepared of persons to be deported to Soviet territory by a series of mass deportations, and to be there confined within Soviet penal institutions. From February the 10th onwards more than a million men, women, and children were so carried off; and many more would have followed them but for the German invasion of Russia in 1941.

The lists included all of university standing, teachers, doctors, engineers, the forestry services, well-to-do peasants and very many very poor peasants, certain categories of workmen, the families of soldiers of all ranks who were thought to be with the Polish Army or interned abroad, refugees from the German-occupied parts of Poland, and 'speculators' – a term applied to small merchants and traders.

Both the registration and the deportations which followed it automatically included the families also of all persons enumerated above, again a perfectly normal proceeding under the Soviet code.

For the manner in which the deportations were actually to be carried out, instructions appeared over the signature of Deputy-Commissar Serov (for the Interior):[11]

'The deportation of anti-Soviet elements is a problem of great political importance. The plans for carrying it through must be worked out in minute detail, and realized by the Executive Troikas of each district. The task must be carried out as quietly as possible so as to avoid demonstrations or panic among the population.' The decree covers about ten pages of instructions describing the minutest details of procedure. 'On principle, the whole operation shall be carried out by the above-mentioned Executive Troikas at night-time'. The deportees at most might be allowed twenty to sixty minutes for packing their things. The weight of the baggage of any family was not to exceed 100 kilos, and might contain only clothing, bedding, kitchen utensils, food for one month and fishing-tackle. Farmers might also take certain simple farming implements, but these were to be loaded into separate trucks so that they might not be used as weapons. Trains must be ready for departure before dawn.[12] Before entraining, heads of families were to be segregated and placed in special cars. After entrainment, the doors and windows of cars were to be blocked up, leaving only an opening for the 'introduction of food and for eliminating excreta'. Shortly after the New Year these arrangements were complete. The enormous number of trains required to move the cargo of human beings were gathered from all over the Union, were assembled and waiting.

The actual dates of the four mass deportations are the 10th of February 1940, April of the same year, June of the same year and June of 1941.

The mass deportation of February the 10th included whole villages of small farmers and farm labourers, forestry workers, ex-soldiers from the last war who had received grants of land, civil servants, local government officials and members of the police forces.

The April deportation of the same year included the families of persons previously arrested, the families of men with the Polish Army, persons in trade (of whom the majority were Jews), farm labourers from sequestered estates and more groups of Polish, White Ruthenian and Ukrainian small farmers and farm labourers.

In June refugees from all other parts of Poland who were in Eastern Poland on the 17th of September 1939 were carried off. The registration of these people had been made particularly easy by an announcement some months previously that all refugees wishing to return to the German Occupation would be allowed to do so upon submitting their names. With them were also members of the learned and professional classes and 'speculators'.

The last mass deportation took place in June 1941 and covered all those included in the previous categories who had so far evaded deportation, children from summer camps and orphanages, persons who had been kept in Polish prisons and not yet removed to Russia, and all persons who had up to now in any way assisted the Soviet authorities. In this way, all members of the so-called Local Committees (consisting of Communists or semi-Communists and all those persons who had supposed themselves to be one or the other and had been prevented by fear from drawing back after they had become aware of what was actually involved), all members of the 'militia' and even A.R.P. workers[13] – in a word, all those who in any way had been in close touch with the authorities, who after witnessing at close quarters what had been done with others had themselves remained behind, and all who had had dealings of any kind with the Red Army – were in their turn removed to the Soviet Union; and there met with precisely the same fate as those whom they had helped to deport on the three earlier occasions. This fourth deportation also included all persons on the files of charitable organizations for refugees.

The February deportation took place in the worst weather anybody could remember. The winter of 1939–40 is remembered for its severity, even in England. These first people to be taken were quite unprepared for the event. Later victims had at least some foreknowledge of what might be going to happen, and many had made what preparation they could in the shape of food and suitable clothing packed and ready to hand. But for the tens of thousands deported in that mortal February no such action had been possible.

From my own notebooks I extract a passage written almost three years later, in which, at the time, I attempted to set down some of the emotions and sensations of this period. In these notes, the confusion and anguish of that time is looked back upon in the light of what has since become known.

'. . . From the place in which we were, there was no view. . . . Each of us inhabited the unlit well of his own heart-sickness. How to eat, where to eat, where to sleep, how to send or get news, whom to see, whom to trust, how to answer their questions, how not to despair; all these things, with grief, devoured what thought we were capable of, day and night. If we heard anything, it was still the voices that had been dear to us. If we were attentive to anything, it was to what of our own had not yet been swept away. The faint fanning sound of the trains drawing out of their immense distances could not reach our consciousness. Violently torn away from our past and not yet having become grafted on to any future, our extraordinary mutilated lives existed in a void. Very likely, if we had been less stunned, if each of us had been able to measure the extent even of his personal catastrophe, if we had been more truly observers and not ourselves pieces of the tragic paper whirling inside the kaleidoscope, we might have already perceived the pattern, for the pattern was there. The fact is that we did not. To us, all was still chaos, without perspective. There was absolutely nothing of which we were yet sure. Of two individuals of identical habits, it was impossible to foretell which might disappear for ever, without hope of return, and which might be told that his case was now completely in order and himself free to go home. Nor, for that matter, whether upon reaching home this second individual might not there be arrested all over again. Far less, as yet, seemed to depend on the unalterability of the new touchstones than on the chance of the day, the hour, the place, somebody's humour, an expression of face or of voice. Those who disappeared simply stepped out of life. . . . Our sources of information were all tainted by emotion. Thousands of persons with infinite difficulty sent messages to tens of thousands of others, and not one of the messages was ever delivered by the person who had heard the original words. It was like a nightmare distortion of one of those games in which a whispered phrase is passed from one player to another down a row, and reaches the last player deformed out of all recognition and often out of all sense. Out of what, at appalling risk, did get through, it was impossible to be quite sure even of the names. Rumour rising higher and higher washed about like troubled water, from the towns to the villages and from the villages back again to the towns. It was impossible to be sure even of bereavement. Who had fallen and where? Who might still return, or be heard of half across the world? Who, even now, struggling to reach the Polish Army in France, had successfully made the night passage through the mountains, waist-deep in snow, trailed by hunger and enemy patrols, beaten to his knees by the gales from the heights, and who had succumbed?[14] The majority of us, too, were hungry, or what seemed like being hungry in those early days; and with advancing winter, cold. Hunger and cold destroy vitality perhaps even more surely than grief. In the struggle just to go on existing, there was little vitality left for seeing into the future. Few of us perceived what was being planned; and if we had, perceiving it would not have helped at all. I am curious now, I would not have been curious then, about the details of so vast an undertaking. Looking back on it now I am able to see a plan. I can see that some objective brain, two thousand miles away, free of all the emotions, beliefs and urgencies which were driving us, must have been intensively occupied, possibly for a very long time, with all the pleasure that comes from concentration and its reward, in working out the trains. The considerations were not at all what they could have been anywhere else in the world. Whatever was decided, nobody would be in a position to complain. Even so, great skill and much brain must have been required for the working out of all these time-tables: all those dates of departure, freights and lines: the number and type of wagons, the locomotives and personnel, the centres for fuelling and refuelling, the strictly necessary trains to be kept running on their side, and the services which could not be allowed to break down – not anywhere or in any way that mattered, that is, for them.[15]

'. . . The faint fanning sound of the trains gathering multiplied, vibrated together high over our heads, approached, almost entered our ears, and then dropped again below audibility. Once over the frontier they slackened speed, damped down their furnaces, slid through the Polish junctions and the great main stations without even whistling; shunted into sidings and on to lost branch lines; stopped finally in the open country, on the edge of suburbs and along platforms where an express used sometimes to pause before dashing into a terminus. The first light snows of the year began to drift up beneath the axles, lay in ridges along the roofs of the cars and melted at first each morning in the noonday sun. Nobody guarded them. Apparently nobody remembered them. So much that was valuable had been pitched down everywhere to lie, rust and rot. Main streets and motor roads still gaped with craters and were blocked by wreckage. Nothing was cleared, nothing renewed. Even the harvest had been squandered and abandoned. Crops had rotted in the earth. Winter feeding had frozen into stinking pulp. Breeding sows and cattle were being slaughtered every day; breeding mares had been harnessed to guns. The whole infinitely costly storehouse of generations had been burst open and destroyed; and not even from any imagined military necessity but from a profound contempt for the care and toil of the individual and for the mystery of man's long husbandry of the soil. Even the village hearths had grown cold. *Izba* after *izba* stood empty.[16] The heart no longer lifted in joy and reassurance at the sight of smoke spirals rising above the village roofs from the glowing stoves. The whitewashed kitchens were inhospitable. No winter stores stood in the larders. The autumn fruits, the melons, cucumbers and tomatoes, instead of being preserved, had turned to frost-bitten masses of corruption. Spring was far off and already there was no salt anywhere. The fields were full of rusting iron, split ears and rotting straw. Even the ricks of the year before had been thrown down, trampled, fouled, often fired. Into this scene – in which everything now spoke of decay and ruin – the idle railway cars, the cold locomotives, the snow piling up under and against the wheels, the uncleared lines and the motionless signals, fitted so well as to be perfectly invisible. . . .

'Some normal traffic still existed. To buy a ticket, it was often necessary to wait days on the station from which you hoped to leave. Nevertheless, trains did run. Some did in fact at last bring in a little food from across the frontier, mostly in the form of tinned stuff (fish and fruit) which the Soviet Union does particularly well. Most of this tinned stuff was destined for the town of Lwów, now a Number One town, Soviet category. These conserves (by those who could by any means pay for them) were bought eagerly. Of those who bought, and those who did not, very many were later to see some of the plants in which these fish had been packed, and to work in them fourteen and eighteen hours a day. . . .

'Other of the trains brought more and more troops and then more and more bureaucrats, and their women and children to be with them. A number of people were allowed to leave for destinations (within the Soviet Occupation) of their own choice. There were even a few days, at the very beginning, when some people were allowed to travel back to the German Occupation. The action of buying a railway ticket and leaving for somewhere of your own choice was immediately consoling. Up to the end of the year, a number of people actually succeeded in returning to their families, or, more often, to the places where their families had been. If they found nobody else, they found at least some former neighbour, some shop in which they had formerly bought goods, or some person who had known them by sight for years. To be greeted by name, to reassemble one's features and personality, to represent for anybody a set of habits, a past, a background – in a word, to recover identity – is for a refugee an experience of extraordinary comfort. But with the turn of the year a change was felt; one of those changes impossible to trace or define but of which everybody is instantaneously aware. Out in the country, at those halts on the edges of suburbs, along sidings and down lost branch lines, the doors of the idle cars were opened. The snow began to be trampled and the engines whistled as the furnaces warmed and the vapour rose. Patrols moved out further into the villages until all the chimneys that still smoked were inside a cordon. In the towns, enormous armoured cars stood in the streets all night. The trains that had come in so quietly gathered again and turned outward. Wherever they moved up from, they were all to go out the same way. They were to go to the Soviet Union. . . .'

What follows is the history and the tragedy, since 1939, of the impact upon each other of two peoples, living side by side, yet culturally, politically and emotionally worlds apart. Of these two peoples, the background and meaning of life for the one has lain altogether in Europe; based on a Latin and European culture, ethic, religious faith and daily habit. For the other, the background has been first Byzantium and then Asia; with a culture, ethic and daily life dictated at all times by the political necessities of absolute government. The one nation, whatever the races assimilated, has been from its inception a cohesive whole; a commonwealth welded together by centuries of shared civilization. The other, under whatever name, remains an Empire, including within its rule some two hundred racial minorities at least. In the presenting of this story the unique task undertaken has been the constituting of a record; and of a memorial. Within these pages are recorded – in words infinitely insufficient to their theme – the lives and deaths of many hundreds of thousands of innocent and hapless persons. Every one of these pages is tragic. Every one is loaded with horror; is concerned with disaster and despair. Yet these pages record also a fidelity of the spirit and a fortitude of the mind which might have seemed hardly within human capacity. They bear witness to the ultimate irreducibility of certain citadels of the human spirit, in conditions through which humanity itself seems at first sight to have suffered irremediable defeat.

Editors' Notes

1. N.'s father was probably convicted after the 1863 Polish Uprising against

Tsarist rule; the area in which the house stood, part of eastern Poland in the 1920s and 1930s, had been occupied by the Germans in the First World War and, briefly, by the Red Army during the Polish–Soviet war, 1919–20.

2. This grandson, the evidence suggests, was the author Zoë Zajdlerowa's husband (see the Introduction, page 1).

3. Józef Piłsudski was Polish head of state 1918–21 and unchallenged ruler of Poland under the Sanacja régime, 1926–35; a Polish hero after leading the Poles to victory in the Polish–Soviet war, 1919–20.

4. Emilia Plater (1806–31) fought in the 1831 uprising against Russia, first as a 'gentleman' volunteer and later as a captain in an infantry regiment, dying at the age of twenty-five. She was immortalized by the Polish poet Adam Mickiewicz in *The Death of the Colonel*.

5. NKVD was the designation of the Soviet secret police, 1934–43; it was an acronym for People's Commissariat of Internal Affairs.

6. This reflects a widespread Polish conviction that Poland was Europe's eastern bulwark against Asia, and that Tsarist Russia and the USSR were essentially non-European societies.

7. In February 1943 a Polish orphanage near Kuibyshev in the Soviet Union was taken over by the local Soviet authorities. Under the new régime, lessons were to be in Russian only. Despite orders and threats the Polish children refused to be taught in Russian and sang hymns and national songs in Polish. See: *Documents on Polish–Soviet Relations*, p. 506.

8. A reference to the scarcity of consumer goods in the Soviet Union in the 1930s. The difference in the standard of material existence between Eastern Europe and Russia, as seen through Russian eyes, is depicted in Alexander Solzhenitsyn's novel *August 1914* and in his poem *Prussian Nights*.

9. For a discussion of Soviet motives, see the Introduction. The significance of forestry workers can be gauged from the emphasis Stalin placed on forests as a major base for the Polish resistance movement against the Germans after the Nazi attack on the Soviet Union in 1941. The specialist knowledge of forestry workers could be very valuable (see *Documents on Polish–Soviet Relations*, p. 491).

10. Camps for penal servitude.

11. Ivan Serov was a secret police official who became chairman of the KGB (acronym for the Soviet secret police after 1953), 1954–8.

12. The instructions were somewhat flexibly applied. From records of conversations with Polish deportees in the possession of the editors, it appears that the NKVD were more rigorous if the male head of the household was present. If only a mother and her children were in the house, more time was allowed for packing, and help and advice were given. Sometimes deportees were encouraged to take simple farming tools, but on other occasions they were told that there were plenty of these in the Soviet Union.

13. ARP, acronym for Air Raid Precautions.

14. After the Soviet invasion of eastern Poland in September 1939, thousands of Polish soldiers crossed the Romanian or Hungarian borders and made their way to France, where the Polish government-in-exile had been established.

15. Doubtless organizational skills were required, but the Soviet authorities had considerable experience of using trains to deport vast numbers of their own citizens, most notably peasant farmers from the Ukraine in the early 1930s. See Alexander Solzhenitsyn (1974) *The Gulag Archipelago 1918–1956*, I–II, pp. 54, 565, London: Bodley Head.

16. Peasant dwelling(s), wood-framed and thatched and, characteristically, unicameral; *izba* in common usage means a room or chamber.

The Journeys

The trains were very long, and seemed also extraordinarily high. This last was because they seldom stood along platforms and the whole train was accordingly seen from the level of the ground. Later, some Polish trains were also employed, but the earliest were all typical long Russian trains brought in for the purpose; dark green in colour, with doors coming together in the middle of box cars as they do in cars on the Underground.[1] In each of these cars, very high up, just under the roof, were two tiny grated rectangles, the only windows and the only spaces by which air or light could enter once the doors were fast. This great length of the waiting trains, always coiling away somewhere and always partly lost to sight, was in itself terrifying to the imagination. Those about to be deported were brought to the stations heavily guarded: for the most part loaded on to armoured cars, but also, when these gave out, on sledges and on little country carts shaped like tumbrils, ordinarily used for the carting of dung.

A woman from the little village of Delatyn gives the following description. 'It was night. The little village, normally so peaceful, on the edge of the forest and muffled in snow, was suddenly filled with loud noises and with the trampling of strange feet. With other persons in the same house, all of them already exhausted by watching and grief, I tossed between uneasy dreams and a tormented wakefulness. Overtaken by these snatches of sleep, it was difficult to be sure how much of all that was happening was real, and how much part of our terrible dreams. After midnight, every few minutes, one or other of us fearfully tested the electric light. Since September all light had been switched off early at the main, coming on again after midnight on nights when patrols were due out in the villages, with search parties in all the yards and N.K.V.D. soldiers bursting into houses and making arrests. On this occasion, a searchlight was set up and kept on all night in the middle of the village street. After midnight, whole convoys of sledges loaded with families who had been arrested went past the door all night. There were thirty-three degrees of frost. At dawn, a sledge went by on which was seated Losia, one of the foresters and a friend of the household, with all the members of his family, and behind them was an N.K.V.D. soldier, holding his rifle and bayonet at the ready. Columns of similar sledges passed throughout the whole of the following day. The neighbours stood outside their houses and prayed. The parish priest stood on a knoll by the church, holding out a great Cross towards those who were taken past.'

The roofs of the cars were piled with fresh snow but the ground all about was trampled and fouled. The trains, after being loaded, often stood for days before leaving, and the tracks along which they stood would become piled with excrement and yellow and boggy from the urine running down off the floors. Against the background of white, the silhouettes of the N.K.V.D. soldiers were shaggy and outlandish. As they paced, they stopped often to stamp their feet, attempting to keep warm by a movement of their arms which is not like ours but characteristically Russian and not easy to describe. Each soldier carried a fixed bayonet at the end of his rifle. Immense crowds of people swayed backwards and forwards. The soldiers with their bayonets forced back all except those who were to leave on the trains. On principle, nobody was allowed to pass the barriers, but many did. The confusion was so great that the soldiers themselves often did not know who the masses of people were.[2] Families were being broken up all the time, husbands and wives separated, children being pushed into one part of the train while their mothers, frantically searching for them, were being herded into another. The stations rang with cries and groans and names being desperately shouted above the din. So many of the accounts I have now before me tell of how the old, dying and infirm, in their ghastly bed-linen, just as they had been dragged out of bed, collapsed in heaps on the ground. Corpses of children froze in the snow and their mothers, vainly trying to restore them to life, covered them with their own bodies and felt the same deathly chill creep up their own limbs and touch their own hearts. There were people who went out of their minds from horror and shock, and their lamentable complaining was added to all the other fearful sounds of woe. Above and through everything was heard the ceaseless shouting out of names, and cries of 'I am here', 'Come to me here', 'Now, now, I am being dragged away'. Baggage of all kinds was piled up and flung down everywhere. Each person had to drag or carry his own. Little children and pregnant women stumbled and fell under the weight of great bundles or bursting suitcases. Roughly speaking, each person was allowed to take a certain amount of baggage; though many, of course, had been arrested in circumstances where they could collect none, and many others had already been separated from theirs on the journey to the trains. It was of fearful importance not to lose this baggage, as it later turned out. Those individuals who survived their experiences in Soviet territory were almost always those who had managed to bring with them something, clothing or other articles, from Poland.[3] But this appears much later on. Fifty or sixty persons were pushed somehow into each car. Those left behind could see a sea of haggard faces surging behind the tiny grated squares. Their own terrible, searching, upward looks strained to meet once more some one pair of eyes behind these gratings. People fought their way towards the cars, with offerings of bread and other food, or to exchange last words. Again and again, relatives, neighbours and friends returned to the barriers, attempting even to take them by storm, with food or a little tobacco for those who were being carried away. The guards drove them back each time with rifle-butts and bayonets. Once or twice it might happen, too, that a guard would let a few of them through. Or, though not often, another might even take a few of the loaves of bread or some scribbled words on a scrap of paper and pass them into the cars. They were not often humane, but they were not often deliberately cruel either: not yet. They were simply indifferent, carrying out their orders, accustomed to such work, possibly even a little taken aback by the intense grief and horror shown by the Poles. One or two, when implored by some frantic mother, or when urging some old invalid or terrified child out of bed, even troubled to mutter, 'Quiet, quiet. It is only being taken to another *oblast*.[4] There will be food for you there and work, and you will all be together again. *Kharasho*, everything will be *kharasho*!'[5] To get rid of these hordes of people with their tears and questions and all the things they wanted to be allowed to do, the guards had all sorts of ruses as well. It was a favourite trick of theirs to tell people that they could not pass now, but that at some hour later in the day, say, at four in the afternoon, if they now went quietly, they would all be let through. The crowd, returning at the time suggested, would find that the train which had been standing for days had got up steam that very afternoon, and had left while they had been away.

As the trains drew out those left behind tried desperately to cling to them somehow, even to hold them back with their hands. There was, however, nothing to hold on to. The doors in the centre of each car closed tightly like a vice, and were secured by an immense iron bar which lay all the way across. The clang of these iron doors coming together was a sound impossible to forget. From the gratings fluttered down showers of white scraps, atoms of paper on which were written names and addresses, last messages begging not to be forgotten, broken sentences and prayers. More than once, as a train moved, as it became clear that fate was irrevocable, that the Poles were again setting out – but this time in hundreds of thousands and in steel-clad and convoyed trains, on the long road which leads from Poland to Siberia and the Arctic North – a few voices first, and then a choir, and then thousands of aching, parched throats, bursting with sorrow, would raise the notes of some pealing Polish song of faith and praise. Over and over again, in the variety of documents before me, one narrator or another pauses to record this same thing – the releasing at such a moment of mass emotion in song. I have heard these Polish songs so many times before and since. They are the songs of the Old Republic, the songs of the Polish Golden Age, the songs of the Partitions and the songs the Poles have made familiar all over the world, since 1939.[6] They are always the same songs and they utter always the same thing; ineradicable love of Poland, proud faith in God, and a passionate determination to be free or die. Those songs are heard everywhere where there are Poles still alive, or with voice enough left, to sing them; and, if not to sing them, to breathe them in their prayers. In camps and prisons, in Germany and the Soviet Union, in internment camps everywhere, in the Polish Army, on Polish ships, in the Polish Air Force, in Scotland and in England, in Africa, in the Middle East, in Italy, at Tobruk, at Narvik, in France, in America and the British Colonies, around Easter and Christmas tables, in factories, in universities, wherever Poles meet together, these songs have been heard during the last five years.[7] Many, upon hearing them, have been much moved. I do not know what they would have felt if they had heard them as they burst forth from those loaded trains leaving Lwów and Stanisławów, Tarnopol, Pinsk, Baranowicze, Wilno, and scores of other Polish towns during 1940 and 1941.

Inside the trains, it was at first almost impossible to distinguish anything. Only a very little grey light crept in, from high up under the roof. After a little while the eyes become more accustomed to this gloom. Certain shapes of things slowly emerged. The fifty or sixty (or more, but this was on the very worst trains: fifty or sixty was the average) persons accidentally herded together in each of the hundreds of cars that made up a train were all dishevelled, travel-stained and, in one way or another, suffering from shock. Many had not eaten for days. Others were distracted by thirst. Many were attempting to support members of their family who might only be ill or who might already be sinking into a coma, prelude to death. People still clamoured for some medical help. In theory, a doctor and medical orderlies accompanied each train. The atmosphere, once the doors were shut, was stifling from the first moment. In winter, in some of the cars, there was a primitive iron stove. These stoves burn wood or coal, but there was seldom, if ever, any of either. Sometimes there was a supply which could be made to last for a day or two; but, then, very often, the doors of the stoves had been wrenched off or the sides driven in by former passengers, and they could not have been lit anyhow. Although the air was so close and foul it was nevertheless terribly cold in the cars; and the children screamed and wept, more, at first, from cold and fright than from hunger. Of course, they were not yet really hungry. None of them ever really comprehended what hunger was until they had been in Soviet territory. A few planks were arranged in tiers around the walls of these cars. There was no bedding of any kind but these planks were intended to be places on which those in the cars could lie down and rest. Probably, when they were first put in, there was a sufficient number of them to accommodate the normal number of passengers carried in the cars. These cars, although we should not have thought them fit for carrying anything but cattle and only then if much more light and air were admitted, are in Russia adapted to the use of passengers by the simple addition of planks and these stoves: and by the opening of a largish round hole in the floor which is intended for the passing of excrement. Apart from the overcrowding and the locking of the doors, there was no special rigour behind the submitting of Poles who had now, according to Soviet notions, become Soviet citizens anyhow, to the same conditions which many other citizens of the same State put up with every day.[8]

In none of the cars, however, were there now enough of these bunks left to accommodate more than about ten or fifteen persons. In the majority, there were none left at all. The extreme filth, recognizably human (for human filth always has something in it which is quite different from the filth of other animals) of the walls and floors, showed that the cars had been long and lately in use, probably for carrying troops. Dust, too, lay along all the folds of clothing and worked its way into lungs whose resistance became weaker every day. This was not so awful a problem in winter as it became in the April and June of the same year, when the roofs and walls of the cars were red-hot from the burning rays of the sun. Space was by common consent allotted first of all to the very old and to the most feeble and to mothers with very young children or women who were pregnant. The hole in the middle of the floor was screened by a blanket or two. This hole was of necessity extremely filthy and repulsive and, from the very beginning, this question of physiological processes loomed larger, probably, than any other. It is a recurring question which it will not be possible to omit from this record. Not only in the trains or on marches, but later in the penal institutions of every kind, the whole endless torturing business of the body's needs, and the absolute lack of any kind of decency or privacy in which these needs could be satisfied, pressed with accumulating cruelty not only on the poor body, but also on the mind.

The first stages of the journey while the trains had not yet left Poland behind were perhaps the most agonizing of all. Natalia C., recounting this parting from the loved and familiar scene, tells how she rose early one morning, still full of sleep, to see her husband off to the town where he had some business. After the cows had been milked, she decided to lie down and to sleep again while the bread rose. As she was pinning a sheet across the window to darken the room, she saw her husband returning in the company of four men. They entered the house, and her husband with a deathly pale face smiled to her and the children. The children were aged six and four, Tomuś a boy, and Wandeczka, a girl. After a pretended search of the premises the family were ordered to leave. The children, seeing their mother begin her preparations, broke into violent grief, dragging at her arms and legs and urging her to stay. When they saw that this was of no use and that she was already seated in the cart, they climbed determinedly on to the cart themselves. 'Crawling to me', she says, 'like worms' over the bundles and baggage on which she was seated. When they reached the station, the father was separated from them and put into another wagon. The mother hoped much that the train would leave in the night, for the track went round a low hill just beside the homestead, and she hoped that the children need not see it and feel all their sorrow freshly burst out again. Unfortunately, the train left during the day. As the homestead came in sight, they saw neighbours and other members of the family standing on the hill and the parish priest with a crucifix in his hand. As the train approached, he raised and held out the crucifix in the sight of the first cars. The wife thought with joy that his blessing was falling on her husband who was in this part of the train. The crucifix shone in the sun. As the chimneys, the orchard, and the trees came clearly into sight, Tomuś cried out in a terrible voice, 'Mammy, Mammy, our orchard, our pond! Mammy, our Gierba [the cow] grazing! Mammy, why do we have to go away?'

At every halting-place still in Poland women and children attempted to approach the cars, to hand in milk or food and to whisper comforting words. Usually they were roughly driven off. The trains travelled slowly and did not gather top speed until they were over the frontier.

With the frontier once left behind, the sharpest wrench was over. There was now nothing loved or familiar to be seen through the inch of grating; and nothing to be wept over, and then left behind, any more. People were struggling all the time to take each other's places at these gratings and to get at least a few mouthfuls of air before they had in turn to give up their place to somebody else. The faint winnowing noise of the trains gathering speed now turned into a tumult and thunder. The rails hummed, the tunnels were full of flying sparks. The men in the signal-boxes worked longer shifts than had ever before been heard of. Bridges and viaducts shuddered through all their length as convoy after convoy of iron-clad cars, loaded far beyond capacity, thundered across them.

At the frontier, trains met and overtook each other. As they drew alongside or past each other, people began the same frantic calling out of names; either their own, in the hope of being heard by those they were seeking, or the names of those they sought, lest there might be somebody on another train who had seen them or knew where they were. The names of the districts from which the deported came, or the stations they had been through, were called out too, without, perhaps, any precise reasoning, but in obedience to a deep instinct to establish some kind of contact with one's own. There was probably also an unexpressed conviction that inquiries must be made; that such countries as England and America, the first of whom was already an ally and fighting in the same war, could not leave these deeds unexamined. There was, therefore, great need for establishing any possible clues to identity. Some time (surely before long) inquiries which could not be ignored would be set going about people of these names, coming from these and other villages. It might mean everything if somebody could say at the right moment that they had been heard of on such and such a day, in such and such a train going in such and such a direction.

From Kiev onwards, scarcely one of the people hurrying to and fro on the crowded platforms so much as glanced twice in the direction of the cars or their freight. The Poles could not get over the sensations induced by the fact that these people, moving about freely themselves, did not appear to feel surprise, compassion, or, indeed, even a mild interest in the convoys. It was still very difficult for people coming from outside the Union to take in that such things could be everyday sights; that members of these people's own families, their fellow-workers or neighbours, might as easily have been transported in similar trains to similar destinations; and that these people having nothing with which to compare such proceedings, did not find them remarkable. It was still some time before they understood that all this was not some otherwise unheard-of proceeding against themselves as foreigners, but that the whole system and the institutions to which they were being taken had, in fact, come into existence and continued to exist as a normal part of life for Soviet citizens. The fact of being Poles was indeed what had brought them to this pass themselves; but similar things had happened to all the peoples within the thirteen republics of the Union. The citizens of Kiev and Kharkov could not be expected to turn their heads because this time the trains came from Lwów or Tarnopol or Stanisławów or Baranowicze or Pinsk, or any other town to them equally remote and unknown.

No regular allowances of food and drink were given out on the trains. Arrangements about this varied. Roughly speaking, it may be said that bread (sour and black and badly baked) was handed out on most trains at intervals of two or three days or so. Occasionally a few buckets of fish soup with fish heads and bones, or eyes and entrails of animals in it, were distributed, but this was very rare, perhaps twice or three times during the whole journey, in all. A number of convoys received no hot food at all, from the time they entered the train until they were driven out at the other end. Hunger was pretty general, but a lot of people did still have some food and hunger was not the worst hardship. The water situation, however, was absolutely drastic. It can be said at once that on no train, at any time, in any temperature, was there ever anything like the lowest possible amount of water which could keep a human being from suffering acutely from thirst.

The callousness shown by the soldiers on convoy to all the desperate appeals made for water is more difficult to understand than anything else. The right of every living thing to drinking water is something so elementary and so universally admitted, even in the jungle, that it seems almost impossible for any human being, when not experiencing any particular sensations of anger or vindictiveness and when not in danger of thereby being deprived of it himself, persistently to refuse to hand in a bucket of water to fifty or sixty human beings, shut in together under such conditions. It is a fact that these men did refuse to do so, and could keep up this attitude throughout journeys lasting four, five and six weeks.[9] There were whole days of twenty-four hours, when not a drop of anything to drink was passed into the cars. There were periods even of thirty-six hours. The allowance, when it did come, would be a bucketful, sometimes two, never more, for a whole car. Even when snow lay deep on the ground and on the roofs of the trains, and could have been scooped up in buckets and passed in without the slightest trouble, they could not be bothered to do it. People went out of their minds from this suffering. Little children could no longer force even a cry from their swollen throats. In late spring and summer, when passing through the scorching land of the Ukraine and the Central deserts, a pitch of suffering was reached which can never be estimated or described. The cars, which no light or air could penetrate, were easily penetrated by sand-storms. Tongues turned black and stiff and protruded from ghastly mouths and throats. To all entreaties, expostulations, outbursts and brainstorms, the soldiers returned only curses or blows. Corpses were thrown out on to the line or put out at the rare stopping-places. Once or twice, some merciful rain fell. On one train of which I have a record, a hole was made, with infinite precaution, in the roof of the car, and a piece of rag stuffed into it and sucked for its life-giving moisture. For this, if they had been discovered, the perpetrators would have been shot. This was one of the worst trains and left Poland in June 1941 after the German–Russian war had begun. Aboard were Polish soldiers who had fought against the Germans and been captured by the Russians in 1939. The train was being bombed all the way. The prisoners, being locked in, remained in the trains. The thirst was so terrible that men were drinking their own urine. There is something more than Dantesque about this picture of men – still dressed in rags of the uniform in which they had fought against the common enemy – now being deported to the Soviet Union, who had to clamber on each other's backs, kneeling up with what strength they could still muster, to suck this rag squeezed through the filthy roof and moistened by a few drops of the rain falling from heaven over an earth upon which other human beings moved in freedom. Many could not raise themselves to put their lips to the rag.

Every few hours or so the soldiers moved up and down the train, stepping on prostrate bodies, thrusting others out of their way and carrying out inspections of one kind or another. This they generally began by beating on the walls of the cars with their rifles, to make sure that no planks had been loosened anywhere and nobody was contemplating escape. These inspections were part of the hell in which everybody lived. The noise alone was torture. The manner of the soldiers was violently overbearing and rough. The number of soldiers in a convoy varied. On most trains there was a soldier in each car, generally on a small platform. But there might be none or there might be more. There might be a platform or not. Always, in the last car of each convoy, there was a mounted machine-gun. At night searchlights were lit on the roofs of the train. I have searched in vain through masses of evidence for records of anything approaching humanity being shown by any soldiers on any of these trains. I have a record of one man passing in an extra bucket of water and five other records of doors being opened for a short period, some ten minutes or so, to let some air in; and this only after the most urgent entreaty and from caprice, not in any way furnishing a precedent for other occasions. This question has preoccupied me profoundly. Throughout my work on this book, work which has occupied several years, I have searched the evidence exhaustively on this point. I have also put the question to every single person with whom I have talked. It has been of immense importance to me, of an importance greater than I can possibly express, to discover that some instinct of humanity did survive, somehow. The answer invariably given me has been that it did not.[10]

Of the doctors who accompanied the trains I have no better account. A very few showed a little more than blank indifference towards the case of some individual child. I have two records of decided kindness. Two – no more. These persons were, in fact, rarely qualified doctors at all; they possessed neither knowledge, medical supplies, nor interest in the matter. At halting-places, an individual here and there was thrust in to join all the others. A woman put on alone at Husiatyn was dying when she was put on. In the night, in the total darkness, while the train was travelling at terrific speed, from somewhere among the piles of baggage she suddenly began uttering despairing pleas for comfort and help. On this train as on all others people were lying in heaps on top of each other on the floor. Anyone attempting to stand upright was hurled from one wall of the car against the other by the speed of the train. When the first grey light appeared it was seen that fountains of blood had been spurting from her mouth all night, all over the children nearest to her, over the bucket used for water, the baskets containing food and the bundles of clothes. The other people in the car implored the guards to let her have a little salt water or even a little snow, but they would not be bothered even to listen. Neither would they, for a long time, consent to call the doctor. When he did come, he looked once at her, to say: 'She is consumptive, and consumptives soon die', and left again. After a few more spasms she did die; too feeble to suffer any more. The body lay for a long time in the bright blood from its own lungs.

This terrific speed of the trains rarely slackened and was least bearable in the total darkness of the night. The most self-controlled persons gave way to hysteria. Children were so petrified with fear and shock that they stiffened themselves in the highest bunks and refused to come down. Their mothers could not persuade them to relax or to let themselves be removed or even touched. In the night their shrieks tore the darkness apart and their water ran down on to the sleepers on the floor below them. Human beings were born in these conditions and lay naked on the filthy bundles on the floor. Two infants were born in one night in the same car, and a third mother, herself in the last weeks of pregnancy, helped to deliver them. Both infants died: one stifled by the atmosphere of the car, the second of brain fever. The mothers lived.

Volumes could be filled with nothing but the story of the trains. And even then it would not have been told, for there are no words which can reproduce the emotions experienced and the sensations undergone. The reader can be given facts. He cannot share the *experience*. He can read about the filth, but he cannot taste it in his throat and feel himself saturated by it, as these people did. He has smelt some unpleasant odours. He has, perhaps, some idea of the faintly nauseating smell of a body which is decently fed, normally evacuated but not really scrupulously washed. His experience is unlikely to go further than this. The atmosphere breathed in by the people in these cars, the condition of the floors, the stench that arose from them, beat off the walls, lay under the roof, filled their hair, skin, pores and lungs, and entered every passage of their bodies, is something of which, even while he reads, he has no conception at all, and cannot have. One can enumerate the horrors. The lack of privacy. The thirst and hunger. The accumulated anguish of body and mind. The *fatigue*. The epidemics. The sores. The vomiting. The diarrhoea, digestive troubles, dysentery and bleeding. For women, menstruation, too, and childbirth, in these conditions. The convulsions of those, most advanced in age, who simply could not bring themselves to make use of the opening in the floor and who strained their bowels to the point of violent rupture. The fevered and broken sleep. The appalling dreams. The nostalgia. The roughness of the soldiers. The language they employed. The agony of mothers over their children. The agony of husbands and wives, brothers and sisters, children and aged parents, at the spectacle of each other's suffering, and before the fear of final separation which never left any of them for an instant. All this can be described. It can even, to some degree, be imaginatively felt. To what degree, depends on the mind and heart of the reader. But there will always be the distance of a universe between this imagination and the experience itself. It will not, therefore, be useful to multiply accounts or enlarge details as might be done. Indeed, although there are thousands of incidents, they all contain the same things. Once you have grasped that these things can happen, you know that they happened to all of these people all of the time. That nobody was spared. That there were no exceptions. There could be only different sets of circumstances, or degrees of sensibility or stoicism in enduring them. Physically, women on the whole suffered less than the men; having far greater physical and nervous endurance, though less strength. The younger the children were, the more easily they adapted themselves: both to the food and everything else.

The old, without exception, suffered most in every way. They felt themselves to be a terrible burden on the young and strong. They were not sustained by the same tenacious instinct of survival, and dreaded above everything the alien and nameless graves which they felt to be awaiting them, and they were absolutely incapable of making the mental adjustment which might have eased their situation even a little. To be forced to perform certain actions before their companions, under the surveillance of the jeering soldiers, to be made to strip naked, to take off their clothes and walk through rooms filled with persons of both sexes, to be derided in everything they did, to have everything they had ever held sacred held up to ridicule, all this was such torture to them that they could not force themselves to any philosophy about it. The younger people and the children, having also refused the use of the hole in the floor for the first few days, perceived that this refusal entailed consequences that were still worse. The result was only that the trains were stopped out in open country, the prisoners were made to get down, to crouch in rows and to relieve themselves without a scrap of cover of any kind, while the soldiers stood on the steps of the train and shouted orders, encouragement and jeers. After this it was simply decided that since the thing must be so it should be so: and that self-respect could be saved only by ceasing to find that it was in danger. Wherever possible, a blanket or something else was made into a screen, but this was seldom practicable. People simply tacitly agreed that they did not see each other, and probably after a time really did not. In fact, it was impossible to keep on being sensitive. People who would not approach the repulsive opening for the first few days, slept with their heads lying in it after the first few weeks. There was nowhere else to lie, and it was impossible to sit or stand. More and more people lay on the floor too weak or too ill to stir. But the elderly and the old never made this compromise. They could not; just as their bodies, which had been cleanly and decently nourished all their lives, could not digest the food. Infants, whose stomachs were still adaptable, digested it and wanted more.

During the actual deportation, and afterwards on Soviet territory (and now in the Union, if any of these aged persons should still be left alive) the tragedy of age has been, and is, the keenest, the most lasting and the most bereft of hope.

At the end of the train journeys, other journeys awaited the Poles. Sometimes, at Kiev or Kharkov or some of the other great junctions, they would have to change trains. To do this, after leaving the first, they might have to wait twenty-four hours or more without shelter of any kind, very often under downpours of rain. Occasionally they were marched through streets, to some clearing centre or to another station. In the streets, they were wretched and dirty, the passers-by sometimes glanced their way, and looked along the weary columns with unexpected sympathy. A few people even turned away their heads to conceal tears. But these feeling people were invariably persons of at least middle age, who could remember another world. Marching through the streets of Kiev some prisoners had to throw away their precious bundles. If they dropped behind they were shot, and if they carried the bundles they could not keep up. Several witnesses have told how people picking up these bundles seemed to look with compassion at the prisoners and watch them out of sight. From some of these convoys prisoners climbed on to the parapets of bridges and jumped over to put an end to their sufferings. The dark water whirled the bodies away, a few shots were fired after them, but the column kept on without breaking step.

The final stages of the journeys (all the scenes of confusion, separation of families and stumbling and falling under piles of baggage, being repeated each time) were covered on lorries, on sleighs or on foot; further treks of twenty, thirty, fifty or even a hundred miles. It all depended on the country the deported were now in, and on what road or tracks had been, or could be, made. Many had to stumble on foot through sandstorms and across deserts. Others had to cut their own way through the forests. Others had to cross swamps, where they slept on the fever-ridden ground, devoured by swarms of mosquitoes. Of those, for example, who had thrown away their baggage in the streets of Kiev, scores died later, during night halts in the swamps. Each morning the bodies were pushed under water and into holes. Those who could not keep up with the march were shot by the guards, often after having been dragged along for some hundreds of yards on face and hands. During eleven days of this, bread was distributed only three times. Their bare breasts, arms and legs were literally roasted by the sun. The flesh hung off them in strips. A nineteen-year-old boy, with blood pouring from his lungs, fell for the last time and was so savagely beaten with rifles that, in the words of the witness reporting it, 'he was beaten in to the ground'. Ditches were heaped with dead and a little grass thrown over them. The soldiers of this particular convoy were irritable and savage. The Germans were already on Soviet territory and there was panic in the air. For nothing but having begged for a little more water, four men had been shot on one train.

There were also the journeys by water. Here is the story of one man's journey. It is also the story of innumerable others. The place-names and the details of embarkation or of the number of kilometres covered will vary, that is all. This river happened to be the Pieczora. In the prison in Kharkov the drinking water was, as always, desperately short. The thermometer was forty degrees C. above zero. At the news that the journey north to a colder climate was going to begin, great relief was at first felt. After a journey lasting ten days they reached Archangel and on September the 17th were embarked on cargo boats on the river Pieczora. The only ventilation was through a door guarded by sentries. On deck there was a single latrine. Within a few days the whole boat stank and all the prisoners were smeared with excrement. Many were violently and lastingly seasick from the motion of the ship. After five days of this they called in at Narjen-Mar, another convict town. In the barracks here the convicts beat each other, often to death, with planks torn out of the floor, to get possession of boots, blankets, etc.[11] Thirty-six hours after disembarkation, small portions of bread and barrels of soup were given out. The barrels reeked of fish and were silted up with sand. Mess-tins and every other kind of tin had been taken away. The soup had to be drunk from cupped hands. One barrel was the allowance for each 250 persons. Half of the prisoners got none. There was no drinking water and, of course, none in which to wash. At the end of September and in early October, groups of 2,200 to 2,400 were put off on to barks (former coal lighters). In these the bunks were in tiers of three and the convicts lay everywhere on the floor. Ventilation came through a sort of gap three yards square. The barks moved very slowly, towed up the river against the current, and the death-rate was very high. The dead were buried all along the shores of the river; all their clothes having been first taken off them, stoppings wrenched out of their teeth, etc.

The wretched convoy of barks slowly made its way up the river. Tugs towed strings of two or three barks. The filth piled up as high as the first tier of bunks. The escort seated in the bows amused themselves shooting wild-fowl and game along the banks, and often held up the journey for hours for some sport or fancy of their own.

After thirty-three days the river became non-navigable from ice. The prisoners were then taken inland. Each group was to establish a new camp in the bush, each new camp being intended to reinforce a camp dying out after one year's existence. Many died every hour. The degree of frost was thirty-five C. below zero. Out of a group of 800, eighty were so badly frost-bitten on the first lap of this new journey that their extremities had to be amputated.

Those under canvas improvised stoves of a kind out of old tins. Digging the graves was one of the hardest jobs there was. The ground was so hard that the digging could last a week. One tent was turned into a 'hospital'. There were no bandages and no dressings, but there was a little aspirin and some permanganate. There was much loss of blood from lice. The very ill, who could not defend themselves against the lice, were literally eaten alive. The water in which a sweater was boiled (in hospital, as an orderly, this man had access to some water) turned to a thick sticky paste.[12]

On another bark, this time on the river T., 1,400 human beings were embarked, of whom 200 were women. After twenty-one days' journey, 710 only reached the first landing-stage alive; out of 200 women only twenty-one survived. Of the Poles in this transport, only one was alive. Buckets of rank soup and groats were lowered into the hold at feeding times (very irregular), and the buckets were hauled up again by means of hooks and lines. At the first lowering, a voice from the deck shouted down that bodies also were to be sent up on these hooks. Within the first few hours the first body was sent up. After a few days they were being hauled up at the rate of ten or more in one day.

Prisoners and deportees were also transported vast distances across Siberia to the Pacific provinces and two descriptions of such journeys follow, one short and matter-of-fact, by a Polish labour-leader; the second vivid and poignant by a young woman whose only child was left behind in Poland.

'In Odessa, I was kept in prison from February the 1st until March the 7th of the same year. The prison at Odessa was full of Poles. I was with thirteen other persons in a cell intended to accommodate two. From the 7th of March until the 17th of April 1940 I was one of a convoy being taken to Vladivostok. [A journey of about five thousand miles – eds.] During this journey, the prisoners now and again received a little bread, but as a general rule nothing but tinned herrings with some boiling water in very small quantities. In Vladivostok there was an enormous clearing centre from which prisoners were distributed among lagiers in the province of Khabarowsk, which are under the supervision of the office for the north-east. There were some 25,000 prisoners camping here in the open. Two barracks were reserved for Poles. On May the 20th together with a large transport of my fellow-prisoners, I was taken across the Sea of Japan to Magadan, and from there, by lorry, to another distributing centre. From this centre we proceeded to Maldiak, 1,700 kilometres away on the river Kolyma. We arrived in Maldiak on the 26th of June 1940.'

The second account begins immediately after the arrest of the narrator in Poland.

'We were taken in a black van to the railway, all herded together to the point of suffocation. It was late evening when they turned us out of the van along railway lines outside the town. Rain fell in torrents. It was positively uncanny how it rained. Everything was slippery and since there was no platform we had to climb up into the train and drag our bundles after us from the level of the rails. One very old Jewess with only one hand struggled hopelessly beside me with a heavy sack. Her peruke had come off somewhere, leaving her shaved head naked and horrible. Unexpectedly and without any abuse, a soldier started to help us. Then another and then a third. These were men of the Red Army, not of the N.K.V.D.

'Mud everywhere and all over us. Searchlights . . . Immensely long, apparently unending trains. . . . One woman cried out, thinking a voice from a wagon which was being filled up with men to be the voice of her husband. I saw her stumble and fall from a blow from a rifle-butt delivered in her back. . . . The searchlight lit up one wagon after another, then came darkness again. The rain crashed down on to the roofs of the cars, like handfuls of pebbles. Our clothes clung to us, absolutely saturated. Some hours later, the train began to move. As it moved, we all with one voice began to sing "*Boze coś Polskę*", and "*Nie rzucim ziemi*" . . . all sang, all moved by the same instinct: Poles, Ukrainians, Jewesses, politicals, prostitutes, thieves . . . songs of Lwów, of Poland, of home.[13] For the time being we went no further than Złoczów where we were shut up in the dungeons of the castle.

'In this prison we were informed of our sentences. I personally received eight years' lagier under the code, for "preparing insurrection arms in hand" and for "membership of the counter-revolution".

'I prepared myself for the journey by sewing together a rucksack of sorts from all the scraps of material I could collect. I cut out these scraps with a sliver of glass; thread I obtained by drawing threads out of what was left of my underclothes, and one of the guards gave me a needle. On our last day we were led through the orchard, among the white and pink blossoms, through the blessed warmth and light of the sun, the young grass so high that a horse was grazing deep in it. We were very sad.

'On the way to the station, my knees gave under me from weariness and light-headedness. The train on which we were put was an N.K.V.D. train. Once on this train we were left all day locked in what is called the "kuriatnik" or chicken-coop, with no latrine anywhere.[14] One of our number begged us to consent to her using the floor, which we did. When the N.K.V.D. soldiers came round in the evening and saw what had been done, one tore off the front of her skirt and ordered her to clean up with that. This was outside Kiev.

'After this, and all the way along the Dnieper, beyond Kiev, beyond Poltava, and everywhere in the Ukraine, there reached us, even inside our hen-coop, the strong and lovely perfume of its black and fertile soil. Ukraine . . . milk and honey . . . extraordinary fertility, loveliness and strangeness . . . clamour of nightingales singing all through the early summer night . . . In Kharkov we lay huddled together in a cell nine metres by four. From the ceiling to floor, all the walls of this cell were thick with Polish names. Whoever passed through Kharkov, and had enough strength left, scratched their name and the name of their native towns on these walls. Kraków, Warszawa, Katowice, Sosnowiec, Dąbrowa, Lwów, Wilno, Kowel, Baranowicze, Lida, Brześć, Łomza, Przemysl, Częstochowa, Tarnopol, Kielce, Tomaszów, Płock. . . . To leave our own we had to climb on to each other's shoulders. To write (or scratch) I used a broken button I had managed to conceal. In Kharkov we were molested by enormous prison rats. Here, too, I met many friends. These women showed a courage, and even gaiety, which can never be sufficiently honoured nor adequately described. One seventy-five-year-old school directress, sentenced for a term of fifteen years, remains in my mind, and so does M. K., sentenced for having wept during the arrest of her husband, thereby "resisting his arrest". There were also many Russian and Ukrainian women, many of these on religious charges.

'The Volga now . . . impossible to tell where the great sheet of water begins and ends. . . . Do the trees grow in the water, or does the water flow into the forest? . . . Bugs, myriads of lice and bugs . . . children in slings between bunks, but the bugs get at them just the same. Their limbs stream with blood, and the mothers cannot feed them. . . . Chelabinsk . . . Ural. . . . All the beauty of the world . . . and all so sorrowful and so grim.

'Novosibirsk. . . . On the stations they turn us out to be counted. Before counting us, they surround us with guards, weapons and dogs. The dogs round us up as if we were sheep; we are all jostled together, stumbling, weak and ill. The guards shout at us "Faster", "Faster". The heat is indescribable. Heat strikes up from this Siberian clay as it might off the walls of a furnace. Every step is agony. Gaol again. Poles, Chinese women from Manchuria in blue silk trousers, a Swiss woman, a violinist. The violinist's husband is a lecturer at a Moscow university. Bugs, lice, lice, bugs. Twice a day we get flour boiled in water. In spite of the filth, the atmosphere is not here so evil and degraded as in that corpse-house in Syzran, where even the floors and walls seemed to be saturated in crime.

'In five days' time we set out again, moved to the station, this time in columns with men. Dogs, guards, rifles, "Faster", "Faster". . . . A fearful hurricane of rain almost sweeps us off our feet. Everything is heavy and bogged down with water; we slither about in a lake of water and a bog of mud. The guards laugh and force us through the deepest puddles, keeping on dry ground themselves. My temples and throat feel ready to burst, there is a noise in my head and a red glare before my eyes. Over and over again I repeat to myself the verses of a Litany. At last the wagon is reached. Bugs again, but now they are a different colour. The struggle for water . . . always this struggle for water. . . . Days and days go by. . . . There swim past me birch-trees, steppe, steppe, birch-trees, steppe; wood, water, steppe, wood, water, and the rising and setting of a strange sun; water, wood, birch-trees, steppe, sunrise and sunset, I have no idea how many; red tulips, irises, grass, and water; birch-trees, hunger and thirst, and all the days growing hotter. . . . The bread they give us is mouldy. . . . The roof and walls of the train are red-hot. . . . Their own food is carried past, we see it through the grating. . . . We are hungry, but still more thirsty . . . the men are silent, they are weaker than we. . . .

'A great river now. A long, long town, all of wood. A port. Figures on the quays; rafts, small boats. Steppe, grass, steppe, birch-trees and steppe. . . . Small stations. . . . Factories. Tankers. Airfields, airfields, airfields, one after another. Cases. Another great river, our hands are swollen from hunger, and our legs from the lack of exercise. Our blood thickens. We can no longer pull off our boots, nor pass our arms through our sleeves. This is Irkutsk. This is Tomsk. . . . Mist constantly before our eyes. Here is a bridge. This is Amur. . . .

'. . . Khabarovsk. We spent some days in a lagier here. After the train the grass on to which I collapsed smelt sweet and was fresh and cool. I was allowed to lie and to sleep on it undisturbed. The prisoners brought me some water and gave me food. The vermin inside the hut barracks were so voracious that I slept all night on this grass. A woman with a child at her breast gave me a cool bodice without sleeves, which I put on with profound gratitude. Others shared their food with me. How I should have liked to stay here! By comparison, this lagier is a haven of rest and humanity. On again. . . . Days pass. Instead of steppe, we now gaze out on dark green hills, the stretches of water have become river, the small woods are now forests. The landscape darkens and becomes grimmer and even quite cold. The clouds are so low they seem to rest on the peaks. Trees have twisted trunks and the bridges are curved. This is the landscape I have been seeing all my life in Japanese prints, only much colder, darker and more forbidding than in my imagination. We live on bread and water. The bread is always mouldy. We are approaching the Sea of Japan. Dunes, inundations and much flood-water, bays, small creeks. . . . This is Vladivostok . . . Vladivostok . . . often heard of . . . a distant, dangerous, uncivilized port known until now only in pictures and books.

'Black-out exercises are going on. We wait all night on the station in torrents of rain. No bread and no water to drink. As we file by him to the latrine, a soldier counts us by striking each woman in the back with his fist. For once, I turn on him, and shout and rave with anger and threaten him with I know not what. This is the only method which is ever successful. It is successful now. He does not punish me at all.

'Bukta Nachodka. The clouds seem to be resting on the earth itself. Peaks, *exactly* as they appear in those prints . . . some volcanic. We are shut up in yet another lagier . . . 230 women with me in one barrack.

'The men were now all being taken away from this camp. They filed away in groups of eight without a break from morning till night. Only then did I realize how many of them there were. One hundred and thirty women were also taken, of whom I was one. In all there were taken five of us Polish women, a few Soviet politicals, and all the rest of that type of criminal which can be most nearly described by the European expression apache.[15]

'The men were put aboard first. Those who were still waiting lit a fire on the shore. Dusk fell, the apache women stirred the fire and began to dance. Others sat around applauding and beating time. The whirling shapes of these women, incredibly coarse and vicious in appearance, were savage and sensual beyond description and beyond forgetting. Their costume was of long, completely Oriental trousers coming down over the ankle and stuffed inside their boots, with over these a skirt and tight fitting bodice; handkerchiefs were tied round their heads and over their eyes; cigarette holders were held between their teeth.

'When at last we went aboard it was dark and I was quite blind.[16] Heavy rain began to fall. Nobody helped me. I was in danger of being left completely alone on the desolate shore. Another blind woman (Soviet) at last came to my aid and finally a soldier. The idea that I might have been left behind amused everybody immensely. I could just see enough to know that a searchlight played over us and over the ship. We were down under the deck. Bunks rose in tiers. I stood in a corner with my fur in a sack under my feet. The boat moved off to the sound of the mournful singing and dancing and the noise of retching. In the darkness hands reached out towards me from all sides. One tore off the shawl, the Polish shawl I wore on my head. Others tried to drag off my sweater and seize my sack. We fought in the darkness of the night and of my blindness. I hit out at random; wherever there seemed to be anything soft. I could just make out the lamp swinging; I could taste blood, and I knew that somehow I must get my back against a wall. I meant to fight to the last. If I once gave in I knew they would murder me. As I reached out and a blow went wide I fell against a door opening, and the commandant appeared. For the time being I was saved.

'. . . Early, very early in the morning, when light came, my very bones saturated with tiredness, I crept cautiously on to the deck. The sea, grey like lead, stretched endlessly away on every side. The tops of the masts were lost in fog; the sea heavy, leaden and still. Seated on a coil of rope, a man in a loose blouse played softly on an accordion a melody which was grey like the sea, like our ship, like the fog. A voice asked me from where I had come. "Comrade, I come from a far, a very far land, my own land, from Poland." We talked, and from the men's quarters came cries which surpassed any I had heard before. The apache men settling a score with their knives. A brigade-leader had gambled and lost the brigade's bread ration at cards. For this he had been tried by the men apaches and found guilty. They literally cut him up with their knives. His brains lay scattered on the decks.

'The ship was now between Hokkaido and Sakhalin. Dark green islands sailed past our bow. We were no further than a gunshot away from the Japanese shore. In the daytime when it was fine, the planks over us were lifted up. Men and women lay together without any kind of shame, but at night, the N.K.V.D. with searchlights made sure there were no men still in our quarters, for this was against the regulations.

'The weather continued fine. In seven days we reached Bukhta Nagaievo. Then Magadan.'

On such journeys, on these trains and to these destinations, were sent those ordinary people from Europe – labourers and journeymen, village schoolmasters and university professors, butchers, bakers, women and children, and the old.

Editors' Notes

1. Solzhenitsyn describes these transports as caravans of red cows (red cattle cars) and is emphatic about the colour. In all other respects the descriptions are consistent. It was in trains like these that the Ukrainian peasants, the Volga Germans and the rest of the exiled nations were sent off to the camps, or to 'places of compulsory residence'. Alexander Solzhenitsyn, *The Gulag Archipelago*, pp. 565–6.
2. The arrests, according to NKVD custom, took place at night. In the Soviet Union the authorities usually took care to load the trains and despatch them at night to avoid scenes like the ones described. Serov's instructions were clear on this point, but unexplained delays prevented immediate departure.
3. Bartering of personal possessions in exchange for food was indispensable for survival in penal camps and places of exile.
4. *Oblast*, an administrative division as in region, province or district in the Soviet Union.
5. *Kharasho* – the Russian adverb meaning 'well', used here in the sense of OK.
6. The three partitions of Poland, which extinguished Polish independent statehood, took place in 1773, 1793 and 1795. Polish self-determination was not restored until 1918. The Old Republic of Poland–Lithuania thus came to an end in 1795.
7. A reference to the deportations and to the dispersal of the Polish armed forces after the military defeat in 1939. The remnants of the Polish Air Force and Navy and the First Polish Army Corps were based in the United Kingdom. The Second Army Corps, formed in the Middle East mainly from Polish soldiers evacuated from Russia via Persia, became part of the British Eighth Army and fought in the North African and Italian campaigns. Most Polish women and children evacuated from Russia with the Polish army were sent to camps in India and British East Africa for the duration of the war.
8. All citizens of the Soviet occupied areas of Poland (in Soviet terminology, the western districts of the Ukrainian and White Russian Soviet Socialist Republics) acquired Soviet citizenship by a decree of 29 November 1939.
9. For a plausible explanation see Solzhenitsyn, *The Gulag Archipelago*, pp. 495–6: 'One has to understand the situation: The convoy staff is limited . . . And then, to go carry water in pails – it has to be hauled a long way, too,

and it's insulting. Why should a Soviet soldier have to carry water like a donkey for enemies of the people?' On some trains, however, deportees, usually one per car, were allowed out at stops to collect water or snow in buckets. This information is in the editors' transcripts of conversations with deportees.

10. But compare the following: 'Some guards were good people, some guards stole, some were nasty. Some gave you as much as they could but they had little themselves. They had no kitchen, their conditions were not very different from ours' (editors' transcripts).

11. These were convicted criminals, usually designated 'non-politicals'.

12. Lice were ubiquitous on trains, in barges and ships, in barracks and prison cells. '. . . the hungry bedbugs assaulted [the prisoner], crawling onto him from the walls or falling off the ceiling. At first he waged war with them strenuously, crushing them on his body and on the walls, suffocated by their stink. But after several hours he weakened and let them drink his blood without a murmur.' Solzhenitsyn, *The Gulag Archipelago*, p. 113. 'I am not kidding you now. If you put your shirt on the edge of a table or bunk or something it would have moved after a few hours because of all the lice and fleas inside it.' (Editors' transcripts.)

13. '*Boze coś Polskę*' . . . a hymn whose first line appeals to God as Poland's guardian throughout the ages. '*Nie rzucim ziemi*' . . . a patriotic 'rota' which begins by declaring the wish never to abandon the land of the nation. 'We could hear such songs, as we waited on platforms, coming from passing trains; we were all Poles linked by song.' (Editors' transcripts.)

14. *Kuriatnik*s were ordinary third class coaches with compartments, but the windows into the compartments had been boarded up and the corridor windows barred. These appear to be the Stolypin cars (named after Tsar Nicholas II's Minister of the Interior who was assassinated in 1911) referred to by Solzhenitsyn in *The Gulag Archipelago*, p. 491.

15. Apache, violent street ruffian. More generally, the non-politicals.

16. Blindness probably caused by vitamin deficiency as a result of prolonged undernourishment. It may also be caused by the bites of gnats or by the glare of the snow.

THREE

Prisons

In the Soviet prisons inside Poland had been detained all those persons on lists already in the possession of the N.K.V.D., leaders of all political parties of all shades of opinion, including leaders of Socialist organizations and Socialist trade unions; all such persons as town councillors, members of trade union executives, members of working-class committees, organizers of working-class, peasant and other youth institutions, civil servents, members of the police forces, skilled workers of all kinds, and very many others – persons on further lists which had been compiled immediately after the Soviet entry and, finally, persons arrested in the act of attempting to pass the new (now Soviet) frontiers or individually accused of any other offence against the (new, Soviet) Law.

Those among the prisoners who had themselves held Communist beliefs and worked, some throughout the whole of their adult lives, for the realization of the Communist ideal, may in many ways have suffered the most. They had lived to see in practice the functioning of something they had been emulating all their lives: and which they had believed to contain in itself sublime possibilities for the betterment and solace of suffering mankind; and the evidence of what they now saw had broken their hearts. Many simply went out of their minds; some violently, others by a rapid progression from stupefaction to despair, followed by profound and incurable melancholia. As well as Polish Communists, there were also many who were not Polish, and who had hurried into Poland after the news of the entry of the Soviet armies.

Among these foreign Communists were men of high character. One of them, falling, after a long period of reflection, into hopeless melancholia, imposed on himself a system of punishments for what he now thought of as the arrogant folly of his life. Another, from Carpathian White Ruthenia, had formerly been an N.C.O. in the Czech Army and was a member of the Party, with Party training. During the Civil War in Spain, he fought in the International Brigade, and received, on several occasions, exceptional mention for courage and endurance. When the brigade broke up, he succeeded in returning to his own district. Upon the news that the Red Army was in Poland, he again crossed the Carpathians –

this time into Eastern Poland – with the sincere intention of further
serving the Party and (as he believed) mankind. At the Polish frontier he
was received with honours by the Soviet frontier guards and passed on to
the N.K.V.D. authorities, from whom he expected to receive instructions
and a programme of work. Instead, he was arrested and thrown into a
putrid cell with some fifty or sixty other prisoners.

In this cell he fell into a protracted silence, until a day when, for no
particular reason that anybody could see, after one more refusal by the
guards of one more request for a mouthful of water for himself or for a
fellow prisoner (I have forgotten which) he could not endure it any more
and his dammed-up feelings sought relief in words. With the breaking of
his silence, he cursed the day he was born, the Soviet system with
everything it meant, with its founders, himself, and the whole of his own
life and all its labours and effort up to now. The tortured heart could no
longer contain its sorrow, its resentment and its rage. The guards, leaping
on to him, beat him senseless with their rifles, before he was taken away to
the punishment cell. His end was in Odessa, in a prison hospital.

The manner in which arrests were carried out was characteristic. In the
houses in which they took place, not only the men whom the police had
actually come to fetch were arrested, but everybody who happened to be
in these houses at the same time. In a house in Wilno, for instance, which
the N.K.V.D. police entered to arrest an old and active leader of the
Bund,[1] named Zeleznikow, who had been an exile to Siberia in the time of
the last Tsar, they found also a man named Rosenstein, employee of a
sanatorium for children of the working class, who was in this house in
Wilno by simple accident. This man was also arrested and also sentenced,
and died in lagier after deportation to the Union. Examples of this kind
could be multiplied indefinitely.

After arrest prisoners were not allowed to communicate with their
families or friends. With very few exceptions, no parcels of food or
clothing were accepted on their behalf. The efforts of families and friends,
indeed, to keep in touch with the accused both exasperated and
confounded the N.K.V.D. officers. One examining magistrate, genuinely
at a loss, exclaimed to the wife of a prisoner:

'What extraordinary women you are here! In our country, when the
husband is arrested, the wife sues for divorce and looks for another one.
But here you come along, begging and pleading on the prisoner's behalf,
which, after all, can only result in your getting sent away yourselves also!'

The prisons and all those other buildings, public and private, which
were made to serve as prisons under the new administration, were more
crowded than seems humanly possible and became more so every day.

In writing of life in these prisons, I shall include passages from documents before me. In making a translation, I have omitted, where necessary, much that was repetitive, all matter of an over-personal and purely subjective nature, appreciations and remarks of a speculative rather than an historical character, all accounts of or even references to Underground and similar organizations and all enumerations of proper names. I have also omitted details of physical torture. This method has much abbreviated the text of more than one deposition; whole paragraphs at times have been condensed into a single sentence. Yet the sense in full of every text has been preserved scrupulously, and no single word has at any time been added, nor anything else, however insignificant, been allowed to creep in, which, to the most minute degree, might have modified this sense.

To begin with, then, here are passages from one man's description of the various cells (chiefly improvised) which he occupied whilst awaiting sentence and deportation. This man, whose experience has no highlights and who received no especially rigorous treatment, was arrested in the act of attempting to cross the Soviet line of demarcation which, from September onwards, had been set up between the Soviet Occupation and Lithuania.[2] A Socialist of note and a lifelong worker for Socialist ideals, this man was in fact not recognized by his captors and was not, as has been said, subjected to any special rigour.

'. . . We were conducted to the nearest post, which had been set up in a farm, and thrust into a shed of sorts, with no windows and no roof. Portions of bread were distributed once a day, and absolutely nothing else, not even hot water. As we were pretty well freezing (ten degrees below zero), we tore planks out of the floor and burned them to keep ourselves from freezing entirely. Our guards did not so much as turn their heads. Nothing could have concerned them less than this destruction by us of "State Property". At the time I was amazed by this. Much later, within the Soviet Union, after my release from lagier, I was able to observe at close quarters the real feelings of Soviet citizens towards the famous "State property".'

On the following day, again with his companion, he was removed to another post, and again thrust into a small space, crowded with other prisoners.

'. . . The atmosphere almost knocked us out. My companion collapsed. The contrast between the atmosphere we entered and the icy but fresh air off the fields through which we had been marching for hours was more than he could resist, and he crashed down in a dead faint on the floor. After a fairly short time, we began to look about and take everything in. The room in which we were was one of three in which, at that moment, were crowded together certainly not less than 150 prisoners: men and women, old and young, and children of all ages.

'In this particular prison we spent ten days. During these ten days nobody washed, still less shaved, once. We received, in all, a quarter of a litre (approximately half a pint) of water a day, and this we drank. Vermin swarmed everywhere. Both men and women spent the whole day catching lice in their clothing. The first day this sight appalled us. On the second day we had to start the same business ouselves. Nor, during the whole ten days, did we once receive any semblance of hot food. Our only rations were a daily portion of black bread, about 700 grammes (approximately 1 pound 11 ounces) for twenty-four hours. Three times in the whole period we received half a herring (either salt or pickled) per head. We could not induce them to let us have even a little hot water to drink, although amongst us were infants of a few months old and one very old woman.

'Every two or three days we were visited by an officer. At each visit, the total gulf between their way of thinking and ours was strikingly plain. The prisoners came from every section of society and to every one of us it seemed clear that, in attempting to slip across a "frontier" (an act which even a few days earlier, before the war, was only a misdemeanour of a fairly harmless kind, and punishable by a fine) – a frontier, at that, imposed by an Army of Occupation, and not in reality one at all – we had been attempting something not only understandable but even right. With a few exceptions all had been wives looking for husbands, mothers looking for sons, soldiers of a routed army attempting to reach home. These others, Soviet officers, listened to such a point of view with sincere amazement. From the bottom of their hearts they considered people who could do as we had done to be genuine criminals. "To overthrow a State frontier!" they repeated after the prisoners. "You wanted to overthrow a State frontier!" It was more than they could comprehend. None of us, of course, had the least idea at that time that for precisely this offence a Soviet citizen gets shot as a deserter . . .

'After ten days, at some hour of the night, to shouts of *"Podnimaisa zvieschchami!"*[3] we were herded out on to the courtyard around which was drawn a heavy cordon of frontier guards. There were at least fifty of these soldiers. Their rifles, as always, were all pointed at us. At least half of the persons thus surrounded were women and young children. After reading out our names, an officer announced that we were being taken to another prison, that we had not more than ten kilometres to cover to the railway line and that *"shag v levo, shag v pravo"* ("a step to the left, a step to the right") would be treated as an attempt to escape, in which event the soldiers had orders to shoot without further warning. We were lined up in fours and the march began. All these people had been at least two weeks without air on a starvation diet, and now they were ordered to set out on a ten-kilometre march, over a road deep in snow. And as always happens on these occasions, the soldiers were shouting "faster, faster" at every step, jostling and shoving along the weakest who kept sinking down in the heavy drifts of snow. . . . The station at which we finally arrived was also heavily guarded by soldiers, on the N.K.V.D. principle of isolating their prisoners and preventing any sort of contact between them and the rest of the community.[4] On the station, it turned out that no arrangements had been made for a train, and that, in fact, nobody had any idea as to when one might arrive. There was, of course, no hope of our getting anything to eat. Mothers again begged for even a little warm water for the infants and younger children, but in vain. In this plight we waited more than four hours, when a train at last came in. The soldiers piled us into two trucks, and other soldiers stood inside these trucks and at all the doors. We were forbidden, on pain of being shot, to look out of the windows. In Lida, when we arrived, we were kept in the trucks for some time and again the station was cleared of all the civilian population and even of the railway staff, which at this time was composed entirely of workers brought in from the heart of the Soviet Union. Again we were warned against glancing at or communicating with anybody, on pain of being shot without warning; again we were surrounded by soldiers, this time of the Lida N.K.V.D., with their rifles and bayonets at the ready, and again, filthy, haggard, hungry and frozen, we were marched away to prison.'

The writer then describes their reception and allocation in this new prison:

'This began by everybody being searched exhaustively. The whole business was very brutal. Later, after a long experience, I came to the conclusion that this brutality when searching prisoners is another deliberately applied principle. The prisoner is to get it into his head as soon as possible that he is nothing but a thing and that nobody has any reason to be particular about the way they treat him. The prisoner is intended to feel that he is absolutely bereft of sanctuary or appeal and of every kind of human dignity; that he is a pariah, outside the community. This is rubbed into him at every possible opportunity. The prison governor tells him so when he visits the cells, the guards tell him so as they hustle him along to latrines whose filth can hardly be imagined or described, the examining judges tell him so during cross-examinations, and the prison barber tells him so again as he painfully shears his head or tears out his beard with his abominable prison razor. . . .

'After this, we were allocated to our various cells. Women with small children were separated from the rest. Possibly they were even freed after a time. We were still in a period of relative tolerance towards "frontier crimes". I and some of my companions were placed in a cell on whose doors somebody's unaccustomed hand had traced a great shapeless "I" in red.

'This was a day of late March in 1940. The sun was melting and drawing off the frost. Snow was lying white and crisp in the forests and on the fields. Out of this bright day I stepped inside the Lida prison. Long moments passed before I could see anything: the atmosphere was so thick. And if ever the words "a human ant-heap" could be an authentic description, that is exactly what I found there, in my cell. The room we were put into had been an office, and was rather a biggish room. At the moment when I entered it, there were already sixty-three persons in it. With our three, they were sixty-six. The fortunate ones were squeezed tightly up against the walls, almost pushed through them. These were in all about fifteen or twenty persons. The others simply stood up on the floor. To sit was impossible and there were no forms and no bunks of any kind. Human cries and groans filled our ears; human exhalations and rank tobacco fumes formed a thick curtain across the two windows, of which one only was a little open. To the right of the heavy doors stood an enormous tub, or rather cask, serving as a pail-closet. Our fellow prisoners were disgusted by our arrival. Each new arrival meant additional misery for the others, and especially so at night when the attempt was made to sleep. For this attempt we disposed ourselves in rows, with our legs drawn up to our bodies. Each row had a prescribed side towards which they were allowed to lie, and to turn on to one's other side meant violent discomfort for all one's fellow-sleepers, protests and even serious quarrels and assault. This first night, we three new arrivals half dozed, half kept watch, standing on our feet the whole night but leaning against the wall in the corner nearest to the pail-closet (called parasha) which was being used by somebody all the time. . . .

'. . . None of the people with us had been really long under arrest. The longest any had been in prison was three or four weeks. Yet all had bruised-looking, livid faces, and the eyes looking out of them were sunk and dim. All were saturated with filth and overgrown with hair. . . .

'No exercise was allowed. Unless the morning and evening walk under escort to the latrines in the yard was to be considered as exercise. Anyhow, that was all we got. Two soldiers with bayonets pointed us towards escorted groups of from three to five prisoners, and the longest period for use of the latrine conceded to anybody was two minutes. We observed that the women in this prison received exactly the same treatment from the same guards.

'No concessions were made to illness. A doctor visited us once, noted the cases of sickness, and never came back. Once, when one of the prisoners had a very severe heart attack, we began to beat on the door with our fists and demand help for him. After a moment, our guards looked in, glanced with complete indifference at the man and having laconically and quite sincerely said, "Let the brute die, then there'll be one less of you!" away they went. What is significant is that these guards were by no means fiends or lovers of cruelty for its own sake. One of them even shared his tobacco with us when he was in a good humour. At the time I was simply unable to take in such scenes as this or to grasp such an attitude to human life. The only explanation I could find was a sort of pathological brutality felt by a warder towards his prisoners, or in the sentiments of a soldier in an occupied country towards those whose country he occupies, and by whom he knows himself to be detested. Later, in the Soviet Union, I understood that this was all wrong. That the explanation went much deeper, and neither began on Polish soil nor was a reflex of prison life and psychology. . . .

'We were not allowed to open the window, we were not allowed to look through the sordid panes, on pain of punishment cell or a simple shot through the head. But in prison the window is all that is left of freedom; and freedom, whatever is said or done, is one of our most normal and most deeply rooted instincts. A great proportion of the tragedies enacted in prison have their origin in that pitifully small, sealed and invariably filthy prison window.

'A glimpse out of the cell window is the highest privilege of which the prisoner can dream. For this privilege he is bound to pay in one way or another; but only a real born coward, and hardly one of those, would for that reason give up the privilege.

'Once, in April, when a breath of spring was beginning to mingle with the dying odour of winter we saw through the window one early morning something we could not at first understand. Hours passed before we understood it. Hardly more than 500 or 600 yards away, along lines exactly opposite our window, was an unusually long train, made up of goods and cattle trucks, and around the trucks was a sea of people. By the coloured handkerchiefs and shawls on the heads of the tallest figures we understood that the wearers were women. The smaller figures were, of course, children and there were figures also of men in uniforms, obviously soldiers, on guard. From time to time, we could see that somebody was being hauled into a truck only by the help of other of the figures, and was obviously ill and infirm. Rising out of the roof of each truck we could see a stovepipe and thin columns of smoke were coiling upwards from the pipes.

'For three days some train was always in view from our window. Whether it was always the same train or whether one would leave during the night and another take its place we had no means of telling. The people themselves were too far away to be recognized again. Of one thing only could we be quite sure: the train, whether the same or one of a series, was encircled all the time by a thick cordon of soldiers. . . .

'Interrogations of prisoners always took place at night.[5] If it ever happened that a prisoner was taken before the judge in daylight, that was a sure sign of some unexpected event, or that something was being prepared in a hurry; for instance transport to the prison in Baranowicze might unexpectedly have turned up. In the normal way life in a Soviet prison begins only late in the evening. When everybody has at last managed to find some sort of place for himself – when the rows of prisoners are at last stretched out for the night on the side on which it has been agreed that they shall sleep, with their legs drawn up under their bodies – the noises and rushing about in the corridors begin. Tramping, heavy movements, rattling of keys, grating of locks. A couple of soldiers with rifles come pushing in. From scraps of paper in their hands, they attempt to read aloud the names of somebody or other. After much difficulty, a decision would be come to as to what the name ought to be. The name read out, there would be no reply; for there would in fact be nobody of that name, or under that name, in the cell. To find the right person, the soldiers would then proceed to waken everybody, cursing as only Russians can. After we have all been awakened and pushed about, they clatter into the next cell, and we hear them beginning the same thing there. In the end, probably, the right man is found. In the search for him, hundreds have been torn out of their refuge of sleep, the only refuge from the horrors of the long, stifling, monotonous and dirt-infested day. The wretch himself is hustled away.'

The writer of this account and some of his companions were actually given their liberty on April the 19th, though all, or nearly all, were shortly rearrested. The reason for their release was an outbreak of typhus in the regular prison at Baranowicze, to which 90 per cent of the prisoners had already been sent and to which this remainder were destined. The prison in Baranowicze, as well as being threatened with typhus, was so swarming with prisoners of both sexes and all ages and in all stages of illness and exhaustion, that the commandant himself refused to take in any more. The prison, which was intended to house a thousand at most, had already been made to take quite five times that number.

The last words of this report are:

'Late in the night an N.C.O. escorted me to the great gate. The gate opened. "Out with you, bastard!" Out I went.

'It was not for long.'

A second account of life in prison which I select to insert here has been written by a young woman. The events which she describes took place in Lwów.

On a night in 1940, soldiers (of the N.K.V.D.) entered this woman's flat, where she was living with her child and a servant. The servant was kept away from her by a sentry with a fixed bayonet and a search was made of all the rooms; it was not stated for what. Papers of every sort were requisitioned; scrap or anything else on which anybody had ever written anything. After this, she was ordered to leave with the soldiers, without waiting to dress, in a thin night-gown. The entreaties of the servant, who kept exclaiming with tears: 'Commandant, be a human being, Commandant, you cannot do such a thing!' at last succeeded in obtaining for her five minutes, but not more than five minutes, in which to get dressed. Two of the soldiers, at the last moment, did turn a little aside, until she had hastily pulled on the first of her clothes. After this she was told to show her hands, in proof that she had no skin disease, itch, or anything of the kind. Her watch and comb were taken from her and she was led outside. The two women were allowed to embrace each other. After being led through the streets, she was taken to prison and marched to a cell.

'The doors opened, then crashed together. Inside were already nine persons. The cell, very small, probably intended for one person. Three and a half paces in one direction, nine in the other. Four planks, a table, a smaller table, a bucket of water and the *parasha*.

'The persons in the cell were: a man of forty-two; a young Ukrainian woman, five months pregnant; a retired Polish general aged seventy-five, with his wife, sixty-five; a girl arrested with her brother in her own house, while her husband was locked out in the street, the brother and sister being accused of distributing patriotic leaflets; an older woman, fearfully beaten, accused of having alluded to a "Western front"; another woman, no accusation; the wife of a policeman; a woman suspected by the other prisoners of having been placed there as a spy; a young girl, consumptive, beautiful, and with a slight limp, from the prison of Zamarstynow.

'Behind these doors, the first strong emotion was an impulse to start screaming. An immense effort was required to master this. The blood beat with great violence in my temples and throat. Finally I fought it down. After this, I gave myself up to trying to think back over the last few hours. I remembered a visit which, as it now appeared, might well have been a police trap. I remembered the street along which I had walked to make it, its apparent emptiness, dirty ice dissolving in the gutter and straw blowing about, and the vanishing figure of a Russian soldier in his spiked cap. . . .

'For the next six weeks in this cell, I endured horrors of insomnia. My fellow-prisoners assured me that this, too, would pass. After six weeks, I was able to sleep as they did. Sleep became, in fact, the only consolation. The inactivity and hopeless monotony of the life exhausted us more than anything else. I learnt by heart whole lists of names of fellow-prisoners who had been beaten and tortured. It was extremely difficult to make even so much mental effort as this. In our cell with us, at one time, there was a Soviet woman. This woman had herself been an interrogating judge. I do not know for certain of what crime she was now accused, but she was a patriot and loved her own country. At times she would weep bitterly, for herself and for all the Russian people. She was ashamed, she said, of what she saw in our faces. Much later, I met her again in the clearing station at Kharkov. . . .

'A cry, a footstep in the corridor, a visit to the latrines – these are the only events in prison. The latrines are the centre of prison life. If anything happens, it is whispered to you in the latrine, or on the walk there. If a message has been got in it can be passed on only there. Friends and relatives who have no other chance of meeting, exchange glances there, before each is dragged away towards his own fate. It is impossible to over-estimate the importance of the latrines in the prison. All news, all exchanges, all snatches of talk between prisoners, are called "latrine news". The regulations allow you to be taken there twice in twelve hours. The time to be spent within is strictly limited. At other times, no prayers, no entreaties, no explanations have the slightest effect. Then after long suppression of a natural urge, the bowels often refuse to function, just when, at last, there is the oppportunity. I have seen the guards look on as a woman writhed in paroxysms of pain, on the floor. . . . "Ah, you want to do it and now you can't do it? Ah. . . .". As a punishment, too, the warders may refuse to take you to the latrines at all. I have known a punishment of this kind to last four days. In such cases, the prisoner has no choice except to relieve herself on the floor of the cell. Prisoners are without exception very pitiful to each other about this sort of thing and never make it a subject of reproach. The guards look on and laugh and make jokes. For some reason, this joke never seems to pall. Very, very great self-control and moral courage are needed to endure this degradation and retain one's self-respect.

'When the pail in the cell is full to overflowing one of the prisoners is generally allowed to carry it away to empty. This chance of walking the length of a courtyard, or even across a passage, is one of the most desirable events of a prisoner's day. Turns are taken to do it. In a cell where the prisoners are on good terms with each other, it would be an unforgivable offence to cheat about this or try to secure it out of your turn. At the latrines, we women often got an opportunity of whispering some words of encouragement to the men, who, on the whole, fell far more easily than we did into the awful depression of prison and even into complete lethargy of mind. It was usually dangerous to risk a smile; a whisper was more easily managed. . . . "It's all right. You will see. Everything will be all right. Only don't give up. Not ever."

'Cleaning the latrines was another of our resources. Those which I helped to clean were used by 200 to 300 persons. A great effort of will was necessary to get you through the work. Yet we all volunteered eagerly. The warders sprinkled the latrines with chloride, three or four fingers deep and then shut a couple or more of us inside. Our eyes and noses streamed. As one scraped, the other would work frantically to decipher the messages left on the walls. The chloride was so strong that foam sometimes rose to our lips. The warder came back to let us out only when it suited him. Once he delayed so long that blood, instead of foam, bright blood straight from the lungs, began to pour out of the mouth of one of my companions. Another time, sixty-seven women were locked in a latrine full of chloride fumes for one hour. Many fainted, but none fell, for there was no room. Though unconscious, they continued to stand upright, propped up by the bodies all around them. The excrement covering the floor rose above our ankles.

'In the mornings we were brought bread for the day and boiled water to drink. Sometimes there was soup and a spoonful of sugar. In the afternoon, the doors would open a little way, a bucket would appear in the opening and the prisoners would crush forward to be given a little water gruel, poured in any kind of receptacle they had. There was no fat in our diet, but we got water and salt. Once, we were given a lot of onions which we ate with joy.

'The regulations allowed a walk of twenty minutes each day, unless you were on a charge. Almost nobody ever got this. I myself was taken out for the first time six weeks after my arrest. My head swam and my knees failed me. Mrs. S., a widow with a child of six months, waited half a year for her first spell of exercise. Children were kept under arrest in this way, exactly like adults, most often for "frontier crimes" and on political charges. But it could depend on the decision of the officer in charge whether a child should be further detained or allowed to go free. I knew cases of children being handed over to family friends or servants, who had successfully begged to be allowed to take them; and even knew of a case of a thirteen-year-old girl arrested at the frontier and sent at the mother's entreaty to friends in Lwów. The mother was even informed by the prison governor that it had been done. In other instances, a mother might be told that her child was safely with relatives or friends who had obtained the right to keep it, and months later it would turn out that nobody, in fact, knew where the child had been sent or what had become of it after it was taken from its mother. The majority of these lost children probably ended in Soviet orphanages, where they would be brought up as Soviet citizens, under a name out of a register.

'Pregnant women were kept till the last moment in the common cells, in the same conditions as the rest of us. One woman (Ukrainian, Katruzia Z.) was only taken to the prison at all because all the rest of us went on a determined hunger-strike, causing a lot of trouble. In this case, the family were categorically refused all access to the child. After her confinement, the mother and child remained together in the nursing cell, as it was called, until the infant died. These infants did very often die, mostly from sores beneath their arms and inside their thighs, caused by insufficient washing, drying, etc. Young inexperienced mothers who gave birth in prison were seldom able to rear their infants for more than a few days or weeks. After the birth of a dead infant, the body was immediately taken from the mother, who was forthwith sent back to the common cell. In our cell there were two women who had lost their children in this way. Both appeared to have become slightly deranged.

'In the prison for politicals, I saw fellow-prisoners tortured. For hours at a time I listened to their fearful cries. After a time I ceased to feel either horror or pity. I remember the exact moment at which this happened, and a clear sensation of something in me having snapped, and all feeling being now over. The cries which we heard were not always even recognizably human. Once, when a man was being tortured, he cried out not like a man but like a slaughtered pig. I did not care. When the tortured fainted from pain, they were restored by injections and questioned further. In support of this, I quote cell No. 46 in the prison at Zamarstynow, in January of 1941, in a corridor off the main corridor. . . .

'Women and young girls were thrown into the cells beaten to pulp. Their hair was torn out from their scalps, their fingers broken, their toes crushed, their teeth knocked in, temples crushed, skin broken open. They were beaten on their heels and kicked in the stomach; their kidneys were laid open by beating. Alanka, the Ukrainian girl in our cell, returned to us unconscious, after having been ill-treated in a special way during menstruation.

'I concluded that the human organism can survive anything. When I had typhus, I simply lay on the floor of my cell with a pair of skiing boots under my head, and once or twice was given aspirin. I had dysentery twice. After seven days of that, a doctor gave me some bromide. I had no other treatment. The second time I was put in the prison hospital, and was put to lie on the straw and rags left by the last patient who had had dysentery. Being delirious, I begged with tears for some soda-water from a siphon on the doctor's desk. A doctor and some of the nurses laughed. "You! A prisoner . . . soda-water! Soda-water is not for you, you filth."

'In the one cell with me were cases of galloping consumption, typhus, inflammation of the ovaries with discharges of pus, and dysentery. In June I was taken out of this cell (political) and put in with thieves, prostitutes and murderesses. Many were very good-hearted. Others were abominable and loathed the politicals and everyone who had had any education. For 130 women in this cell there was one parasha, and of the 130, at least seven were officially syphilitic, stinking horribly from open sores and putrefying all over; and very many more were in the same state, though not certificated. Later, a second parasha was supplied. Once in this cell we were given salt herrings for dinner and then no water during twenty-four hours. This was a punishment for some breach of discipline. We were constantly being searched, in the most intimate ways. The death rate was high, and the deaths, on the whole, were fearful to witness. In this cell with its appalling scenes, venereal diseases, abominable language and corruption of all kinds, were many very young girls of about fourteen and fifteen years of age. What these scenes were, and what are the personal habits and the conversation of these professional criminals, nobody who has not heard them can have the smallest conception.

'Helen Z. in my cell, was seventeen. Her mother was killed in Tarnopol, during an air raid. With her brother, she was arrested in trying to get from Lwów to Cracow. When I came into the cell she was a skeleton. Once when, during exercise, her clothing had become saturated with rain, she was ordered to wait in this rain and not return to her cell. Within a few weeks she was seized by open tuberculosis. This child slept among all the worst syphilitics, and for some time alongside me. She then passed into a phase of constant haemorrhages, but she was still not taken out of the cell. Finally, after a haemorrhage in which she completely lost consciounss, she was taken to the hospital. In this hospital, I met her again during my second attack of dysentery. The condition of this hospital ward was indescribable. Four of us were lying side by side; one, also a young girl of seventeen, was a Jewess from Cracow who, with another student, had come from Cracow to Lwów, expecting to study and follow the Communist programme, and instead was lying dying in this ward. Miserably ill as I was, I could not at first bring myself to lie on the straw I was given, and from which another dysentery patient had just risen. Nothing under me was changed during the whole week that I lay there.

The doctors, Jews, one from Lwów, the other from Cracow, and the two nurses from the Lwów Jewish hospital, were absolutely powerless to help. In these conditions, my little companion died. Before her death she again appealed to the N.K.V.D. to transfer her, at least for a time, to some better conditions where she might regain her health. The child passionately desired to live. Before she lost consciousness she begged for a priest, a request which heartily entertained our guards. She was buried, none the less, with a prayer book which she kept concealed all the time, and which one of the Soviet nurses laid in her crossed hands.

'In the spring of 1940, in Brygidki (where my own cell number was at that time 14), a number of Polish children were in No. 17. The guards told us, after endless questioning, that the youngest of these children was turned thirteen. This was not true. There were boys among them of not more than eleven. During the moment or two when we were scrubbing that part of the corridor and the warder could be tricked into looking somewhere else, we talked with them once or twice through the cracks in the door. Three were aged eleven, one ten. The oldest (Jewish) was sixteen. All the others were between eleven and fourteen. These children were "politicals" (accused of distributing leaflets or carrying food to prisoners, etc.); "frontier offenders" (arrested at a frontier with their parents) and "speculators" (accused of selling tobacco and other articles in the street). Cell No. 17 was very dark and very airless; the children slept on the floor and few had coverings or comforts of any kind. Nevertheless they were being treated with relative mildness. Their food was much better than ours; there was sugar in it, even a lot, and plenty of fat. These children had all been dressed alike, in school uniforms, blue with yellow trimming; obviously all taken from some Ukrainian warehouse. Their heads had been shaved. Books too, were allowed them; lives of Stalin and Lenin, anti-religious tracts, Soviet history, etc. All of them were very brave. Each of them declared at every conceivable opportunity that he was immovably determined always and in everything to remain what he was, a Pole. During cross-examinations, only one was badly beaten and a second struck; another was threatened with beating and dog-bites, but threatened only. None of the children would tell anything, if indeed they knew anything to tell, which is most improbable.

'After their cross-examination, they told us how we ought to behave, and what our duty was. Older children were locked up in cells in Brygidki No. 1 Block. These older children also had books, pencils, etc., and comparatively good food. Much later, on the station at Zlocozw, through which I passed with other prisoners, I saw a little boy of twelve in school uniform, quite alone in a transport of men; no coat, no stockings. I spoke to him and he was at great pains not to break down, turning away to hide the tears of which he was ashamed. His little frame shook all over. To be spoken to by a woman, making him think probably, against his will, of his mother or sister! His name was Stanisław and he was then twelve, he told me. Tried for a political offence and sentenced to deportation.

'In Zamarstynow with me were girls (Ukrainian) of eighteen and nineteen. If I had not seen it with my own eyes, I would not have believed it possible for young girls to be beaten as they were. All were condemned to death, and when this was repealed, to ten and fifteen years of lagier. One of these girls after being raped was carried back to the cell and laid beside her mother. The mother herself told me this. One young girl was so beaten that she died. In Brygidki a second young girl died from the beating she received.

'On November the 12th I was removed to Zamarstynow to a political cell. This cell was three metres by two and a half; there was one bed, a hot stove in one corner, a parasha, and fourteen women. We had to pack ourselves, quite literally like sardines, head to foot. It was impossible for any one person to turn alone. We had all to turn at once. I was three months in this cell and we were all very united. Christmas was passed here. We passed it even with joy, profoundly convinced of God's grace over us and of the ultimate restoration and divine destiny of Poland. We sang carols all through the night and comforted and upheld each other. On this occasion, even the N.K.V.D. gave us up! The prison staff peered at us through the grating from time to time, but hardly attempted to silence us. In Brygidki, the carols were taken up from one cell to another, until the whole prison rang with the sound, and the street outside was filled with it too. In Zamarstynow it was the Ukrainian women who sang, but the men did not take it up. In this prison, they were too physically exhausted.

'After this, I was sent back to Brygidki. For several hours I waited in a large room with a lot of men. The men were almost all naked. All were being searched. The N.K.V.D. soldiers near me insisted on finding this funny. Neither I nor the men paid any attention to it at all. A doctor whom I succeeded in seeing gave me some ointment for my arms and legs, which were covered with abscesses. The holes from some of these went right down to the bone. This ointment at once eased me. In Zamarstynow, I had been given an ointment intended for itch, which had terribly inflamed the sores. In the cells where I now was, urine ran in all the time from the latrines next door. I lay on a plank soaked and running with urine, wrapped in the sodden caracul coat in which I now lived. Two days later, I was moved from this cell to one which was terribly small but full of old friends. Many of the women in this cell had been fearfully tortured.

Zoë Zajdlerowa. (Source: Phoebe Winch)

'Looking through photographs of these children . . . is like looking through a register of human skeletons . . . [they] had to fight . . . the long, losing battle against cold, hunger, heat, disease, terror, Sovietization and their own growing exhaustion, for now more than three years.' Photograph of a Polish girl taken in Kazakhstan in 1941.
(Source: APUST)

'The invaders – and not only the rank and file but highly placed officers of the N.K.V.D., the most privileged caste in the whole Union – were seized with astonishment and admiration at the sight of . . . articles offered for sale . . . [and] would rush into all the shops in a street and come out again after having bought up literally everything in sight'. Photograph of Soviet soldiers sporting watches, taken by a commercial photographer in Lwów, October 1939. (Source: APUST)

'We lived in tents without floors. The tents stood on frozen mud.' Interviewees remember the makeshift stove(s) as illustrated. (Source: APUST)

'The wretchedness of the prisoners' clothing is unimaginable. . . . The rare footware is made of felt or cloth . . . the usual course is for the prisoner to wrap his feet and legs in plaited straw or in rags.' (Source: APUST)

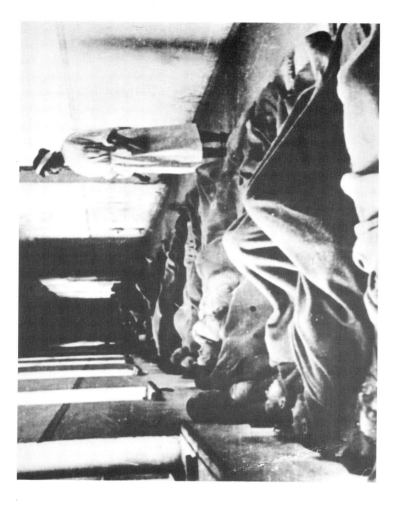

'The patients lie about the floor, sometimes covered by a piece of blanket, often not covered at all.' (Source: APUST)

'Not far from the lines of demarcation I was pulled up and arrested by a frontier guard who asked me at once by whom, and for what purpose, I had been sent to cross the frontier.' Photograph of a border post on the Nazi–Soviet frontier in Poland near Małkinia, September 1939. (Source: APUST)

Reunion in the Middle East. Photograph taken in 1942 outside Tehran.
(Source: APUST)

Mother Witer, superior of the Greek Catholic Convent, was there
with three nuns. The Mother had been hung on a hook for three hours.
The examining judge had had her mouth forced open and then spat into
it. There were many, many others. I remember them all. One who was
young and very intelligent was there to spy on the rest. May God forgive
her. . . .

'The warder here was a woman. On all occasions she went out of her
way to say to visiting officials, "Oh, how I dislike them!" (almost as
though she feared she might be suspected of leniency), "I cannot like them
at all!" To this, the woman doctor returned, perfectly sincerely, "How is
one to like swine?"

'Sleep and the hope of dreams was our narcotic against everything.

'In a sense all our waking hours too, were filled with fantasies. We spoke
endlessly together of the past and the future (never of the present) and of
the Polish Army – our thoughts followed our Army ceaselessly throughout
the whole world.

'All of us repeated for all the others everything that we knew by heart;
films seen, books read, music heard. We composed whole odysseys and
romances; recounted *Potop* and *Quo Vadis* from cover to cover over and
over again. *Quo Vadis* was told four times in that one cell.[6] We lectured,
taught each other morse – all in whispers.

'On the 20th of April 1941 each of us examined her conscience, and
made confession within her own soul. A priest imprisoned in another cell
gave absolution and benediction, turning himself towards our window.
On the way to the latrines and during exercise pieces of dried bread which
had been consecrated by this priest were smuggled to us. For many, this
was the last Communion of which they partook on earth.'

Persons under examination were beset with inquiries and deluged
with accusations which did not make the most elementary sense. An
examining judge would produce such phrases as: 'Come now, confess the
whole of your activities. Confess everything counter-revolutionary that
you have done in the whole of your life. Throw all this foul weight off your
soul. Admit all you have done, all your life long, against the cause of the
workers and of the working people!' The impression made on the Poles,
addressed like this, and conscious in their own minds that they had at no
time attempted, or done, anything at all against the cause of the workers
(and very often that, as leaders and members of working-class movements
themselves they had spent the whole of their adult lives in doing exactly
the opposite), was often of having fallen into the hands of a fraternity of
sinister lunatics.

These Poles in prison and awaiting trial were not told of the paragraphs
in the Code which concerned them, nor even (before cross-examination)

what they were accused of. All requests to see the Code were met with astonishment and refusal. With very few exceptions, none of these Poles did, in fact, ever have a trial. The examining judge reported the alleged facts. The Moscow body known as OS[7] pronounced sentence, and the prisoner, having been led into some disused privy, barber's shop, or similar black hole of the prison, had a paper read aloud to him stating that a 'special N.K.V.D. body in Moscow, after examining the affair in question, had pronounced sentence of a term of hard labour of five to eight years, etc.' After this, he was deported.

Five to eight years was classic. A few prisoners, caught attempting to cross the Soviet–German line of demarcation or the Polish–Lithuanian frontier in either direction, received as little as three years; but never when there was a further charge (as there almost always was) of speculation and espionage.

One testimony from a young girl called Irena, sixteen years old in 1940, describes the arrest and imprisonment of her mother and herself after they attempted to cross the frontier en route to Wilno in Lithuania. After a period in prison they were sentenced to three years corrective labour. Her account of this experience follows.

'In April 1940, after the first deportation, we decided to go to Wilno also. We had no means of livelihood. Everything we owned had been taken away from us. The farm-hand I mentioned above used to steal our own meal from us from the granary. On the way to Wilno we were arrested by a frontier patrol, searched, and kept for the night in a kind of cell, and on the following day we were taken to Murowana Oszmianka. Thus began my long journey to Starodub, in the Soviet Union. In gaol, my mother, who had a bad heart, had an attack. When I asked for some water for her the guard swore at me. Two days later we were moved again and placed in a temporary prison, located in the cellars of an ordinary house. A corridor ran down the middle; around it were the cells, seven and a half feet by six feet, without any windows. In a terribly stuffy atmosphere and in semi-darkness, a small lamp was burning all day and all night long; there were eleven of us, all women. The door to the corridor remained open, for otherwise we would have been suffocated.

'Then the investigations began. These were always at night time.

'On the 16th of April 1940 my mother and I were taken to a prison in Molodeczno. This was also a temporary hastily set-up prison. Eighteen women slept in a small cell, on the bunks, under the bunks, and on the floor. The window was covered but a little light came through, though no air. That enemy of prisoners – the lamp – was kept burning all day and all night. During the long months I spent in prisons and in a penal settlement, my greatest desire was to sleep, for at least one night, in complete darkness. I used to tie a handkerchief round my burning eyes, but the light managed to penetrate even that.

'For a whole month we were allowed no exercise. Once in twenty-four hours we were taken to the latrines; always at a different time. Five in the morning, or at midday; one was as likely as the other. We used all to volunteer to carry out the buckets to the latrine. Those who were never in a Soviet prison will never understand what happiness it was to carry out this otherwise loathsome task. We all dreamed of seeing the sky, the sun, the green trees; of breathing some of the fresh air which came in from the neighbouring gardens. We did it in turns, and waited eagerly all day for this opportunity, which lasted two or three minutes. When we returned to the cell, the atmosphere there seemed even more lugubrious, and the air fouler than ever.

'The food in the Molodeczno prison consisted, in the morning, of 600 grammes of bread, very weak tea or hot water with no sugar. At midday, we got a pint of smelly soup made from putrid tripes, eyes, jaws and teeth and full of boiled flies. We got the same soup again in the evening.

'After a month of waiting the interrogations began again. When the statement I had made previously was read to me, I understood that the authorities had taken advantage of my ignorance of Russian and my consequent inability to check what they had taken down to change the meaning of what I had said. When they read my statement to me, they had left out the paragraphs which they themselves had added. I had signed it, however, so I was responsible for its contents. I protested categorically and explained the actual state of affairs to my new judges. I do not know whether they believed me.

'In our cell were four wives of officers from Molodeczno, arrested for reading, and allegedly spreading, a rhymed horoscope about the future of Poland (the one that says that "the hammer and sickle" will collapse) and W.G., a typist from the School Inspectorate, arrested for copying this horoscope on her typewriter. All of them were accused of agitation and of being counter-revolutionaries. They were told to confess their guilt for then they would be able to see their children, who otherwise would be deported to Russia.

'It was very difficult to get any medical aid. One woman suffered from shingles and had very frequent attacks, during which she used to scream with pain. I could not bear listening to her and used to cover my head up and stop my ears. The guard in the corridor was less susceptible and never paused in his pacing, walking up and down in his linen footwear. He never called a doctor, though we implored him to do so. Mother fell ill again and her heart attacks grew increasingly frequent. At first I could get no help for her. Once, when I thought she was dying, I fell into such despair that I made a row, the equal of which I think I shall never again be able to make. I screamed, wept, stamped, and banged at the door. It had the right effect. The Governor of the prison came, called a male nurse and said that in the event of another attack Mother was to be given hot water and a doctor was to be called.

'On the 29th of June 1940 we were transferred, this time to Soviet territory, to Polotck. In Polotck were placed those prisoners from Wilejka, Molodeczno, Berezwecz and Oszmiana whose cases had already been investigated. Here we felt as if we were in a comparative paradise, though we were continually being told that *"Vam tut nie kirort"* (this is not meant to be a health resort for you). It was quiet here. The cell was well aired though, of course, as always, it was fearfully crowded. The food was not plentiful but fresh and decently prepared. There was a ten-minute walk every day, and even books to read.

'On the 3rd September 1940 our sentences were read to us. They had been made "in absentia". In the prison garden, representatives of the N.K.V.D. and the prison governor sat down at a table standing beneath a lilac tree. Their faces were kind enough and they spoke politely. I was told that I was sentenced to three years of *"trudovoy ispravitielnoy kolonii dla niesovrshennoletnikh v Starodube"* (corrective labour-settlement for children) in conformity with Article 120–2, for an attempt to cross the frontier. Mother got three years in a corrective labour camp in Tiemlag, Mordovska, U.S.S.R.

'We knew then that we were to be separated. We determined not to break down and to trust that we were not parting for ever. But what was going on in our hearts was another matter.

'We started on our journey on the 17th of September 1940, after having been searched for I do not know which consecutive time.

'The journey to Orsza passed fairly rapidly, for the conditions were bearable. While we were in Orsza, many transports arrived from other prisons, including Luck and Kowel. The prisoners were reshuffled here and trains regrouped. It seemed like a rally of prisoners from all parts of Poland, prisoners whose ultimate goal was Siberia or Kamchatka.

'Mother and I were separated. The guard called me out, with the now familiar *"Z vieshchami"*.

'Our time had come. As I walked out I looked back for the last time at Mother, whose face had become perfectly bloodless. As the doors of the freight car clanged between us I saw her conjure up for me a last smile. I myself concentrated every bit of will power and courage I had on holding back my tears.

'They now took me to prison in Orsza. Before it had been a prison it used to be a convent. It looked terribly sinister with its great iron doors, dark cells, damp walls and sealed windows. I was squeezed into a cell where there was not space enough to stand. Seventy women, almost naked because of the unbearable heat, screamed and stewed in the small cell. I spent the night in the corridor. All night I could hear the wild cries of Russian women all round me. In the morning a man was led out of another cell. His clothes were torn and wet, his face bruised and marked all over with fresh blood. He staggered as he walked down the corridor. His eyes, out of which he tried to peer, were swollen and almost closed. The guard with him kept prodding him to make him pass me as quickly as possible.

'Once, during the daytime, I heard shouts of "Don't beat me, you swine!" then groans, and what sounded like the sound of someone being kicked. Then a door banged. I began to cry then and to bang on the door, too, because for a minute it seemed to me that this had been my brother's voice.

'In our cell there were five of us "under age": Maria S., aged seventeen, Irena C., aged fifteen, Jadwiga W., aged fourteen, Basia T., aged sixteen, and myself. Each of us had been sentenced for an attempt to cross the frontier. Nothing was being said about sending us on to Starodub. One day, having been allowed out for exercise, we met the governor of the prison. I asked him why we were still waiting. "A good thing you reminded me," he said. "I had forgotten all about you."

'We left on the following day.'

Editors' notes

1. The Bund, or Jewish Workers' League, was an internationalist Marxist organization formed before the First World War and active in the inter-war period.

2. Demarcation line, not frontier, because this was the line marking off the Wilno district, transferred by the Soviet authorities for a period of months to the Lithuanian government in Kovno. The whole of Lithuania, including Wilno, was incorporated into the Soviet Union in 1940.

3. This phrase, left over from the Tsarist period, was engrained in Russian prison usage and had a familiar ring in the ears of the Poles. The invariable first words, meaning 'get going' are followed by others varying with circumstances. In this case, the whole phrase is 'get going, with things', which in Tsarist days was the recognized prelude to execution. In 1940, however, it was more often the prelude to deportation to the Soviet Union. The continued use of these terms, so reminiscent of persecution under the Tsars, profoundly affected the imagination of the Poles and an allusion to it formed a part of almost every

deposition examined by the author. This point is also borne out in the editors' transcripts.

4. The normal procedure in the Soviet Union but not followed when the trains were first loaded up in Poland. See Chapter 2, 'The Journeys' above.

5. 'First of all: *night*. Why is it that all the main work of breaking down human souls went on at *night*? . . . Because at night, the prisoner torn from sleep . . . lacks his normal daytime equanimity and common sense. He is more vulnerable.' Alexander Solzhenitsyn, *The Gulag Archipelago*, p. 103.

6. *Quo Vadis?*, a novel, was written by Henryk Sienkiewicz (1846–1916). It won him the Nobel Prize for Literature, adding worldwide fame to a literary career widely recognized in Poland as brilliant.

7. Actually OSO, Russian acronym for a three-men board of the People's Commissariat of Internal Affairs, with powers to sentence 'socially dangerous' persons without trial.

FOUR

Penal Camps

A ll lagiers are solely and absolutely under the control of the N.K.V.D. Administrative posts in all lagiers are filled by officers and N.C.O.s of the N.K.V.D..

In every group of lagiers a central administrative office deals with the planning of programmes, the transfer of prisoners, questions of internal economy, etc. The executive posts in these offices, again, are all held by N.K.V.D. personnel, but clerical work may be done by the prisoners. Individual camps inside groups are known as kolons, and the head of a kolon is often a civilian, specially engaged for the purpose. This head man, or commandant, appoints for himself a sort of staff to look after internal arrangements and to be overseers generally. These men (called in slang pridurki by their fellows) are chosen from among the convicts and have a privileged food ration. The lowest functionary in the hierarchy of this general staff is the brigade-leader, but he is also probably the most important. Unlike the other functionaries, brigade-leaders are not nominated by the commandant but are chosen by the convicts themselves. The privileged convicts are employed as overseers to the other prisoners and are also the only authorized mouthpiece of the prisoners with the commandant.

All work gangs are split up into brigades, the number of persons in a brigade depending on the type of work done and the conditions for doing it; brigade-leaders distribute and superintend the work done by their brigades and are responsible for the return of figures.

The system by which officials take little or no part in internal affairs within the camps but delegate to a cross-section of the prisoners themselves what amounts to absolute power over all the remainder – a power against which there is no appeal – is a system theoretically admirable and just. Nevertheless, it is the factor which, more than any other (not excluding the climate), makes of these institutions the peculiar hell which they actually are.

In the first place, all these positions of power are of necessity held by what in our language would be called common criminals. The regulations (which, it must never be forgotten, hold these criminals to be infinitely

105

less depraved than the 'politicals') lay this down absolutely. No politicals are allowed to hold a function of any kind (though in a few of the remote lagiers some clerical posts may be filled by them, against the regulations).

These common criminals must almost all have been sentenced for crimes with violence; since so many of the milder crimes, such as 'speculation', 'sabotage', inefficiency, and crimes connected with employment, all tend to be grouped under 'political'. In consequence, absolute power over men of less violent dispositions is delegated to men who must have been guilty, at the least, of housebreaking, assault, hooliganism, robbery, and even murder; and still more often are simply members from birth of the professional criminal class.

Payment is made for work in the sense that for work done each convict is credited with an allowance of food. If he fails to work he acquires no credit and consequently receives no food. This credit is calculated on the basis of an imaginary unit of measurement, called the 'norm'. For every type of work a 'norm' of output has been laid down, and the regulations demand that each convict, in the course of each working day, should accomplish as his *minimum* the norm which is obligatory to his task. In actual practice, as we shall see, almost nobody ever comes within miles of accomplishing this norm at all. The brigade-leader assesses how near to, or how far from, the norm the individual convict's work has come and the resulting allowance of food. Distribution of food is done by '*kettle*', of which the following are the most generally employed. The quantities given are all as in peace-time and have become less since 1941. Some supplement to these *kettles* is prescribed for camps in the Arctic Circle.

Kettle No. 1 (for those who accomplish above 50 per cent and less than 100 per cent), 400–475 grammes (14.1 ounce to 1 pound 2 ounces) bread for the whole day, and very thin soup three times a day.

Kettle No. 2 (for those who accomplish 100 per cent), 600–650 grammes (1 pound 5 ounces to 1 pound 10 ounces) bread, the same soup three times a day. Some spoonfuls of barley or groats at night.

Kettle No. 3 (for those who accomplish more than 100 per cent – called *Stakhanovtsy*),[1] 750–1,200 grammes (1 pound 10 ounces to 2 pounds 10¼ ounces) bread, soup and groats, and probably fish or a white roll at night.

Kettle No. 4 (for pridurki), more than 800 grammes (1 pound 12 ounces) bread, and three full meals a day.

Punishment *Kettle* (for those who do less than 50 per cent of the norm), 300–400 grammes (10½ to 14.1 ounces) bread with one meal of the worst quality soup once a day.

In some camps there can be further variation of *kettles*, but the five quoted are the commonest.

The regulations provide also for payment in cash, but exclusively for work done *in excess* of the norm. Further, of this cash payment one-third is first to be taken in taxes, one-third to be put into a savings account (to be paid over only when the convict regains his freedom) and the remaining third only to be payable cash down. As stated already accomplishment of the norm is almost never a genuine possibility, and the question of payment in cash remains almost entirely academic.

In the establishment of norms, marked preference has been given to labour requiring skill and previous experience. The most unskilled and most exacting types of labour carry the most exacting norms. The result is that the less previous experience of manual labour a man has, and consequently the less he is fitted for it, the more he is required to do. Not only is the norm for specialists markedly lighter (partly, very likely, because they often help, in the designing-rooms and places where the programmes are planned, to set their own), but their work, too, is quite differently looked upon. The toiling masses are the victims in every case. Of these, almost nobody at all, though working continuously and for very long hours, ever honestly accomplishes more than 50 per cent; and for the old and infirm it is impossible to accomplish more than 10 per cent. In setting these norms no allowance has been made for conditions. Workers in free employment, if their norm itself is not very much lower, yet work only six to seven hours a day (since 1941, eight), and in lagier the same rate has to be kept up for perhaps twelve hours on end; with this further difference also that the distance between the camp and the actual work site often adds as much as several hours each day to the time the convict is on his legs, working, marching, answering roll-calls, etc. under armed guard.[2]

In many lagiers, one day free of work a month was allowed, and in some others one day in ten, until 1941; since then, no free days are allowed at all.

The professional criminals, once turned functionaries, are themselves the victims of one panic obsession. This obsession is their fear of failing to obtain the maximum output from the masses of other prisoners now put in their power, and the consequent loss of their own privileges – the outstanding and quite inestimable privilege of their new state being, in fact, the power to fill their bellies a little; to eat to some degree like men. The kettle from which a functionary eats, though it is still nothing like an adequate diet for a man working twelve hours a day and often on his legs in the open for at least sixteen, is unimaginably in excess of the kettles from which he would again eat if he lost his position. Of all these functionaries the brigade-leader, though the lowest in the hierarchy, has the most real influence on camp life. The provision of food allotted to each kolon is calculated on a basis of the work accomplished by the kolon as a whole. This food for the whole kolon is again shared out between brigades in proportion to the amount of work which each brigade has done. But within the brigade it is the brigade-leader who has sole power to decide what proportion of the norm each man shall be said to have accomplished, and therefore what proportion of food he shall receive. The less the brigadier has to distribute to each man, the more is left for himself. In such circumstances, the slogan 'as you work so shall you eat', admirable in itself, becomes an instrument of blackmail of which the full cruelty can never be adequately described. The power thus given to the brigade-leaders (and the inevitability with which they must proceed to abuse of this power) is equalled only by the dread of losing it under which they labour themselves. It is impossible for them, under pressure of this fear, to do anything but slave drive their fellow-prisoners more ruthlessly even than they are slave driven by the N.K.V.D. It is impossible for them to feel pity or to show mercy, and, when the inevitable corruption of all life within lagier is admitted, this can neither be wondered at nor can it be condemned.

The nature of the work itself (that very element in which the seed of regeneration is supposed to be contained), the climatic conditions and the scale of the contracts undertaken by the N.K.V.D., are all such as to make the accomplishment of the programmes impossible by any methods which are employed. In earlier days, when slavery had a legal existence and slave-labour was brought to Europe and America from Africa, a slave at least constituted a valuable piece of property. Also the reserves from which this slave-labour could be drawn were restricted, and the furnishing of the market required considerable effort and involved a high element of risk. The replenishment of slave-labour for the pioneer work done in lagier presents no difficulties like these. A convict in lagier represents no money value at all; and in fact, after a certain inevitable stage of exhaustion and physical deterioration has been reached, may even be considered a liability, and is all the better for being finished off quickly – as then happens.

All this being so, there is one factor only in the camp life which makes individual survival at all possible. This factor is graft: in Russian 'blat'.[3] This Russian word is extremely difficult to translate, and really signifies the relationships which exist between anybody and everybody else – between prisoners and each other; between prisoners and pridurki; between pridurki and the authorities; between the kitchens, the office-staff, the guards, the N.K.V.D., and everybody else. If you have good blat, you may survive. If you have not, you must inevitably go under. Blat can be won uniquely by the conferring of an obligation, and it is almost impossible to say what forms this obligation may take; in the nature of things, it must invariably be something unimaginably humble, but if it is an obligation at all it entitles you to some degree of blat. Blat is the basis of the whole internal system; and the whole basis of blat is the fact that everybody, from the top to the bottom, theoretically, has an interest in ensuring to the community the highest degree of production possible – again an ideological conception; again, theoretically, both humanitarian and just.

In practice, the whole of life in lagier from top to bottom presents one vast labyrinth of cheating. The camp heads cheat the convicts, recurringly promising them better food and better conditions, and none of these promises are kept. The more plentiful rations, the often considerable supplies of fats for the Arctic regions, the white flour not infrequently ordered in Moscow, never get further than the top. Whilst cheating the convicts, they cheat also their own superiors, reporting to them that schedules are being kept and programmes carried out. These programmes in point of fact are eternally in arrears. The brigade-leaders and accountants in their turn cheat the camp authorities, to make sure of their own percentages. At all times, there are two great currents of cheating in operation: one flowing up, the other down. Each party realizes that the other cheats; both keep quiet, for obvious reasons. In this, and in this alone, there is solidarity between the convicts, even between the professional criminals and the politicals.

In this business of cheating too the pridurki have much the best of it, as compared with the mass of their fellow-prisoners, who almost never have any such opportunity. Even the N.K.V.D. on the spot are in conflict to a certain extent with this battening by one group upon all others. Periodically, attempts to cope with it are made, but without lasting result. In 1937, for example, many pridurki were shot in the presence of the other prisoners, or were condemned to appropriate punishments; but this too remained without result. While the conditions last, *it is not possible to get results*. Every single one of the other prisoners would do as the pridurki do, if they could only get the chance. That the abuses should be checked is no part of the plan of the bandit elements or of the functionaries who hold closely with them and who have themselves inevitably been chosen from their ranks. A camp commandant who falls foul of these elements is certain to be denounced by the prisoners themselves for subversive ideas, and for favouring politicals; and this again must to a certain extent explain, and even excuse, the fact that commandants as a rule do not attempt improvements. It is difficult indeed not to see the whole of life inside these camps as one monstrous merry-go-round. At the centre of it all sits the commandant, responsible to his own superiors. The commandant slave drives the prisoners, and is himself driven to this slave driving by the forces which drive him. The convicts turned functionary slave drive the other convicts, slave driven by fears of their own. The speed has always got to be increased; because, however fast it all goes, they are never quite able to keep up with the day's programme; the next day's programme accordingly keeps going faster too. The slaves, if only they need not go so fast, if there had been left to them even a little strength or health or hope, might even keep abreast of the programme. . . . It is this having to go so fast that makes it all so slow. . . .

One Polish male prisoner gave the following account of his experience in the camps.

'We arrived in Maldiak on the 26th of June, 1940. There were four camps there, each containing 2,500 persons, and we lived in huts covered by tenting, 100 prisoners in each hut. We slept on bare bunks made, not of planks, but of logs. Everybody slept in their clothes. In the summer there were sudden changes of temperature and very light nights. The summer was short, with great heat in the daytime. But even at its hottest, the smallest cloud would cause an instant change in the temperature, and it would then become intensely cold. Swarms of flies, a kind of mosquito, very tiny and very blood-thirsty, caused us great misery, getting into our eyes and biting us to the bone.

'By the middle of September, the snow was up to our knees. At Magadan, we were given winter jackets, and in the camp a few received felt leg coverings and another type of warm jacket called bushlaki.

'The whole region about the camp was utterly deserted. Apart from the prisoners and the administration no one lived there. The native inhabitants moved further and further into the taiga at each Soviet advance into the interior of their country, keeping always as far away as they possibly could from the intruders and living by breeding animals which they graze in herds.

'Reveille was at 5 a.m. Before going to work, the prisoners got a piece of bread each and a portion of gruel. After this, and in a column four across, we were marched under escort to our places in the mines. The mining was for gold. On our way to work, an orchestra sometimes played. The work on the surface consisted of digging earth, often mixed with gravel. We dug with crowbars, picks and shovels, and in winter when the ground was frozen, with gouges (chisels). It was indeed convicts' work. The daily norm was 125 barrows of earth dug, which had then to be pushed to a distance of from 300–400 metres. Below the surface these mines were 120–150 feet deep, and accidents below the surface were frequent, as many as five or six a day. The underground corridors were narrow and the ceilings not propped. The unfortunate victims of accidents were hauled to the surface, their hands cut off in proof of death (to be shown to the authorities) and the bodies then thrust below the brushwood. At 12.30 there was a half-hour break and we got our dinner, consisting of 150 grammes (5.25 ounces) of bread and a portion of thin skilly; occasionally a piece of fish. After dinner we kept on uninterruptedly until 8 p.m. The prisoners who had not by then accomplished their norm had to work two hours more. After the return to camp, there was still a lot of things to be done. Bread had to be brought from a point five kilometres away, the firewood too. Supper consisted of a piece of bread and the soup again. The ration of bread varied between 250 and 500 grammes (9 ounces to 1 pound 2 ounces) a day, according to the norm accomplished. The prisoners were of all classes, representing a cross-section of the whole of Soviet society, and not only of all the nationalities of the Soviet Union but also of the states who are her neighbours.

'The orchestra very often played while the prisoners were at work. To the accompaniment of this music, the guards would fall out prisoners whose work was especially feeble and shoot them, there and then. The shots rang out one after another. The bodies of the murdered men were also buried under the brushwood on the surface of the mines.

'A Jew from Lwów working alongside me was so exhausted that he repeatedly fainted at work. The guard ordered him to fall out, took him to a nearby shed, and there he was shot. I heard the shot and saw his body a few minutes later.

'The same fate overtook prisoners for the slightest breach of regulations, especially for moving even a few steps away from the spot where they were at work or for not keeping in line when they were marching. Everybody was pitilessly robbed the moment they arrived and all the prisoners were utterly demoralized. There were frequent fights, mutual denunciations, and at work no pity of any kind was shown by one prisoner to another. The whole inner functioning of the camp depended on present criminals or ticket-of-leave men. There was nothing they would not do to secure for themselves a larger piece of bread. The more intelligent among the prisoners were perfectly open-eyed about the functioning of the régime in the Union and were hostile to it, though quite powerless. Their only hope was that something might happen from outside, under the impact of which the system would come crashing down.'

Each convict, if he has none of his own, has the right to the following garments: two shirts, two pairs of pants, one vest, puttees, one pair of trousers (linen in summer, wadded in winter), a cap with ear flaps, a wadded short jacket, one pair of boots, and in winter, one other warm jacket and felted leg coverings.

Visits to the bath house are compulsory. These visits are always out of working hours. In the bath house are cauldrons of hot water and benches on which stand wooden troughs. Each convict has the right to six to eight litres of water. Before going to the bath house the convict is shorn and shaved, his outer garments are taken from him for disinfection and clean underclothing given (this last only if he has, in fact, state clothing – private clothing is not washed).

The whole business of the prisoners being supplied with clothing is as much of a fraud, in practice, as the rest. The majority of prisoners would be extremely lucky if they had one garment out of the lot. The wretchedness of the prisoners' clothing is unimaginable. The column as it marches to and from work, and assembles for food and roll-call, is made up of apparitions simply not of this world. The rare footwear is made of felt or cloth. Some attempts at soling and patching is occasionally made with perished rubber from disused tyres. The usual course is for the prisoner to wrap his feet and legs in plaited straw or in rags, if he can get them, plaster the whole thing over with mud and then plunge the limb into water. The coating of ice which in the open air instantly forms over all this may protect the limb inside from frost-bite. The trek (sometimes as long as for ten kilometres) to work and back again involves, besides all its other miseries, the lifting at each step of these feet and legs, first plastered with wet mud and then coated in ice. A prisoner who, by blat or by any other means, in fact, receives any piece of clothing, is bound to have it taken away from him again when sent to another kolon; and this transfer from kolon to kolon is perpetually taking place. No camp commandant will allow any recognizable piece of State clothing to leave his own camp. Clothing, like every other necessity of life, has an enormously high money or barter value in the Union, and the outfits prescribed by the regulations are no more likely to reach the helpless slaves for whom they are intended than are any improvements or additions to their food.

Working very often for weeks on end above their knees and up to their waists and even up to their armpits, in snow, mud or water, the convicts have no means (and if they had the means, no time) for drying what clothing they have, between one shift of work and another. In practice, the only time the clothing is even partially removed is during the compulsory weekly visit to the bath-house; and this visit, like everything else that is intended for the relief or hygiene of the prisoner, is also a farce and largely impossible, since the better part of any clothing given up for disinfection is certain to be stolen. No convict will willingly be separated from his clothing at any time, and all this clothing is literally alive with vermin. Water in which such garments are washed turns to a blue paste; this paste is coagulated blood. In the worst camps (and the the worse climatic conditions are, the worse all other conditions become) weaker inmates are constantly being stifled or beaten to death under cover of darkness to gain possession of something they have about them which still has some resemblance to human clothing. The Poles and other foreigners who were brought into the camps in 1940 and 1941, and who still possessed a part of the clothing in which they were arrested (army greatcoats often and underwear and boots of a quality and material never seen or imagined by the mass of the citizens of the Soviet Union), kept themselves alive on the capital which these things represented. Even the N.K.V.D. officials bought eagerly at nominal prices, and the blat which these things represented was fantastically high. Many even possessed bundles containing similar things, riches which cost not a few of them their lives. A Pole records how he and a fellow-prisoner slept with wire bound about their bodies and outside their clothing, to prevent it being pulled off them as they slept. Even this was not sure to be successful. If the owner was physically weak and had poor blat, he was simply done to death in the darkness. In the morning there was nobody to say, and indeed nobody to inquire, how the deed was done, and the clothing thus obtained would be worn without the slightest concealment by its new proprietor.

One such prisoner states: 'We lived in tents without floors. The tents stood on frozen mud. To the place where we worked in the forest we walked about six kilometres a day, there and back. When we returned at night, chilled and soaked to the bone, we sank up to our knees in mud inside the tents. The stoves, such as they were, thawed out the ground under canvas. We lay along the shelves in all our clothing, and in this way, in a sort of feverish sleep, succeeded by morning in drying out on our bodies a portion of our clothing before the guards with their dogs came to drive us out to another day's work. When one of us died in the night, we concealed the body beneath the bunks for as long as we could endure the stench so as to receive the dead man's ration of bread.'

The medical officer can free a convict from work for a period of days, but not unless he has a temperature rising to a given number of degrees, nor may he thus set free, in any one day, more than a given quota. There is also a quota for those he may order to hospital. In theory, the doctor also divides into categories those convicts fit for hard labour, for slightly less hard and for light labour, and the unfit. The unfit are to be employed on other than manual labour.

Out of all those who, in one form or another, have power for evil or good over the lives of the convicts, it might possibly be said that the medical orderlies and officers do at times make a certain attempt to bring some measure of relief to the sufferers. Every kolon possesses a medical officer of some kind; much more often a medical orderly than a qualified doctor or surgeon, and most often what in Poland and Germany is called a felczer – hard to define, but something between a cow-doctor and the old barber type which in England and France over 100 years ago used to be called in for jobs like the letting of blood, lancing of boils, etc. These men have an enormous number of handicaps against which to struggle; of which the least, probably, is their own lack of medical knowledge. The camp commandants control them very strictly. In no circumstances are they ever able to exempt from work more than a given number of prisoners in one day, whatever their own feeling in the matter may be. They are always out of material and have practically no drugs. In the majority of camps, if they have a stock of permanganate and a Soviet aspirin product they are well supplied. In the severest winters, a doctor may very well be without a single bandage or piece of clean rag for dressings, while the frost-bitten legs and arms of half the prisoners are filling with pus. Vitamin-starvation and scurvy are the great scourges. On principle, the doctor may prescribe the so-called 'scurvy ration' of sour cabbage and preparations made from the iodine-filled berries in which the northern forests abound; he may prescribe, but he is not able to get it. In practice, no such rations are ever genuinely available. The lack of iodine preparations, in particular, characterizes the whole system. Not only do the forests among which the camps are situated abound in berries, but further anti-scurvy draughts of great efficacy can also be made from the cones of certain pines. No argument has ever been found (even the obvious one of raising production) to convince the heads of camps of the utility of devoting even one day's work out of a whole season to the harvesting and storing of these fruits. To a great extent, this can be laid at the door of the guards, who simply will not turn out to escort the convicts to work of this kind. Exactly the same thing happens about fuel for use in the barracks. The convicts work all day from dawn to dusk in the heart of the gigantic forests. The camp itself is within the forest, and yet there is never anything like enough fuel for even the meagre stoves provided. The guards who will not turn out for the work of collecting camp fuel will not consent either to the prisoners being allowed tools (saws, axes, etc.) without their supervision, and the question of fuel ends there. Cases have even been known of sharp clashes between camp commandants and the guards, and the clashes have invariably ended in capitulation by the commandant.

Just as he may free only a certain number from work on any one day, the medical officer may also order only a stipulated number to hospital or rest points.

After scurvy and all the vitimin-starvation diseases, kidney and skin troubles of a very advanced kind are common. The patient with the kidney trouble swells monstrously, first in the legs, then in the upper part of the body, until the disease reaches the heart and the miserable victim dies.

The progress of disease in these extremes of climate, and in organisms so undermined, is terrifyingly rapid. Diarrhoea, a sort of bloody dysentery, typhus, and lung disease are common. Scurvy breaks out not only in rotting gums and falling teeth, but also in deep body wounds generally and on legs and arms. The first outbreak is in the form of a tiny pimple, then the surrounding flesh reddens and the pimple begins to fill with pus until the whole thing looks like a carbuncle and finally becomes a widely diffused wound which never heals, though a scab may form. The flesh below this scab is always soft and shifting. The agony of walking and of working in the open is very great; it is in fact agonizingly painful to use the limbs at all. Another sort of sore is set up by the bites of poisonous gnats. My close friend, Olga L., tells how her two-year-old child was bitten in the head by gnats,[4] and how a sore formed and poured out matter for three months before it, surprisingly, healed. Each morning when the child woke, her head was tightly bound in what looked like a close cap of matter. In the undernourished, ill-used and vitamin-starved bodies of these victims almost no wound will heal. Sores remain open and no new flesh will form. Any scab that forms is always breaking again and always releasing a new discharge.

Frost-bitten extremeties also putrefy. Itch forms between fingers and toes and on the upper parts of the breasts from contact with the sodden clothing. Incontinence of water is another misery from which nearly all, in a short time, become sufferers. The ruined organism has no control over its muscles, and this, too, helps to keep the clothing permanently sodden and filthy.

The rapid deterioration in the health of the camps' inmates and their desperation to be declared sick is vividly described:

'As a result of the twelve- to fourteen-hour day, with no day of rest in the week, and of the quality and quantity of the food, after a very short period in the camp the prisoners suffer from exhaustion, and are easily attacked by disease. A prisoner gets sick leave only when he has at least forty degrees C. of temperature, and then only if the quota of sick leave for that day is not filled. The exhaustion of the prisoners brings about a slowing down in the output. When the output goes down, the guards begin to beat them with their rifle-butts, put them into solitary confinement, and finally shoot them. Those who are in the lock-up (called tubes) also work under incessant supervision, and get only 200 grammes of bread and 100 grammes of soup. Dysentery and tsinga are endemic.[5] Out of a camp of 10,000 men, some 2,000 die every year, a considerable proportion of these from exhaustion. Every morning there are some prisoners who cannot be roused. They have died during the night. In the first two-and-a-half months of my time in the camp on the Kolyma, out of the total of twenty Poles in my group, sixteen died. Four, including myself, survived.

'The prisoners' one dream was to get away to hospital. The hospital was run by medical orderlies, all prisoners or former prisoners, and the equipment was extremely primitive. Nevertheless, life in hospital was incomparably better than everyday life in the huts. Self-inflicted wounds were universal. A prisoner willingly chopped off his fingers in the hope of getting thus admitted. I myself, with another Pole, shortly before our release, decided to cut off fingers and toes. We had come to the end of our endurance.'

Incontinence of the bowels is also common and greatly afflicts the old. Olga L. observes how this latter affliction, in women of a certain age, was often the first precursor of a rapidly progressive mental failure. The sufferer advances fatally from a sort of mental oblivion, often appearing half-unconscious of her terrible surroundings, into a galloping senility, and dies without a struggle and equally without relief. The disturbance in these women's minds is seldom violent or apparently painful and resembles more the decay of organic matter than the death of a human being. The whole process seldom takes longer than a few months.

An exception was the case of one woman, probably more than seventy years old, in this same settlement, who, though incontinent and senile, remained stubbornly alive.[6] In the same hut were Olga with her child, this woman with her daughter and son-in-law and their young children, and some other families, and the disease was so advanced in her that there was no possible means by which she could be kept even relatively clean. No change of clothing was possible; no soap, no paper, no clean rags, and water was still more precious than any of these. There was simply nothing at all that could be done, and nothing was done. Even the daughter in time abandoned her efforts at least to remove and renew some part of the rags in which she lay at night. The atmosphere inside the building was so foul that nobody would willingly cross the threshold in winter, when the doors had to be kept shut. In summer it was perhaps a little better, for the doors could be left open during some part of the day and even at night. The horror was increased by the fact that this woman was repugnant in mind as well as in body, quarrelsome and obscene, with sexual obsessions, and death would not come. Nobody within the hut was capable of feeling for her any of the emotions of charity. Her own daughter grudged her the crusts she gnawed and which might have been given to the children. (She grudged them, but they were not withheld.) Whenever the creature appeared out of doors, everybody scattered away from her. When, in her deep distress, she attempted to approach the well which supplied the settlement's precious allowance of water, she was driven away from it with threats and blows.'

Listening to this story in a room in London, I could not at first assimilate it, as perhaps the reader cannot assimilate it now from this page. Over and over again I asked: 'But did you feel no pity? No pity at all? Was there no desire to help her? Was there no feeling of that kind at all?'

My friend said that there was not. Life reduced to these levels does not leave room for pity.[7]

'We were conscious only of what we ourselves suffered through her. In our hearts we cursed her. We cursed her because she would not, or could not, die. I am sure that her daughter and son-in-law cursed her too. When I returned each night, after fourteen hours' hard labour in the forest, all that I was able to feel was a furious resentment that she should further contaminate the only corner I could call my own. I loathed her because my child had to be in her neighbourhood all day. I loathed her with fresh fury every time that child (who was at this time only two years old and who waited fourteen hours every day for my return from work, and for whom, whatever my physical or mental condition, I was always able to force a smile; to whose education – in the sense that she should never forget Poland or the Polish language or the father who was absent with the Polish Army, I devoted every ounce of the strength and every minute of the time left over from my work, from standing in queues for food and roll-calls and from the hopeless struggle after some sort of cleanliness inside the hut) innocently repeated in my hearing the obscene and crazy language and the revolting sexual images which were never out of the madwoman's mind.'

Failing sight, falling sickness, and blindness are all results of prolonged undernourishment. There is also snow-blindness, and the blindness of those who work in the mines. In regions where ferocious winter cold turns to equally intolerable summer heat, the straight rays of the sun can be a cause of blindness, too. Blindness may follow the bites of gnats. Human beings and even animals attacked by hordes of these pests can lose so much blood that they die within a few minutes. In the forests, these gnats settle on faces, legs and arms, or any other exposed part of the body, and devour the flesh to the bone. The formations in which they move are often so dense as temporarily to obscure the light. The regulations lay down that workers in these gnat-infested and malarial regions are to be supplied with a special netting, designed to cover the whole of the body. Naturally, this protection is almost never available, and when it is, is more often than not withheld as a disciplinary measure; just as in extreme cold convicts are made to stand naked or almost naked in the extremes of frost as another kind of 'discipline'.

Doctors vary immensely. In the hospitals, both doctors and nurses are often excellent, but they too are fatally hampered by lack of material, lack of room and lack of beds. If drawn from among the convicts, they may be medical men of the first rank, professors of medicine, surgeons, etc. On the other hand, these are constantly afraid of being sent back again to the convict life, or even sent to punishment cells, for any real or reported over-indulgence of their patients. A doctor who is not himself a convict is in a stronger position, but he is just as much tied by the quota system, and just as much handicapped by the lack of supplies. A patient ordered to hospital by the camp doctor may be sent back again when he gets there, having failed to pass the hospital commission. The hospital authorities in turn cannot help turning patients away when they have absolutely not got a square foot of room even on the floor. Although there are very a large number of hospitals, the general level of health is so appalling that there are never anything like enough, or enough beds or blankets in those there are. Beds are made of planks, as in the camps and elsewhere, are in tiers, but nowhere and at no time can those bunks accommodate all the patients. The patients lie about the floor, sometimes covered by a piece of blanket, often not covered at all. Whatever the disease, from pneumonia to a putrefying limb, patients on admittance to hospital must be bathed, and from this rule there is no appeal whatever. The results are mortal. First the patient, often in a high fever, waits for the bath. After the bath he waits, perhaps the whole day, for a bed, or for lying-down space on the floor. After this he waits for a blanket. The only thing he does not have to wait for is death. In cases involving high temperature and collapse, the death-rate from this factor alone is very high. Very often, the doctor reaches the patient only in time to express his disgust that a piece of already lifeless flesh is taking up space for which, in their turn, those who are to die within a few hours are still waiting. The doctors and nurses who have to struggle with this sort of thing are themselves often reduced to despair. Many, however, are callous to a degree; in part, perhaps, because, like the convicts, there is little else that they can be, but many more, undoubtedly, because of the particular mould into which the minds of Soviet citizens have been so attentively and so successfully forced. In considering this account of what can happen, even in the medical profession, and before deciding that it simply cannot be true, it will be well constantly to keep in mind how all who are sentenced under Soviet law, being in one respect or another displeasing to the régime, must, in consequence, be thought of by the orthodox as very great sinners indeed, and quite unworthy of compassion. The Christian of the Middle Ages – who very often had not many bowels of compassion either – was at least required by his religion to pretend that he had; the extension of mercy and loving kindness to publicans and sinners being an essential part of that religion which not even the least merciful of churchmen ever quite succeeded in explaining away. The Soviet citizen receives precisely the contrary injunction from his religion. To feel compassion for the sinner must be thought of as a condonation of the sin, and as a sin in itself. Those who have in any way whatever offended the régime, must almost certainly be felt by the Soviet orthodox to have forfeited all human and even animal rights. This is at least an explanation which can be made to cover the facts, and they have somehow to be covered, for, incredibly, they exist.

Medical commissions visit the camps from time to time, or some of the camps; especially the clearing centres from which labour is distributed. In a camp on the lake Vanz, about forty-five kilometres from Miedvieyegorsk, a medical commission arrived while Poles were there, and began by separating from the rest persons over fifty and the incurably infirm. This commission was composed of persons who were themselves serving sentences and who understood camp conditions, and who did attempt, as far as their very limited power went, to be fair to the convicts. One doctor on this occasion exclaimed despairingly: 'What can they want of people in such a state? What more can be got out of them? The only possible thing would be to open a hospital unit for the lot!' This doctor did, in fact, succeed in getting a sort of rest-point opened in which there were always at least eighty persons out of the 400 in the camp. Later, a second commission, composed of two young women doctors, arrived, and refused sick status to half the persons already in the hospital.

In September and October 1941 a medical commission from Magadan visited some of the Kolyma mining and lumber camps. A long procession of human phantoms appeared in the town and were put into ships. Those who saw them go aboard could hardly believe they were human. 'It was a procession not of human beings but of corpses and trunks.' The majority had neither noses, lips, nor ears; very many were armless and legless. Among these was a handful only of Poles. The rest were all Soviet citizens. The Magadan commission had recognised them as being unfit for work! In Magadan, it was said that, once aboard ship, they were taken out to sea and drowned, but there is not any proof of this.

Here is one account by a woman prisoner transported to a penal camp in north-eastern Russia.

'This lagier is exceptional in that there are more prisoners than there is work. Without work there is no bread. The commandant is, therefore, besieged with requests for work. Prostitution is the only means the women have of keeping alive. By now I am half-blind from hunger, and seriously afraid of losing my sight altogether. Nobody helps me. I stumble over everything. Every few minutes my body goes into a convulsion from hunger. A man in the male quarter sends in a piece of paper "for the Polish woman". This man is Moniek, husband of Salka, who was the head of our cell in Brygidki. Moniek and Salka are professional thieves. I dragged myself to the wire enclosure through which I was able to talk to Moniek. When I told him that Salka and I had been together, that she was well, that she talked of him constantly, that it was I who had knitted a sweater for him, his joy was intense. After this, my position was different. The commandant asked me why I had not said at once that I had friends of this kind. I was given work, a very great favour in the circumstances. All the time I was here I was befriended by Moniek, who also sent me tobacco, and money whenever he could. He was disgusted with his Soviet associates. He wanted to organize them, but what was the use of it, he asked? Such a pack would never be self-respecting thieves. Any of them, he said, would thieve a piece of rag or an old stick and run to him with that, expecting approval. He had had to give it up.

'While we were in this lagier we saw thousands of Poles being taken yet further away. Whenever we could, we exchanged signals with them, and tobacco and messages. I have no idea what became of them. Perhaps they too went to Kolyma. There were rumours of Polish-Soviet talks, at the thought of which we felt both joy and fear.

'I worked all day on the heights, among fields of vegetables. In spite of my attacks of blindness, I could see fairly well during the day. As I worked I gazed far across the bay. Great peaks rose out of water, the ships came and went. The colours of everything changed with bewildering rapidity. At one instant the whole world would be the colour of sapphires, changing in the next, through a whole spectrum of dark greens, blues, greys and a mist of blue. The temperature changed in the same way. At one moment it would be unbearably hot, at the next I shivered in all my clothes. I still had my immortal caracul coat and my sweater. I kept pulling these on and off and I was always too hot or too cold. My arms and legs were so rotten with scurvy that it was agony to use them. We had to carry water a whole kilometre uphill.

'At dusk, and during the night, I was perfectly blind. The women would purposely lead me into barbed wire, water, and filth of all kinds. A few became friendly. I remember among others Anieczka, deported, as she said, for a waltz. In some hall in Moscow she had won a prize for dancing. The wife of an Italian diplomat had congratulated and talked with her. A few days later she was arrested for "contacts with foreigners", and was now in lagier. A Don Cossack, an old man, also showed me kindness. In 1914 he had fought in Poland, and he said that no women in the world were better or more faithful. From him, too, I had both scraps of food and, what was almost better, "blat". From a scrap of my skirt which was still whole I made him a pouch and embroidered it with his monogram. One of his sons was a lieutenant in the army, another was an airman; and here was the father in lagier and delighted beyond words at so valuable a gift. Some of the women in the barracks offered to pay me if I would do the same work for them. I was able to do it in the daytime when I could see.'

Later she was sent north by sea.

'At Arman, we saw a camp on a naked shore, with no trees. A few wooden huts stood together, the barracks further back, and, dominating everything, even the sea, the huge Ryb-Prom.

'A Ryb-Prom is a fish-packing plant. All the year round the workers are salting and packing salmon of every kind, according to the season. The Ryb-Prom is always streaming with water. Our clothes, our blankets, even the planks we slept on, were always streaming too, and full of salt. Our boots, if we took them off at night, were shapeless and sticky like gloves washed on the hands when we came to put them on again next morning. Our clothes came off only once a week, when we went to the bath-house. The weather, too, was sodden, wet, grey and cold, with fog out at sea, and the melancholy Okhotsk stretching into infinity; rain sliding past all day in great grey sheets and, very occasionally, a grey sail or a naked mast drifting by.

'Two women working together are supposed to pack and salt away 6,600 salmon in one day. In itself the effort of reaching down to the bottom of the great kegs is enough to exhaust the strength of a healthy woman properly fed. The pain in our arms and shoulders was excruciating. We felt as if we were being flayed by the salt, the water and the movements we had to make. We worked a shift of twelve hours inside refrigerators. Scales lay about our feet in drifts. The whole Ryb-Prom, the ice-house, the packing-sheds, the gutting-alleys and the yards flashed with them. Great backbones of salmon rose in mounds of flashing sapphire blue. The scales were rose-pink, blue and white, like porcelain; the barrels grey and the salt a sparkling white. Outside, were the grey Okhotsk, the grey rain, the grey sails, and the grey-green uniforms and steel-grey bayonets and rifles. Among the barrels, a few couples were always lying in hurried, sodden and animal embrace. After some days I was moved from the kegs to the gutting-alleys. I forget exactly how many I was expected to gut in a day. I think it was 1,700. The doctor was a kind woman, herself serving a sentence of twenty-five years. She spoke French, but in secret only. It was to her that I owed the change of work. Apart from the actual nature of the work (which was the most exhausting I experienced anywhere), this was not the worst lagier one could find. Our commandant was young, and had himself been a convict. (Not that this was anything to go by. The commandant at O— was also young and an ex-convict, and was hellishly hard and bad with the women prisoners.)

'The men and women had separate barracks and common eating-rooms, yards and work. The food, too, was good by comparison. Soup made of fish-heads in the morning, kasha with pieces of fish at noon and salmon fried in seal-fat for our dinner. The star workers got a kilo of bread, but few of us ever passed 50 per cent of the norm and got only 500 grammes of bread and small portions of the other foods. Those lower than 50 per cent got only 300 grammes of bread, with soup. After June 1941 not to complete the norm for a period exceeding a week was officially sabotage, and the offender could be tried and then shot. Copies of such death sentences hung in our eating-rooms. In Kolyma, the signator was Drabkin. The tremendous difference between us and our fellow-convicts was very clear to me here. In spite of everything the Poles waited with hope in their hearts; hope of something, belief in something, and this something was the survival and final liberation, if not of themselves, of the nation and of Poland.[8] Our fellow-prisoners hoped for nothing and had faith in nothing. They moved about in a haze of exhaustion and with a film of semi-insanity glazing their eyes.

'Just then more workers were needed in the kitchens, to cook for the night-shifts. But the cooks would have only Polish women, they said. Even they were appalled by and afraid of the apache viragos. For the sake of extra food I volunteered, but I could not keep it up. After our twelve-hour shift in the sheds we stood till one in the morning gutting agian, slicing and scalding, breaking and carrying wood and boiling and carrying water; then, more dead than alive, to lie on a sodden plank bed till six, when we had to be up again and back on our shift. The pay was pieces of fried fish, real tea with sugar and white bread, but still I could not get on with it. At this time I had an extraordinary experience, perhaps the worst of my life. From exhaustion I began to lose all conception of time. I would find myself brought up short and thinking: "Has this just happened, or is it only about to happen? Has what is being said to me already been said, or is it only going to be said now? Am I speaking Polish, Russian, German or French? Have I been asked this question, or do they only intend to ask me?" I felt as if everything outside me was behind one sheet of glass and I myself behind another. To answer these questions I had to make a conscious effort of mind, as I might have had to make a conscious effort of body to move my feet in walking, were I losing the power to do so. I felt a distinct physical sensation of breakdown between the functioning of my brain and my limbs and my senses.'

After a breakdown in her health, she was given somewhat lighter work in another camp in the same area.

'The site of the camp in Talon is very beautiful. Meadowland, ringed in by vast forests, one side bounded by a chain of mountains, the other by a wide, slow-flowing river. The air fresh and keen. Beyond the forest, swamp. The tilled land produces potatoes, turnips, cabbage, low-growing oats. Here order was kept in the barracks and the "politicals", incredibly, were better thought of than the apaches and other criminals. This is the only time I experienced this. The barracks are roomy and light, with pallet-beds. Between the beds are empty packing-cases for lockers and some chairs. Here I met Helena, the granddaughter of a Polish exile deported in 1863. The exile married . . . died. His son, born in Russia, never saw Poland with his own eyes. To Helena, his daughter, the son passed on recollections of his own father; what little he could remember of the tongue his father loved. Dying, he begged her to remember too; to keep Poland in her heart. As she talked, it all seemed such an old tale, long told; and yet, to her, it was still a bright dream. Between 1936 and 1938, very many Russians of Polish origin, like Helena, were "liquidated" by being sent to lagier.

'We worked long shifts in the fields, cutting and loading sackfuls of cabbage. With my terrible discharging sores, it was very difficult for me to pack, sew up and load the enormous sacks. Hands and arms were covered with blood; the cold entered all my open wounds. The apache women lit great fires in the fields, but they would not let us other women near.

'On the horizon the mountains were always sapphire blue, never seeming to change. There was a feeling of timelessness and of extreme isolation. More and more snow fell. The silence and oppression weighed more heavily on us as time went on. Among these mountains thousands upon thousands of Poles were at work.

'On good days we were sent out to pick berries. A pail was put into our hands and a piece of bread for the day; the doors were opened; out you go. No guard was sent with us, escape being quite out of the question. My companion sometimes was a woman who had lived in Shanghai. During the revolution she had escaped from Soviet territory through Vladivostok, and had earned a good living selling fashionable clothes in Shanghai. An intense longing for her own country brought her back to Soviet soil. To live in Russia she was willing to do any work she could get, and to submit to the régime; but they accused her of something or other and sent her to live, and die, in this northern lagier. On such days we had a sensation almost of freedom. The guard led us as far as a clearing and after that we wandered all day with our pails among great perfumed expanses of damp grass. The forest itself was voiceless and sullen; with evil swarms of mosquitoes and gnats. The only small beasts that moved through it were occasional ermine, of a dirtyish yellow. We were free even to wander away from each other; we feared only wolves and bears. Great trunks of trees rose about our heads like the masts of ships; their crowns low and spreading and their immense gnarled boughs a dark, poisonous green. The moss was white and in it grew carmine berries on bushes with purple leaves. These berries were enormous; sweeter than anywhere in the world, berries of Kolyma. Great trees lay crashed on the ground, their roots in the air; the crater left by their fall filled up with thick, tarry water. Bears too, coveted these carmine berries. We saw one, now and again, lumbering across the prairie, towering up like a peak. My legs and hands now became so full of pus that I was put to work with old Jaga, plaiting straw slippers. Four of us worked in a tiny log hut, with a stove in the middle, minute windows, a wooden wheel, and straw stuffed between the logs in an attempt to keep out the bitter wind. Jaga was very old. All day long she sang and told tales; old tales of the time of the Tsars, full of magicians, bishops, enchanted wolves, sunsets and moonrise, sleigh rides and Easter joy. . . . Only the very infirm were allowed to do this work. Among us were a former colonel (Tsarist) whose spine had been permanently injured during interrogation, a former noble who had been educated in Warsaw, a former engineer (Soviet), blinded in a gold mine, old Jaga and myself, a former human being and a Pole.'

The organization inside the camps which looks after what is called educational and cultural life is known as the K.V.C.Z.[9] At its head is almost invariably an official from outside. This organization provides books, newspapers and radio. Films are shown and music and amateur acting are encouraged; everything seen and heard and read being, naturally, totally along the lines of Party doctrine and propaganda. It is obvious that, unless they are driven to it, as to everything else, the enormous majority of the convicts in the majority of camps are far too debilitated mentally and physically to interest themselves in this so-called culture. The cultural evenings are simply further circles of the merry-go-round. Convicts, of whom very many in their former life may have been lecturers, teachers, university professors, barristers, consulting engineers and so forth, are huddled together, fainting from exhaustion and starved of sleep, at the end of their day's work, to listen to the blitherings of young cultural workers who often cannot read so much as a simple passage aloud without stumbling over every fifth or sixth word of it. On these occasions, a voice from the audience pronounces the difficult word, or finishes the passage, or even takes up the explanation or supplies the troublesome fact (generally a slurred date or a distorted historical happening, or simply a name) – anything, everything, to get on quicker, to finish, and to be able to lie down and sleep.

Yet, of all the 'cultural' provisions, the most gruesome is surely the orchestra. In many camps, it performs even at the work site. The music has its own rhythm; the rhythm of gangs bowed by labour, who may not pause in that labour for the shortest breathing space. Like sailors hauling on ropes and singing as they haul, yet not joyfully, as sailors are said to do, but sorrowfully and in fear, the convicts wield their picks and bars and pile their burdens, to its beat. All Russian music is haunting and sad, but there can be no other Russian music quite the same as this. The forest echoes from one site to another, not only with the chink of axes and picks and the shouting of commands, but with the point and counterpoint of half-stifled voices, swelling into sorrowful choirs and dying away among the infinite sombre ranks of the northern pines. This is a Soviet opera, unknown to the rest of the world.

The story of the camps would be incomplete if it omitted the treatment of Polish, and Soviet, adolescents. A sixteen-year-old Polish girl, deported to Russia, provided the following account, emphasizing the re-education programme which was more intense for young inmates than for older camp residents.

'Finally we arrived in Starodub, in the Orlovskaya district. . . .

'The penal settlement occupied the premises of a former seminary for priests. There was a huge two-storey building situated in an old park. In the front of the main entrance, in the centre of a flower-bed, stood a statue of Stalin. This kindly guardian of youthful offenders hugged a child in his arms. Over the entrance door there was another huge portrait of Stalin. The day after our arrival the wind tore the linen across the middle of his face, which made us dance with joy.

'There were 500 girls in the settlement, aged from thirteen to eighteen. Of these, twenty-six were Polish, aged fourteen to eighteen. Sixteen out of this twenty-six were serving sentences of three to five years for attempting to cross the "frontier", the others were politicals.

'Władysława K., aged sixteen, had tried to escape to Poland from northern Kazakstan, where she had been deported with her family. She got stuck in the snow and was arrested. Her family managed to hide.

'Tamara N., aged fifteen, Franciszka Z., aged sixteen, and Janina O., aged sixteen, had all been arrested for belonging to the P.O.W. (a Polish military organization). These girls were serving eight-year sentences. They had had to go through many severe interrogations. Every kind of method had been employed to make them divulge the names of members of the P.O.W. They had been locked up in a cell which could be filled with water, dressed only in their chemises. Frania had been beaten. One examining judge had started to undress in the presence of Tamara and had threatened to rape her.

'Weaving, knitting and sewing were done in the colony, all by machinery. At first we used to work in three shifts of eight hours, and later in two eight-hour shifts. The work was difficult and heavy and we were unfamiliar with the machines we had to manage. Our ambition was to work well. We were Poles, and Poles would be judged by the way in which we behaved.

'Conditions in the weaving department were very bad. Cotton dust blew round the whole room and got into one's eyes and lungs. Krysia Ch., who was fifteen, soon fell ill and spat blood. Little fourteen-year-old Władzia F. worked over molten lead which was used for needles for the machines. She went quite yellow like a lemon and her big eyes shone feverishly in her thin face. She often suffered from haemorrhage. I once did her work for her, when she was too exhausted to get up and (although this might have meant being locked up) remained lying in her bunk. The smell and vapour of the lead were so terrible that by evening I went off in a faint.

'The Polish girls were dispersed among the Soviet girls in the various dormitories. At first we slept two in a bed, later we got a bed each. Until the spring of 1941, the food was not bad. We got 400 grammes (14.1 ounces) of bread and three meals a day, with a three-kettle system, according to the standard of work. If your standard of work was below 75 per cent you were entitled only to the "punishment kettle" (200 grammes) (7 ounces) of bread and a half-litre (approximately one pint) of soup. If this failed to increase your output you were locked up in gaol, though you still had to work. Similar punishments were given for spoiling the machines (the machines kept getting out of order, which was really no fault of ours) and for refusing to work. You could remain in bed if you had a temperature exceeding thirty-eight degrees C. Anything less did not count.

'There were only a few political prisoners among the Soviet girls; Belova Klava, sentenced for ten years for distributing anti-Communist leaflets in Rostov (influenced by her lover, a film actor); Anna Voseskaya, sentenced to eight years because her grandfather had been a landowner. Her father was also under detention. There were also others who were sentenced respectively to three or five years, for making counter-revolutionary statements. There were also about fifty girl refugees from Latvia, Estonia, Bessarabia and Hungary. These girls had tried to get to Russia, full of Communist enthusiasm, surmounting many difficulties and crossing many frontiers on the way, but they were arrested and sentenced to three, five, eight years. Some of them still remained enthusiasts, or at least appeared to be so on the surface. Most of them, however, had lost their former fervour, were homesick and wept a lot – especially on the non-working days. The rest were recruited from the underworld of

Leningrad and Moscow: prostitutes, murderers, thieves and hooligans. Perverted types all of them; most of them with syphilis (and we slept, bathed, and ate all together) and some – only fifteen years of age – serving their third sentence. As children they had been in a children's penal settlement (where the work was for four hours only and fairly light). They were all tattooed. On their arms and backs they had indecent words and on their cheeks their lovers' initials. One had "Stalin" tattooed on her left shoulder and "Lenin" on her right one, and a complicated design depicting pigeons on her chest. Some had fan-shaped cuts on their cheeks. It meant that their lovers had taken them as their own, they explained. They looked simply terrible; they had boils, some were swollen, and one had no forehead at all. All of them made up terribly. Make-up, eau-de-Cologne and hair oil could be bought at the canteen in the settlement. They especially liked to drink this eau-de-Cologne and hair oil. Their indecent vocabulary and conversation went on all day long. Many of them were Lesbians, and some became the sweethearts of the education officers. When talking with them, these officers always employed the most atrocious vocabulary. Being in their company and having to endure this talk made us completely wretched and was fearfully hard to bear.

'Sixteen-year-old Koltchanova, sentenced to five years for taking part in safe-breaking and the murder of two persons, used to talk with an uncanny sort of satisfaction about cases of assault, murder, and her lover. Her father, a N.K.V.D. official in Tashkent, was shot in 1936, and her mother had died earlier than this. Having no means of livelihood, she hitch-hiked to Moscow, where she fell in with a lot of street-walkers and joined a gang of bandits. A great famine in Tashkent in 1933, when people ate their children, was one of her reminiscences.

'The worst of all was Anna Guseva, aged seventeen, the sweetheart of a gang of burglars, and sentenced for strangling children.

'All of them tried to get out of work, cut themselves on glass, etc. One even swallowed glass. She was taken to prison and we never saw her again. They stole all our things and our food, but this we minded least of all.

'All these girls were very loyal to the Soviet Union. The Governors always told us that from the "national-patriotic point of view" they were "all very healthy". They might not, perhaps, have been so bad but when they scented victims in us they started out to take advantage of it. Once they were given a lead, we were for it.

'In May 1941 the fifteen-year-old daughter of a Soviet dignitary arrived in the settlement. Her real name was not divulged and she was pledged not to give it away. In the settlement she was known as Lola Gavronska. She was brought up in the Kremlin and spoke fluent French and English; she had been abroad with her parents. Her father had been executed, her mother had been sentenced for fifteen years and Lola for eight. She was very nervous and frightened and was treated worse than others. She was often locked up, sent out of the dining-hall and treated unjustly in her work. When I got to know her better, she told me about how she had been questioned. She was locked up in a cell for three days without food or drink and kept in a state of terrible nervous suspense. They were continually telling her to get ready for being questioned. She was beaten. I saw unhealed wounds on her back. I believe everything she told me. And even if I found it hard to believe, her completely grey pigtails proved she was telling the truth.

'There was a school in the settlement, where there were three hours of lessons daily. We were put in the fourth form as we did not know Russian. We were taught the history of the Union and the history of the Party.

'We were forbidden to speak Polish. At first the explanation of this was that we would learn Russian all the sooner; in the end we were just categorically forbidden. But we did not care what they did to us; we simply went on speaking it. Once during a lesson I asked Ivan Ivanovich Pizin, the political director, whether it was in the interest of the Internationale that we were prevented from speaking Polish. He replied by asking, "Why do you dislike the Russian language so?" Then a long lecture ensued, to prove that the Polish language as such did not exist, and was merely a dialect of White Ruthenian!

'Our life was continually being made unbearable by "educational work". A large team of teachers and political officers tried to make us into loyal citizens of the Soviet Union.

'There was also a club in the settlement, decorated with enormous red flags and colossal portraits of the Leaders. In it, meetings were held daily, of the dramatic and dancing groups and of the choir. They told us we must join this club. When we did not do so they got impatient and did it for us, putting our names down for the choir. We invented thousands of excuses, occupations and duties, to avoid going to the rehearsals. Nevertheless, they forced us to go. Concerts were arranged in which we had to take part. Once, a representative came from Moscow and a concert was organized, in the course of which the choir was to sing the "Internationale". We stood in the first row with our mouths shut. There was a terrible row afterwards and we were publicly reprimanded, but there were no further repressions, for they laboured under the delusion that they would yet educate us. Then there were daily propagandist lectures. This was torture. I could not keep quiet and had to tell them back what I thought and felt. Our lecturers seemed to think different things at different times. Sometimes the Germans were a great nation, bound to the Soviet Union by sincere friendship, and sometimes they were Fascists who invaded other people's countries. It was on one of these occasions that I said ironically, "It is only you who free other people's lands". It was this that drew their attention to me.

'The political director, Pizin, once read to us a poem by Mayakovski, entitled "Passport". Explaining this poem, Pizin said that Poland, "a geographical novelty", consisting of fragments of the White Ruthenian, Ukrainian and German nations, had ceased to exist. "And you", he said, "think that Poland exists and will continue existing?" We could not stand this any longer and, with tears in our eyes, we said that he was lying. From that time on, they kept an eye on all of us. "Those damned Polish girls are organizing themselves", they used to say.

'Raja Khripun, a Jewish girl from Saratov, was ordered to spy on us. She was serving a six-year sentence for undressing children in the streets and selling their clothes. One day during a break in our work Raja came up to me and asked me why we had attacked the Soviet Union. What was the social system in Poland, were we happy, and what was it possible to buy in the shops? I drew a map of Poland on the table and explained what everything was really like. Just as I was telling her that not everyone in "Western White Ruthenia" greeted the Red Army with enthusiam, the director came into the room. "Well, what is it now?" he said. "Are you agitating? It is your business to keep silent." I said that I could keep silent but that I would not lie, and if I were asked anything I should always tell the truth. . . .

'The cinema was another nightmare. Every Sunday they showed us propaganda films. One Sunday we had a film called "Men of the Frontier". The education director came to our dormitory and told us to go to the club. It was a terrible film – against Poland and the Poles. The director sat next to us and observed us all the time. Afterwards Raja asked me how I liked the film. "You poor, silly things," I said. "How they are making fools of you!" On the following day I was called before the director, who reprimanded and warned me.

'One of the teachers, Mikutina, an elderly lady of the pre-Revolutionary days, liked us. She asked us to subordinate ourselves to the will of our superiors, and to be careful, for they were watching us. She said that they even had hidden microphones. Hidden microphones? Wonderful. . . . We began to search for these on trees and in bushes, and especially when the education officers could see us. They realized that we were making fun of them, and this annoyed them most of all.

'The school, the lectures, the cinema, the propaganda, and the education so distressed and exasperated us that we wanted to be transferrred to a camp for grown-ups where we would be spared all this. Our applications to this effect, however, were refused.

'The 1st of May 1941 was by way of being a crisis in my stay in the settlement. We were told to assemble in the club. The club director was already there and was engaged in a loud and boisterous conversation. He was extremely glad, he said, that today it was a liberated White Ruthenian nation that was celebrating May the 1st. He recalled, he said, how workers had been starved, how the "masters" had all ill-treated the peasants, how the peasants, in despair, stole soil from the landlords' fields in sacks, and how officers had beaten the soldiers (in Poland of course). It was only when the Red Army came that freedom had been introduced, brothels and prostitutes liquidated. This was particularly painful and hateful to listen to here, among the Soviet girl criminals. A heated and fierce discussion ensued. Suddenly the club director came up to me and, pulling at my collar, cried, "Remember, you have no army and never will have one!" I retorted that there was a Polish Army and there always would be.

'After dinner I was again called before the director, who again reprimanded and warned me. I was accused of being an agitator and of demoralizing Soviet youth. The Soviet girls wanted to kill me, he said, and if they did this, they would be acquitted by the Court. I said that I had not been able to help reacting like that, and that I knew I must be prepared to suffer the consequences. . . . In the evening we went into the garden and sat down on a seat. We were sad and dejected. Janka began to sing. Suddenly I heard a voice behind me and turned round. There was a group of Soviet girls, and one of them stepped forward and spat in my face.

'At nightfall I was again called before the directors.

'The days that followed were quite normal. Only the "patriotically healthy" Soviet girls threw hostile looks at us and used to push us about. In the dining-hall some of them complained that we were eating Soviet bread and yet agitating against the Union.

'After this there was the showing of a film entitled "The Wind from the West". The director said, "We have succeeded in getting this film here to show you the real life of the subject nations. This particular film is an illustration of life and 'freedom' in former Poland. Your presence at its showing is compulsory." For some time now I had been keeping away from the club. Nothing could put me in worse odour than I already was. So I did not go to the club, but lay on my bed waiting for my colleagues to return. First the Soviet girls came back, full of enthusiasm about the film, full of compassion for the Ukrainians and White Ruthenians and swearing at the Poles. Then Marysia returned. Her lips trembled and her eyes were full of tears. The Soviet girls around us swore at us and threatened to smash our heads at the first opportunity.

'On Sunday the 22nd June 1941 at twelve noon, Molotov announced on the wireless the outbreak of the Soviet–German war. Surprised by this information, and feeling hundreds of eyes cast on us, we displayed no emotion whatever. I can repeat this with a clear conscience: we showed absolutely nothing of what we felt: sad thoughts chiefly occupied our minds. War again in our country, new bombardments of our towns! The settlement itself was panic-striken. Everyone walked around with pale and terrified faces. It is possible that our self-control was too outstanding amid this general despair. "It is their fault," someone cried, pointing to us. We stood together and looked with amazement in the direction from which the cry had come. What was this fault and why was it ours? Had we not up to now been accused of disloyalty to the Soviet Government whenever we spoke of the crimes of their German allies? We could not understand these accusations. We had not succeeded in putting in a single word when we were called before the director. There I was told of the charges now brought against me. When the terrible news of the outbreak of war was being broadcast over the wireless, I was said to have been glad and to have clapped my hands, and to have cried "Long live Germany", and that the rule of Communism was over.

' "What have you got to say in your defence?"

' "Nothing, for all this is not true."

'The infuriated Pizin banged his fist against the table and shouted, "Then perhaps you will allege that you cried 'Long live the Red Army'."

' "No, I never did that, nor ever would, either in honour of the German Army or yours."

'I was surrounded by all the directors. There followed a long conversation, with a threat that I would get fifteen years' "political camp". In the evening there was a meeting. I stood in the door of the club. There were speeches, clapping hands, speeches, more clapping of hands, and cries of the Soviet girls. In conclusion one of the prisoners asked whether she might speak. It was Raja Khripun. Dressed in a red frock, she mounted the stage and awakened enthusiasm among her colleagues. She was very noisy and knew how to speak at great length about the Party, the Comsomol [sic], ideals, etc. She had strong fists, and friends among the directors. The others were frightened of her. Her speech differed little from the preceding one. She concluded it by addressing the directors in the following words, "We demand that, at such an important moment, such harmful defeatists as L., Ch., K., and Z. be eliminated from our midst." These last words had an extraordinary effect. All eyes immediately fell on us, and hands reached out to grab us, tore our hair, and beat us. The directors managed, though with great difficulty, to master the situation. "Leave justice to us," said the political director. The "Internationale" was sung and the meeting came to an end. We sighed with relief.

'In the evening I went into the garden. I wanted to be alone in order to compose myself. Then suddenly I heard voices and movement behind me. Before I had time to see what was going on, I was hit in the back. I was surrounded by a group of Soviet girls and every one seemed to think it was her duty to hit me. Then my head began to turn and I felt a kick in the stomach. I recovered consciousness lying on my bed. Marysia was weeping and washing the mud off my face and hands.

'Three nerve-racking and exhausting days went by. The Soviet girls constantly persecuted us. The directors saw it all but did nothing.

'On June the 25th I was sitting in the dormitory with all Mother's letters and her photographs unpacked. I was writing to her, though I had no hope that my letter would be posted. There was now a war on, and a "counter-revolutionary" would certainly not be allowed to write. I was called to the director. He said that the "Plenipotentiary" was going to speak to me. L. was also summoned. An armed guard took us in the direction of the gates. We were searched in the guard-room, and anything we had which was made of metal, was taken away from us. A few minutes later we were in gaol. On the following day J. and N. joined us and the others later, so that there were eight of us in a small cell. The directors were very mysterious, often visited us, but never gave us an inkling of what was going to happen to us.

'The settlement was a branch situated at the other end of the town and located in the premises of the real prison. Five days later we were taken there. We were placed in one small cell. Knowing that we were being observed through a slit in the door, and wishing to show that we were not frightened, we pretended that we were in high spirits; we laughed and danced. The governor of the "branch", Salomon Simonovich Hin, the worst of the whole lot in the settlement, ordered us to be transferred to another cell, and looked on while this was being done. Our new narrow cell was dark, with streams of water trickling down the wall. With a sarcastic smile on his lips, the governor remarked politely, "This is the death cell".

'The whole cell was covered with beds – there was not even a narrow passage between them. We only got palliasses for the night and at day-time we sat on the beds, which were fixed to the floor.

'Then the questioning began. This was always at night-time and was conducted by a large team of "investigators". Again they brought forth absurd accusations and never-ending discussions on the subject of Poland and my alleged pro-German attitude. During the last questioning I told them, "I know that you think me guilty. You will, however, punish me not for being pro-German but for being Polish."

'J. and I were charged with agitation, counter-revolution and organization. "Your case has been transferred to the military tribunal which, for offences such as these, accords the severest punishment." Outside the Soviet girls were screaming, "Shoot J. and Z."

'On July the 1st Starodub was for the first time bombed by the Germans. Air raids grew increasingly frequent. The girls from the settlement proper hid in ditches during alerts, but we remained in our cell. We were not scared of the bombs. In the bottom of our hearts we expected to be shot anyhow.

'On July the 22nd there was terrific rushing about. Amid much shouting and disorder everything was packed and loaded on to carts. Then all the Soviet girls were led out of the premises. Evacuation. We were the last to be taken away, and they put us into a special carriage with the worst type of female criminals. The education directors kept with us all the time. "Political work" had to go on, even in a train. One day Pizin said that Soviet victory was a certainty, despite the Germans' momentary success. "You may not be there," he said to me, "but the other girls will see a Soviet Warsaw."

'Our journey was a long one. We were going in the direction of Siberia.'

Editors' Notes

1. Stakhanovtsy, an allusion to shock workers, usually called Stakhanovites in English, named after the first and most celebrated exceeder of norms, the miner Aleksei Stakhanov who, in August 1935, is said to have mined 102 tons of coal, instead of the usual seven, in a single shift.
2. 'The main thing is: avoid *general-assignment work* . . . that is the main and basic work performed in any given camp. Eighty per cent of the prisoners work at it, and they all die off. All. And then they bring new ones in to take their places. . . . Doing this work, you expend the last of your strength. And you are always hungry. And always wet. . . . The only ones who *survive* in camps are those who try at any price not to be put on general-assignment work. From the first day. At any price!' The words of a *special-assignment prisoner* in Alexander Solzhenitsyn, *The Gulag Archipelago*, I and II, p. 564.
3. Stems from the Yiddish word cognate with *blud* in German and blood in English, in the sense of the saying 'blood is thicker than water', as understood by nepotism.
4. This was in *posiolek* or place of compulsory residence, not in fact in *lagier*, where children were not sent.
5. *Tsinga* – caused by vitamin deficiency resulting in haemorrhaging, especially in the joints.

6. Again, this particular incident occurred in *posiolek*, not *lagier*, but this does not affect the relevance here.
7. Compare also Gustav Herling (1987) *A World Apart*, Oxford: Oxford University Press, pp. 245–8.
8. 'It was a terrible life. But it took the Jews 2,000 years to get back to the Holy Land and some are still going back. So long as you have that dream to keep you going. At that point I believed that sooner or later I would go back home.' And again: 'Once we were brought to Siberia, commonsense told you that you never got out from there. But people talked and said, "Don't worry – we won't be long here, we always get out." And eventually we did. It was some sort of wishful thinking' (editors' transcripts of conversations with two Polish deportees).
9. This should read K.V. Ch., Kulturno' Vospitatelnaya Chast (Culture and Education Section).

FIVE

'Free Exile'

Between the institution of lagier and the institution of 'free exile'[1] there is in normal Soviet usage a wide distinction. Further, those penal settlements indicated under the expression 'free exile' may themselves be of two kinds, from remote outposts organized into labour colonies, closely guarded, and ruled over by a commandant, who is usually an N.C.O. of the N.K.V.D., to others where the system of surveillance is chiefly local and even comparatively mild. Under the exile system, the deportees may be placed out in kolkhozy or sovkhozy and similar State enterprises. In the case of the Poles the distinction existed only formally. In the great majority of settlements for Poles the conditions barely differed from conditions in lagier. In kolkhozy, sovkhozy and factories also Poles received specially rigorous treatment.

In the narrative which follows, a young woman, whom I shall call H., has written of life in 'free exile'. This young woman, a lecturer at the University of Lwów, widely travelled, a remarkable mathematician and an excellent linguist, in the first few months of Soviet administration in Lwów had been admitted to the category (extremely honourable in the Soviet Union) of 'scientific worker' and assigned to a new post, also in the University. In the course, however, of the 'reorganizing' and reshaping of the Polish universities which took place, the possibilities of this new assignment turned out to be non-existent. Within a short time she had been suspended. Shortly again after this, her father having already been arrested and taken to prison, H. too, her invalid mother, and her younger sister, were arrested in their home, and deported to Kazakstan. Of the husband and father no more was ever learnt. So very large a percentage of the deported Poles ended the long journey in just such a settlement as this, so very many women, children, and old infirm men from all over Eastern Poland were being handed over by the N.K.V.D. between 1939 and 1941 as cheap labour to the native workers on these farms, that within the pages of this single history – a history which contains absolutely nothing to mark it off from all those others which might equally well have been reproduced here – may be found resumed, even to an incident or a phrase, the experience of hundreds of thousands of other Poles from Lwów and elsewhere.

There is no doubt that within the Soviet Union there exist some collective and State farms which are better managed and better exploited than the one described here and than all the others of which the following pages might equally serve as the description. Some travellers from Europe, in fact, have visited such farms. Nevertheless, in the mass of material at my disposal, material supplied by those who throughout long weeks, months and years, have actually lived and laboured on these State and collective farms, I have absolutely no evidence confirming their existence, and I am therefore not able to present any such evidence in this book. In the accounts at my own disposal, the only divergences are between the sizes of given settlements, seasonal and regional occupations, categories of work undertaken, etc. In all the essentials, these farms are all as like as each other as a lot of peas. On some, the death-rate was more alarming than on others; there was less epidemic infection, or there was more; the proportion of those totally unfit for work, and thereby ineligible for any food cards at all, was higher, or lower. There are no differences other than these. Those settlements to which Poles were consigned lie chiefly in the Soviet East; the great majority are scattered throughout the steppes of Kazakstan beyond the Ural Mountains and down by the edge of China. Much of this country is beautiful, but infinitely oppressive and sad. The steppe rolls away on all sides like a sea. Not a tree or a shrub breaks it vertically anywhere. There is almost no life. A few mournful birds pass rarely overhead; lapwings and bustards, with sometimes a wandering pigeon. The sun is an enemy; the habits of the native populations, unaccustomed to life between four walls, primitive and repellent beyond words. These native peoples, Kazaks, Khirghizi, Uzbeks and others, forced out of their natural nomadic and shepherd life into the alien state of settled farmers, contrive only the most wretched of livings on these collective farms. Their living and sleeping quarters, in clay and mud huts and in degenerate forms of their own native yurts, are infested at all times by vermin, and are shared by them with their equally wretched calves – as rickety and diseased as themselves – and fowls. Their diet, very limited in quality, is little more than thin gruel, with whey. Wild garlic or a few berries gathered from the steppe constitute a feast. The exiled Poles, squatting in corners of these same huts, worked as many as fourteen and sixteen hours a day, gathering and mixing with bare hands the dung collected from the steppe. This dung, shaped into small bricks and dried in the sun, is the staple fuel of these regions. Besides baking bricks, they guarded cattle at long distances from the settlement, dug and carted manure, built irrigation ditches and reclaimed the desert, and still could not earn by their labour sufficient food to keep themselves and dependants alive. The breadwinner, too often, succumbed the first; from exhaustion, and from having, quite literally, taken the bread, such as it was, out of her own mouth to put it into the mouths of those she loved. With the disappearance of the bread winner, the right, even of unemployed members of the family to receive bread disappeared too. Children in their first teens and even much younger, exempt under the Soviet code from the obligation to work, were yet turning out to labour of all kinds in the desperate attempt to feed whole families of still tinier brothers and sisters after the death of an exhausted mother had orphaned them all. The ordeal by privation and want undergone by women and children on these grain, milk and butter producing farms, was equal at least to the ordeal undergone in lagier. These were the conditions up to 1941. After 1941, and the war with Germany, they became even worse. In the struggle for existence, before and after 1941, the foreigners from Europe naturally went to the wall. The natives, wretched enough themselves in all conscience, yet had the advantage over them in numbers of ways, and used their advantage. For this form of 'free exile' the control of an overseer, with irregular visits from officers of the N.K.V.D. was sufficient for policing purposes. The absence of roads or of any other communications, the impossibility of anywhere procuring food, the infinite expanses of desert and the hostility of the natives, made any ideas of escape perfectly futile.

On their way to these settlements, after twenty, thirty and sometimes forty days spent on the N.K.V.D. trains, hundreds of thousands of these exiles from the green fields, friendly towns and ancient parishes of Poland waited whole days on the naked steppe for the convoys to take them on the last stages of their route. Ragged, emaciated, filthy, prisoners of the Soviet East, they gasped under a pitiless sun all day or shivered with cold, without food or covering, all night: never again, at sunrise or sunset, to watch with joy the scented wood smoke rise above the Polish villages, the windows of Polish homes beckon with hospitable lights or the great white, fraternal Polish storks sink down upon or rise from their roof-top nests with serene and fondly familiar deployments of their immaculate wings.

This narrative begins on the 29th of April 1940 (after a fifteen-day journey) at Ayagouz – a day's journey from Alma-Ata – at four o'clock in the afternoon.

'. . . Here we were ordered to climb on to high lorries. It was very difficult to do. Many could scarcely crawl, from general exhaustion, cramp, dysentery, etc. and from natural infirmity. One man was eighty-four, with his wife who was eighty, and there were many other aged persons who had been bedridden and infirm before ever the journey began. All these persons had now to make the immense effort of climbing, with their baggage, on to the high moving lorries. Families and groups of friends were again broken up and separated from each other in this way. The immensely precious baggage was lost and mislaid too. People sat, or lay, with heavy baggage on their feet and legs for hours at a time. A woman holding eight-month-old twins was seated on a trunk which lay across my own legs for hours. For all this there was no help, in the immense confusion and given the impatience and violence of the escort and the drivers of the lorries. At first there was a road of sorts. After that, the whole journey lay across country. Everything was unspeakably desolate; there was no track; the whole country stretched out grey and flat, without a single tree, cut by small streams and ditches, all of it saturated and sodden under the rapidly melting snow. The lorries kept sinking down into morasses of mud, and were drawn out by others which threatened to sink hopelessly too.

'During the whole journey, only one human settlement was seen: a huddle of dirty mud huts with a few ragged, dirty and unfriendly Kazaks standing at the doors. At last a second settlement (the one at which we were to remain) was reached. This settlement was bigger than the one passed on the way. In all, there were ten small, very dirty huts, no garden of any kind, not a single tree. The Kazaks were repulsively ugly and very unfriendly. Again the same confusion reigned. Persons were dragged down from the lorries, apparently at random, and the baggage was treated in the same way; pieces of it were just hurled to the ground. About 200 persons were unloaded here and were told nothing and given no instructions. Too tired even to be hungry, we simply sat and lay on the bundles and other baggage and waited, for hours. Our companions were taken on further, we had no idea where. The natives spoke little Russian and greatly resented the whole arrangement and the new mouths to feed; and would at first sell us nothing, nor help us in any way. The next day, after much persuasion and in exchange for things which they coveted (almost anything we Poles still had about us, in spite of all we had been through, was unimaginably better and finer than anything which these people had ever seen or handled or even heard of before) they traded with us a small jug of thin whey, the only available food. No quarters of any kind had been provided. The natives, who were abominably overcrowded themselves, were expected to house us in corners of their huts. Nobody was satisfied with this arrangement, and we least of all, for the natives were not only repulsively dirty but also syphilitic; many of them with missing lips, noses and ears. By dint of bribery and great determination, an empty hut was finally made over to the use of our group. In this hut were four little rooms, like cells, with earthen floors. Sticks had been fixed into the spaces intended to hold windows and a few pieces of glass had been laid between, it would be hard to say why, as they served no purpose whatever. Ten of us had to live together in a room three metres by four. Everywhere was absolutely alive with bugs and other vermin. In this room there was an enormous kettle embedded in a rough bed of clay and beneath this was an aperture filled with ashes. Beds of a kind were rigged up from suitcases, balanced on large stones. The nearest water was a brook running over stones, but this was half a mile away and there were no vessels in which water could be carried.

'In all, about 160 Poles (six of these very old) remained at this farm. For fuel, dung was collected from the pastures and shaped into small cakes, which were then baked in the sun. These cakes give off very little flame but much heat. In the co-operative shop belonging to the farm, about the size of a cupboard, we were able to buy a lantern, a packet of apple tea and some copies of a geography book. The men, of whom one was a judge and another a university professor, both over seventy years of age and totally unaccustomed to manual labour, were set to digging latrines and to ploughing with oxen. All this unaccustomed work was most unskilfully performed, to the malicious pleasure of the natives, who followed them about with jeers and mimicry. We women attempted to construct stoves from clay and old tins. On the next day we, too, were sent out to work. Only two out of all the pitchforks they gave us were anything like serviceable. My mother, who was bedridden at the time of our arrest, was ordered to work also; but my sister, who was under working age and need not yet have gone to work, was allowed at our request to do so in her place.

'The first work was digging over and shifting an enormous pile of dung. This pile was frozen so hard below the surface that what was really needed was to break it up with picks. When the sun got high, the ice melted, and the workers were then knee-deep in sticky, stinking, ice-cold dung. This work went on for days and was perfectly useless, as with the implements supplied it could neither be properly dug over nor shifted. After a few days, the pile became quite fluid and the women simply churned about in the brown swamp during shifts lasting eight hours, doing nothing to it that was of any use at all. This state of things, though quite obvious, was permitted by the overseer, who did nothing to remedy it and merely saw that the women remained there and kept moving. The waste of time and labour, apparently, did not interest him in the least. In all, there were four farms composing this sovkhoz. Bread came from the bakery at the Central, where the post office also was. Only those who went to work were allowed to buy bread, and a quantity of (roughly) two pounds was the maximum which might be bought by one worker in one day. This bread supply came only very irregularly. Days could pass and no bread be bought at all. For some pieces of cotton ribbon (with which in Poland pairs of sheets used to be tied together in shops) found in our baggage, we were able to buy some eggs and a glass of flour from a Kazak woman. None of these women wanted money, but were now very eager to barter and almost dragged our possessions away from us, although we were very unwilling to give them up. Inside the huts it was intensely cold. There was no fuel and nowhere to keep it, had we any. Rain fell in torrents and poured into the tiny room in which we lived.

'The N.K.V.D. called frequently at the farm. Each time we were put through the same round of questions, but they never wanted to answer any of ours. We could never find out, then or later, to what rate of pay we were entitled, what the regulations about the work actually were, how much bread we were allowed to buy, or how to secure it, and generally what our position was according to the law. In fact, we were altogether in the power of the natives, of whom one or two became a little more friendly as time went on but who had never wanted us there, and still did not; and who were, in the main, utterly hostile, not only to us but to the collective farms, the N.K.V.D., the Russian language and everything else which had been imposed on them by the régime. It was natural that we, who had been brought there by the N.K.V.D., and were under N.K.V.D. surveillance, and whose presence brought N.K.V.D. officials still more often to the farms, were included in the hostility. I do not believe that our being Poles, any more than any other kind of foreigner, had anything to do with it. We were simply part and parcel of everything also that had come from outside, and our arrival, like all those other things, was not likely to signify anything good. Nothing good had ever come from outside yet. As time went on, and we became a little more proficient at the work and could be made use of, and whenever we had anything which could be used in barter, our relations with them improved quite a lot; but there was never anything like mutual trust or even goodwill (except with one man who showed us genuine kindness). By bribing, a great deal could be done, but once the bribe was used up, you were back where you were before. Tea was what they coveted more than anything and, very fortunately, we had a little in our baggage, and later some began to arrive in parcels from Lwów. For a screw of tea, even the overseer would excuse you from work. In this way we bought respite at least for our mother, who was totally unfit even for the task she made hers, of providing us with at least hot water to drink after work, and of sometimes even cooking for us a few wild roots gathered with infinite labour from the steppe.

'Our main food was always the same thin whey that we had had for our first meal. At times we even had quite a lot of this. At others the natives would overturn the tins in which we were trying to collect it, and push us about and even knock us over in spite. This fluctuation in their treatment of us depended largely on our bartering capacity at a given moment; also we did not always want to part with our property, which, after all, was our only real means of existence (for what we earned was, first of all, infinitesimally small, and secondly, always in arrears and always having deductions made from it for taxes, war loan, and the like), and when this happened, our attitude displeased them very much. Also the N.K.V.D. visitors told them all the time how bad and dangerous generally we were, and that we should be kept in our places and shunned. There was also always the danger of this bartering business being denounced as "speculation", and there were periods in which they, themselves, from fear, refused to trade with any of us any more.

'Visitors from the N.K.V.D. were always the signal for mass meetings, rows, exhortations and sessions of "political education". At these meetings the programme for the coming season would also be talked over; the Kazak overseer generally doing all the talking. This man was a liar and a frightful bully. At the first meeting of this kind we listened with great attention to everything. Later, we got to know it all by heart, and we thought of other things while he expounded and raved. Part of the talk was always addressed to us. "You must suffer as we do for the greater glory of the Idea," he always began. "For five years, maybe ten years, you must get used to hardship and suffering. You will suffer, you will not get bread, you will not get milk, you will be kicked out of your lodgings. After this, you will get used to our life, and you will be citizens of the great Soviet Union." When he was going on like this, his voice always took on a certain note. Clearly he was repeating a whole set of spellbinding phrases which in their day had been used on him. There was always a point in the speech when one knew he was now going into one of these trances. His voice would become different; nasal, churchy. The words would come tumbling out exactly as if a gramophone record had been put on to say it all. After a certain time he would snap out of it, lose his whine and begin talking again in his normal voice about what we were going to do for the season ahead of us. For the summer, the younger people were to be sent haymaking, and a troop of women were to leave with the cattle for the summer pastures. Asking for volunteers, he held out inducements of much better lodgings, priority food, a permit to buy flour, and a choice of lodgings when we returned to the farm. All this time the N.K.V.D. kept on also promising me "scientific" work which, of course, was the purest nonsense.

'The idea of leaving the dark, ruinous huddle of huts where we had been so wretched, and of moving to summer pastures on higher ground, seemed in our circumstances even attractive. We were deceived, heaven knows why, into thinking that some of the advantages held out by the overseer might really turn out to be genuine, and we volunteered, quite eagerly. Even if we hadn't, of course, we should have had to go in the end. The usual indescribable mix-up took place over getting away. After innumerable false starts, disappointments, delays and fallings out, we started. The carts on which our utensils and other goods were piled kept on falling to pieces on the way. Where they were mended at all, there had been nothing stouter to do it with than ropes made of straw. Everything kept falling off and having to be picked up again in an even worse state than it had been before. The oxen (for us anyhow) were almost unmanageable. We had to keep pulling and pushing them along by their enormous horns, wounding our hands painfully in doing so. Our hands, in any case, were always very painful and covered with scars. At the Masloprom (dairy farm, where the butter was made) we attempted to buy a little butter, but we were told that no one at all, much less unprivileged persons like ourselves, might buy any. The whole of the farm's output was reserved for Germans (this was still in 1940).

'When we reached the summer ground the only accommodation available was a scherbak (shed plaited from wicker). Small green leaves still sprouted on the canes; the shed was plaited all in one piece and the roof was curved. The floor was a piece of meadow and a flower or two still grew in it. Writing it down, it sounds almost pleasant, but it was, of course, mouldy, decayed, bug-ridden, and mournful beyond words. The milk-farm was composed of three "courts", lying about half a mile distant from each other, and each run by a "court ouprav" or overseer. Each court had a "tyelatnik" (shed for calves), 120 or so cows, out at grass all summer, and a certain number of these wicker scherbaks. In each shed lived a milkmaid and a herdsmaid, and their pay (theoretically) was in proportion to the amount of milk they daily delivered to the creamery. The native milkmaids naturally took care that we should get the worst cows; poor milkers, with faulty udders, etc. Each of us had fifty or so calves also to tend. These calves, though, I suppose, charming, were possessed of devils and ran almost wild up and down the hills. The scherbak we eventually got turned out to be a new one; through the roof I could see leaves and blue sky, it was not yet verminous and I was inclined to like it. Our ouprav, who was pleasanter physically than most Kazaks and had blue eyes, said that it was "kharasho", but that if I did not at once smear it with dung we should be drowned when it began to rain. I still did not know what he meant and he was amused at my incompetence. In a quite friendly way he explained to me that I must follow a cow about until she made a dropping, and then with this absolutely fresh dung I must smear the walls and the roof of the scherbak to make it proof against rain.

When dry, the dung would have no smell. I did as he told me, and in time succeeded in smearing over the whole surface, which, of course, I could do only with my hands, for we never had tools for anything. The acid in the dung was very corrosive and took most of the skin off my hands. After I had driven a few stakes into the ground to act as hangers for our clothes or pots (all of us now had something to serve as pots, either received in barter or made out of tins of conserves which had been in the baggage) our home was complete. Outside the scherbak was a dyuroshook. This is an oblong hole dug in the earth, about one yard long and a foot and a half wide and two feet deep. Along the bottom the earth is all dug away and on the surface a sort of bridge of earth is left. This is the stove. The fuel (little bricks of dung) is burnt under the bridge; the vessel for cooking is balanced and made secure any way you can contrive. The longer part of the hole forms a sort of chimney and furnishes the draught. This chimney can function in one direction only, so you choose one most likely to be right for the chief winds. The natives lent us a little fire to get started with, and we began by cooking a sort of flour paste which, for us, was a very good meal.

'Now we had to learn to milk. Everything was very dirty. I began by washing the udder of my first cow, but this was considered so idiotic and so "Polish" that I gave it up at once. We had no stools and had to cower down under our cows which was very tiring, and of course we had the kickers and bad starters, but there was no help for that. The calves were most difficult to manage. My poor little sister cried bitterly at not being able to manage hers, and in fear of the ouprav. My mother was the happiest of us all, for a native neighbour allowed her to use one of her pots, in return for a coloured rag, and helped her a little on the first day.

'We milked three times a day: at 5 a.m., at noon, and at 8 p.m. I can see quite well how irritating our incompetence and bad work must have been to the other workers. I always did see this. The court ouprav was quite tolerant. Actually, he got many cigarettes for me and used to question me about home and Lwów (our home town) as I crouched under my cow. Once he mended my shoes for me. Some of the women learnt to milk very well. Mrs. R., who was of Russian origin, stood up for herself and threatened to report to the N.K.V.D. that the natives would not allow her to work unless she gave them bribes. This was true. At this dairy farm we received a letter from Poland, which was brought from the post office to Farm 4, and from there to the Masloprom, and which the man who collected the cream then brought to us. We also saw a Soviet newspaper for June 1940.

'Here, too, the natives would sometimes be quite friendly and at other times hostile and vindictive. The ouprav would sometimes be

quite decent, and at other times would accuse us of being counter-
revolutionaries and threaten us with punishment, as proguls.[2] It was
impossible ever to establish any sort of order or sense in our lives or to
count on anybody, or even to understand what they had in their minds.
My own mind tended more and more to take refuge in fantasies. I did not
want to think about reality. I thought constantly of the past and repeated
over and over to myself things learnt long before; books read, people met
and known, pictures and places seen. When any of us talked together, we
always chose these same subjects. Of the present, none of us desired to
talk. It was altogether too difficult. On fine days, when I took my herds far
from the settlement, life, in this queer, doped condition, was almost
bearable. I collected and carried fuel, in bundles of fifty pounds on my
back. Among the hills we discovered a sort of wild onion, mushrooms, and
a herb like spinach. This improved our diet enormously. Salt lay about in
plenty for the cattle, and we stole some of this. A parcel arrived from
Lwów. The contents were, of course, a sensation. The natives wanted all
the tea in it; they even threatened us to get it. We decided to use it all for
bribes, and to go on drinking and smoking dried herbs and leaves
ourselves. Like everybody else, we had packed nothing really useful in our
baggage when arrested; the things we had brought were almost sinister in
their unsuitability. Nevertheless, they were of great value. For a lunatic
pair of violet crêpe de Chine evening shoes I obtained a pound of butter
and a teapot of sorts. When the paymaster came, I and my sister received
two roubles, 18 kopeks apiece. The native milkmaids were earning 120 a
month. Each of us now had 150 calves. Our ouprav explained to us that in
the Soviet Union the amount of milk a cow gives had been established
somewhere (I suppose in Moscow) and the milkmaid who hands in less
than her quota has to be fined. No wonder we earned so little! In July we
found some berries. Our courts now moved to other ground, and the same
wild confusion had to be lived through again. The chief event of this, to
me, was that the dung on the new ground was better. I could now
distinguish qualities. . . . Everything went on as before. Backbreaking
work, little or no pay, constant hunger, bugs, lice, dysentery and no
medicines. A few goods, such as cloth shoes, occasionally became available
in the Co-op., but they would not let us Poles buy them. I now had pains
and fever almost all the time, with a high temperature. When the
nightmare of moving came round again I hardly knew what was going on.
The carts shook us almost to pieces, the instructions were changed every
hour. At the last moment we were told that our scherbak also had to be put
on the cart, as it was "State property". The track led us through rivers and
ditches; pushing, leading and urging forward the unwilling oxen. Several
times we got lost. Once we were taken past our own farm and had to

return. When we did get there, we found our rooms had gone to someone else and there were none available anywhere. The ouprav, as always, denied having ever promised us anything. All responsibility, as always, was shifted on to somebody else. Finally, after much heartbreaking negotiating, bribery, etc., I succeeded in buying a mud hut. For this the present tenant required no money, which was just as well, but demanded a suit of clothes. Up to now we had struggled to keep our father's clothes which we had with us, in the hope that he might yet be alive and that we might some time find him again, but I now decided to part with the suit. The hut was near the river and was made of mud, held together here and there, by pieces of wood. Inside, there was a sort of passage and byre, both roofed with wicker, and two tiny rooms or cells. The floor was the ground, and there was a slit for a window and a chimney of sorts. It was not possible to stand upright. The tenant said we could buy the "furniture" too, if we wished. This was a bench and a "hanger" like I had made up in the summer pastures.

'Our work was now quite different. Great piles of grain had to be shifted and stored. To do this we carried it from the piles to the magazine in a sort of wooden chest with handles, and of course, had always to be pushing it back and struggling to keep the piles from collapsing and running away. Nobody but ourselves found this method primitive or wasteful. The dust almost stifled us, and, standing inside the magazine, one had to be careful not to get smothered under the grain. Everything we did cost far too much time and labour; we were everlastingly carrying things backwards and forwards over the same ground.

'The rains now began again. In our hut the water rose to our knees. I suffered very much from my old fevers and from lumbago. We worked at the sunflower harvest, extracting the grain, and among the mangolds, cutting off the leaves and the roots. To do this, we sat long shifts on the sodden ground. All of us stole the mangolds when we could, drinking the sweet syrupy water which came off them when boiled; we also used the water for soup, and we smoked the leaves. The craving for tobacco tormented us all the time. As we sat at this work, we all told stories and recounted endlessly everything we knew by heart and could remember or imagine. I was always being asked to tell about my travels, the people I had met, the meals I had eaten abroad, the journeys by plane, in Poland, Italy, Hungary and France, that I had taken. The only journeys we did not talk of were our journeys across Asia, in locked trains. As we talked we were wearing skirts and bodices patched with the wrappings in which our parcels had come, and our shoes were tied on to our feet with string.

'Two of us were sentenced about this time as proguls; for this the punishment was six months' compulsory labour and twenty-five per cent only of money earned – in practice, this made little or no difference. The work was scarcely voluntary at any time, though we did honestly do our utmost to learn and to become proficient, and our pay was always short. I dug out 150 buckets of clay between shifts, and put it all on our roof. Out of tiny pieces of shattered glass, picked up over a long period, I pieced together a pane, bordering each fragment with rag and joining these. Of this I was very proud. The N.K.V.D. officers, however, at their next visit, reproved me for owning so much, and said that we were here to atone for the lives which Polish workers had been made to live, not to live well ourselves. I kept on, however, and actually succeeded in baking a kind of brick from clay, to make a stove. A Pole from another farm helped me when he could.

'The bread supply was more irregular than ever. Men came sometimes from other farms, offering to sell stale flour, spoiled groats, etc. Sometimes the ouprav allowed these sales, sometimes not; but never, now, to us. The thought of winter was terrifying. No work, our reserves almost exhausted, my health gone, nothing with which to bribe the ouprav. I was constantly unhappy about my little sister. Parcels now scarcely ever came through. Even when we got word that something awaited us at the post office, we were seldom allowed to fetch it, and if you did not go yourself and sign all the necessary papers you could not get your post at all. Then for a while the ouprav became rather milder to us again, though never for long. There was a story that the N.K.V.D. during one of their visits, had reprimanded him for starving us, spoken about the possibility of defeat of the Germans and advised all Poles to send a petition to Moscow to be allowed to return home. At any rate, he now allowed us to buy some flour at Ay, and even gave us a permit to go and fetch it. We spent two nights at Ay, waiting for mail, sleeping on the floor by the kindness of the postmaster. This man was good and kind, but terribly frightened of getting into disfavour. Kazaks and Russians lay all about the floor all night, some sleeping, others talking. The scene was still extraordinary and unreal in our eyes. To our great surprise they talked politics. Perhaps they had forgotten about us. Anyhow, we said nothing. This talk went on all night, in their low, resigned voices. Trotsky, they said, had governed far better. These Russians, of course, had also at some time or other been deported, and were probably also farmed out to kolkhozy. Towards Christmas, the weather grew more and more severe. The buran blew,[3] full of snow; soon the snow was as high as our house and the cows walked about over the roof. We had to keep digging ourselves out. This was a terrible addition to our labour. The door was so made as to open outwards against the full weight of the snow. The whole thing was one long inferno. Bent double with lumbago, I had to hack out steps up and down to the hut every day. I now trembled all the time and ached all over with pains and fever. In the New Year our work was changed again. I had to go out with a gang (all men) spreading out for many miles across the fields and cutting a sort of brick out of the frozen snow of which we later built low walls. This was for irrigation. The walls all followed a careful plan. The norm for this was 750 walls a day per person; each wall being three yards long and one high. This would have meant building a wall in thirty-eight seconds. Of course nobody could do it. In fact, between six of us, we did about forty walls a day. Our clothing was cruelly unsuitable. How we longed for anything durable and warm! The snow stopped what communication there had been with the other farms. We had no bread and could not get at the fuel I had stored. Inside the huts, everything was streaming wet, mouldy, and green. There was no post. We lived chiefly on bran. The one Kazak who I have said was friendly to us was indeed, under the circumstances, heavenly kind. He helped me with digging out the hut, shared his food with us, lent us fuel and even money with which to buy flour. The natives had veered round again now and demanded money for everything, instead of an exchange. One young Polish girl of eighteen stole two pounds of wheat for her old sick father and was sent to prison. I myself developed pleurisy, and as, to get excused from work, I had to walk eight miles to a doctor, it was easier to go to work than to stay off. The sun now reappeared but of course thawed everything. The river rose in flood, and all the workers were called out to save the sheds and other State property. With my sister I worked knee-deep in icy water to save our own hut. As spring advanced we were sent to dig out the agricultural machines which had been left out under snow all winter. Nobody knew where to start looking for them; no note had been made of the places in which they had been left. The same round of meetings, with the same talk of programmes, transport and seeds, began again; but in practice it all went on in the same hopeless muddle, waste and confusion. The ouprav promised that we should be able to buy bread again, and some sugar and sweets; and these things actually appeared in the shop but we were not allowed to buy them. Our Kazak friend brought us some sweets and some lumps of sugar as a gift. Agricultural work did not really begin again before April the 20th. Very often we worked all day in the fields and at night on the farm. The shifts and hours of work were more irregular than ever. I was very unhappy when my sister had to work all night with a tractor-crew out in the fields; especially as she herself very much dreaded being alone with Kazak men. The tractor crews were a very tough lot and got better food and lived better than other workers did. Sometimes there were Poles among the crews. There was more work to be done too in the same old heaps of grain, and all of us contracted coughs from the dust.

When there was nothing else to do, they sent us back to the old dung-heaps, which by now we rather liked; for at least, there they left us alone. So long as they could see that we had not left the spot, they accepted that we were at work. The sun warmed our weary and feverish bones and we slept, lay, talked and daydreamt on the now familiar dung.[4] We were no longer squeamish. I now began to prepare a new supply of the little dung briquettes for the coming winter. The help which Lwów had been able to send us was now exhausted. We could not hope for any more parcels and our own strength was running out.

'I pursued the ouprav with demands to be allowed to plant a small plot of ground near the river with seed potatoes, and got his permission. I bought two pounds of potatoes and planted them with great care, watering them every day. I don't know how I managed all the work I did. The summer programme was announced. It was to be gigantic, they said, and even the old and ill would have to work; which meant that mother would have to. The taxes increased still more. Nobody ever came within miles of reaching any norm. With the heat, the flies again tormented us even more than hunger. One after another of us would break out in a fit of hysterics from their attacks. The shift I was on now worked from 2 a.m. till four in the afternoon. By again bribing the ouprav, I was able to get my sister off work with the tractor crews. Then rumours of war began to reach us. Our shift was changed again and still longer hours were set. Those who had been working in towns were sent back to the farms. The barns, sheds, etc., were repaired and set somewhat in order. Our part in this was to carry clay and bricks and to plaster. We also worked at a grain machine which was visiting the farms. The engineer in charge of this machine was a Pole. The machine was kept working right round the clock, in three shifts, and the same engineer was responsible for it in all three shifts. If it had broken down, he would have been guilty of sabotage. He used to fall asleep when he sat down and even when on his feet, but if the machine made the slightest change in the rhythm of its running he woke instantly. Rumours gathered and everyone was nervous and jumpy. Finally newspapers reached the farm with the news of the German–Russian war, and reports of Stalin's speech in which he said, "We are fighting on the side of Great Britain and the U.S.A. for the victory of Democracy . . .".'

From 'free exile' again, but this time from Soviet Europe, from a camp in the Komi Republic, up by Archangel, in the frozen North, come these details of categories of labour to which the deportees from Poland were set. The writer is again a woman.

'In the beginning we were put to grubbing up tree stumps with very heavy crowbars; afterwards we were put on to lighter work. All day long we hacked off young branches with knives. The boughs after being cut down had to be packed into a sort of trench, two to three metres deep, filled in with earth and well beaten down. This was what they called light work. After that the trunks of the trees had to be rolled down to the water. The tree had to be carried on a sort of raft and flung far out into the water, so that there was no piling up and no blockage along the banks. The water was not very deep and very often we had to get down and wade, for the tree would stick fast. For getting the wood away, we had long poles forked at one end, called "bagors". We had to take care that the wood kept level when going under the bridges and into a sort of machine, which bound them into bundles of ten or more and then sent them on further. This is how our "stanol" was constructed. The whole thing was a rectangle made out of bridges whose ends only were made fast. The water went under the bridges carrying the wood and the wood was guided from long narrow rafts running out into the middle of the river. It was much more dangerous and much more disagreeable to stand on the rafts than on the bridge; for one thing, they were always half under water and slippery; lots of the planks were missing and the timber in them was quite rotten. People were always getting drowned off these rafts. We also had to unload great rolls of barbed wire and steel cabling; pushing and dragging the enormously heavy rolls ashore over very narrow gangways. Very often the rolls fell in the water, to the fury of our commandant. When the barbed wire and the steel cables were being fired we worked during the night. Getting the lumber out of the forest in the dark was much more difficult. We also had the furnaces to tend and the immense tangled roll of wire to get on and off the fires. The skin used to be all torn off our hands.

'After this we had potato digging and collecting of moss (nine kilometres away from our posiolek). For the potato digging we were paid in kind, one bucket out of every ten dug went to the digger. (This was exceptionally good pay.) Other work was forest clearing, which entailed among other things making great piles of lumber and burning branches and boughs from early morning until dusk.

'A winter occupation was making strong slippers. First we had to collect old cord of various kinds, then unwind it; then from the unwound string make plaits; and out of the plaits shape and sew the slippers together, using an enormous needle. For some sewing privately done by one of our group for a Komi woman, the Komi promised bread. After delivering the work, and as she was carrying off the promised loaves the woman who had done the sewing ran into one of the militia. The next day she was told by the Komi that the soldier had asked how it could be that one of the workers had so exceptionally large a portion of bread, and advised her, should there be an inquiry, to say that she had stolen it. Working for a private profit would certainly be considered a much more serious crime than theft. Some days later she was in fact summoned by the militia and interrogated about the loaves of bread, and, in panic, said that she had stolen them, for which she received a warning, but no immediate punishment. . . .'

Another passage shows the tigerish determination of mothers to protect their children from the dangers of Sovietization.

Since 1939 these mothers had been struggling single-handed to keep their children alive and to keep them Polish. The majority of families deported had been made up of families of women and children and very old persons only. . . . These women had had to fight single-handed the long, losing battle against cold, hunger, heat, disease, terror, Sovietization and their own growing exhaustion, for now more than three years. Too often, aged and invalid parents and other relatives were also dependent on the same one woman's pitiful earnings; on her courage, resource, and the efforts of her despairing love. Besides everything else, these same women had struggled with no less determination to care for their children's minds and souls. In letters written by children themselves at this period – children who looked on at the mounting exhaustion and martyrdom of their mothers with no less anguish than the mothers at the Sovietization and moral disarray of their children; an agony to which, in the children's case, was added a panic fear of losing their last and only protector and the only thing remaining on earth which was familiar and dear – I find a reiterated cry; almost as if one of them were passing it to the other, a cry as of a creature only then coming to full consciousness of his state, a cry swelling and mounting and mounting in volume: 'Where, where are our daddies?' writes one child after another, 'We want, we *want* our daddies.'

Olga L., writing of an earlier period, before she had been released from 'free exile', writes:

'Our children had to be abandoned to their own resources. Mother and all adults were away from dawn to dusk. In certain posiolki crèches had been organised where the children could remain the whole day, and sometimes for whole weeks, if the mother was sent to very great distances from the settlement, as in the hay-cutting season. In these crèches the children received real food, with butter, sugar, milk, etc. But everything that went with it was forcibly entirely Soviet; the children were exclusively under Soviet influence, and in speech, and worse still in outlook, began to pick up Soviet ways. . . . In our camp no such institution existed and we fought tooth and nail against any such plan, preferring that our children should be hungry and vagrant rather than that Soviet influence should set its mark on them, perhaps for the rest of their lives. Older children in any case were obliged to attend Soviet schools.'

This extract sums up clearly the attitude to Soviet institutions for their children which dominated Polish mothers during the periods of deportation and imprisonment, and which did not change after the amnesty. These mothers had all seen such institutions for themselves. They knew by experience the teaching, the attitude towards religion and the ethical standards enforced in them. This friend, when speaking to me of the matter, further said: 'It is possible, I suppose, for persons who have never been put to the same tests to feel that we were to blame for such an attitude; to say that as mothers we were asking too much of our children; that no mother is justified in condemning her child to hunger and even vagrancy for the sake of an ideal. To that, I can only reply that Polish mothers throughout the whole of Polish history have always asked much of their children and have persistently taught them to believe, as they had been taught themselves, that there are worse things than physical hunger, ill-treatment, solitude, or anything else that this world can do; and that it is first from these worse things, from perversion of the mind and abdication of the spirit, and not from the pains and fears of the body, that a Polish mother strives to safeguard her child. This, however misguided, is what we did feel, and what we continued to feel about the effect on our children of institutions utterly alien to us in character and officially atheist in programme. And I think it cannot be true that we mothers loved our children any less than those mothers love theirs who think first of what they can do for them in this world. I think that no woman who has not been faced with the same choice on this matter may presume to give any opinion.'

To this there is nothing, it seems to me, that I can add. This then is what it meant to the women of Eastern Poland, who at all times and most literally took out of their own mouths the bread they earned in such sweat and anguish and put it into the mouths of their dependants, to know their little children subjected to these Soviet influences. They preferred even that they should starve, that they should wander over the face of the earth, that they should die in want and fear. That even the children themselves thought and felt like this was irrefutably demonstrated in 1943, at the time of the forced issue of Soviet passports to Polish citizens, when it was attempted to bring influence to bear on Polish mothers who refused these passports by confronting them with their children in the hands of the N.K.V.D.; when these children themselves cried out to their tortured mothers not to be brought by this or by anything else to surrender those things in which they believed.

Editors' Notes

1. Remote outposts, called *posiolki* (singular, *posiolek*), far from railway lines or towns. Referred to by Andrei Vyshinski as 'places of compulsory residence'.

Documents on Polish–Soviet Relations, p. 180. The deportees were put to much the same type of pioneer work as in penal camps, but were paid for their labour on a system of piece work and bought their own food in shops, owned and kept for this purpose by the NKVD.

2. *Proguls*, persons criminally evading work.
3. *Buran*, a snowstorm in the steppes.
4. 'Dung was a staple commodity; a necessity for life. Even now, though I detest the smell of cattle, sheep and goats, I instinctively regard each cow-pat and dropping as a life-saver' (editors' transcripts).

SIX

The Release

On the 22nd of June 1941 Germany attacked the Soviet Union. This first German attack was, of course, launched over Polish territory, across the demarcation line agreed upon between the German and Soviet Governments in 1939 at the time of the new partitioning of Poland.

Support of, and alliance with, the Soviet Union was immediately declared by Great Britain. General Sikorski, Polish Prime Minister and Commander-in-Chief since 1939, immediately opened negotiations with the Soviet Government. On the 30th July 1941 a new Polish–Soviet Pact was signed in London, at the British Foreign Office, in the presence of Mr. Churchill and Mr. Eden.

This Pact contained, among others, the following clauses:

'The Government of the U.S.S.R. declares its assent to the raising on the territory of the U.S.S.R. of a Polish Army, whose commander will be appointed by the Polish Government in consultation with the Government of the U.S.S.R.'

A note appended to the Agreement further declared:

'The Government of the U.S.S.R. will grant an amnesty to all Polish citizens at present deprived of their liberty within the territory of the U.S.S.R.'

In the whole history of nations there was no parallel to what had now happened. The population of almost one-half of Poland, since 1939, had had their homes burst open and destroyed, their families and friends deported, everything that was most dear and most sacred to them cut down and rooted out, by order of the Soviet Union. The Polish Forces everywhere, fighting on the Continent, in the Battle of Britain, in Africa and on the high seas, were fighting to liberate not only the people of Warsaw and Cracow but also of Wilno and Lwow. It was not a simple thing now to turn and once again hold out hands in friendship to the men who had ordered and done these things. But this act of immense national discipline was undertaken. For the second time in just over twenty years the offer of friendship was made. The war aims, the articles of faith, the great Christian principles, so often invoked, from platforms of every description, by the Western Allies, blazed forth for a few magnificent seconds into passionate life and reality; and that within the almost fabulous territory of the Soviet Union.

To the Polish Ambassador and his meagre staff fell the gigantic task of organizing civilian relief. The earliest conversations between the representatives of the two governments covered not only plans for the organization of this relief, but – before the plans themselves could have much meaning – the actual steps to be taken to *find* the Poles. The difficulties to be surmounted were so numerous and so great that it must often have seemed as though the plans that were being made simply could not be carried out. Nevertheless, relief in various forms, food, clothing, medical supplies and money, was distributed by Poles between October 1941 and April 1943 to the amount of 5,000 tons in material and 110 million roubles in cash. In the course of 1942, and up to the early months of 1943, about 800 Polish relief stations – orphanages, feeding centres, hospitals, schools, and other institutions – functioned throughout the Union. The words 'orphanage', 'feeding centre', 'hospital', 'school', and many others must not be given their usual connotation here: something infinitely more primitive, and often without food or resources for the current twenty-four hours, must be conjured up. Nevertheless, such as they were, in contrast with the conditions of Soviet penal institutions of all kinds and of the purely Soviet communities upon which, after release, the ex-prisoners were cast, they meant the plain difference between life and death to the men, women and children who found shelter in them. They meant in fact much more than this. But once again I am brought up short by the inadequacy of all words to express certain experiences. I do not know any words in any language which I can make express for me the emotions aroused in the Poles by, first of all, the conception at all of a Polish Army forming on territory which until now had been to them only the territory of an unspeakable captivity; and afterwards by the returning sight of Polish uniform, of Polish soldiers and the Polish flag and by the arrival on Soviet territory and the presence amongst them of General Sikorski.

In the last days of November 1941, the Polish Prime Minister and Commander-in-Chief, Władysław Sikorski, arrived within the Union.[1] Few statesmen before Sikorski can have assumed for their nation a heavier or more exacting burden than the Polish–Soviet Pact of 1941, whose weight – more and more overwhelming – he carried about with him until the day of his death in 1943.

Amongst the Poles of the deportations generally the arrival, and presence, on Soviet soil of General Sikorski – upon whom, throughout years of tragic adversity since 1939, the unanimous summons of the whole nation had fallen – struck down to the very source and floodgates of emotion.

To them, throughout a span of years not to be reckoned by any ordinary measurement of time, day in and day out, wherever they turned, by whomsoever addressed, the very existence of a Polish Army, of a Polish Government or of a Polish State, had been denied, with oaths. Morning, noon and night, throughout those intolerable years, it had been droned over and over to them that all three had 'ceased to exist'. And now, on this same Soviet soil, received with the highest honours by these same Soviet chiefs – and moving amongst themselves, concerning himself with the smallest details of their lives, of all that they had endured and of all that they were now permitted to hope – was the one man who, for the whole world, symbolized in his own person that Polish Army, that Polish Government and that Polish State.

To these intense, but predictable, sensations, were added the tremendous effects of the General's own personality. In his presence, one felt oneself at once in the presence not of Sikorski the man, nor even of Sikorski the Prime Minister or General, but of that Polish nation for which he stood before the world, and which was bodied forth in him; and it was this quality, perhaps, more than any other of his many qualities, which made him great and which called forth from the Poles of the deportations, whose national pride had been exposed to so many inconceivable humiliations, so passionate a response.

Individual emotional experience in all this is well illustrated by passages of a letter received from a woman who was at this time in Kuibyshev.[2]

'I remember as if it were yesterday the moment when they told me that within two weeks the General would be in Kuibyshev. I went back to my own room feeling the same wild rush of joy that I would have felt had I been told that some remnant of home was on its way to me. Or perhaps not quite that either. Rather as though someone were on his way who would bring with him, and as part of himself, that assurance of calm and support which one feels only in one's own home. . . .

'At this time I was working in our Embassy. As I passed in and out each day I drank in the preparations which were being made to receive him as if every one of them were being made for my own nearest and dearest. . . . I rejoiced over every strip of carpet the N.K.V.D. sent in to smarten up those little rooms on Chapskaia Street, over every crock of shabby flowers placed in his room. Out at the evacuation centre everybody was making his and her preparations, too; by desperate attempts at getting rid of vermin, rearrangements of personal rags and a general frantic effort to establish some kind of order, in his honour.

'When we knew for a fact that he was really in Kuibyshev every one of us was convinced that now all that had been cruel and bad in the past was over and done with – left behind for ever. Out at the centre I had to describe over and over again to each person I met every single little thing I knew about him: how he looked, moved, spoke. I described him as I had seen him last – before the war; pacing up and down with his light quick step in the living-room of my flat in Cracow, unable to keep still even for a minute, as upright as an arrow.

'In the meantime, there was that evening a great gala reception given in his honour by the Soviet authorities. I decided to slip in after it had begun, to look at him from a distance myself remaining unseen. As I entered, a play which was being given had just begun and so I remained standing, inside the doors and opposite the box in which he had taken his place. I remember so clearly how I stood there, and how I had to accustom my eyes to all the heavy marks of suffering and fatigue which were now in his face, and which I had never seen there before. I remember the deep pang with which I thought: those dark pouches beneath the eyes, those lines, those marks of toil and heavy care, have all been for us. I remember the strength of feeling, absurd even, which almost swept me away.

'Seated in the box, he was looking straight ahead of him, somewhere into space, as though there had been no stage and no play. Only when the Professor[3] leaned towards him and said something in a low voice did he begin to look at the stage and to smile – then it was the same smile, clear, strongly magnetic, full of vitality. Immediately I thought, "It is all right. Everything, *everything* will be all right now," and I went out, carrying away with me the strangest sensation of being cared for and safe.

'On the day following, he came out to the Centre. Some of the youngest children greeted him with a recitation of verses made for the occasion. The verses were painful, naïve, and far too adult in sentiment for the children who delivered them, themselves little higher than the ground, skeleton-like in appearance, with dreadful green pinched faces. I shall not ever forget how they lifted those faces towards his and how they looked up into his eyes, drinking in his look in return, and never turning their own away again. It was as though they were seeing at long last a hero who had come to them out of a legend upon which they had been kept alive – and this, of course, was just what was happening.

'The General stood stock still as he listened. From my place in the crowd I, too, watched his face; and I thought that I detected in it an expression of quite especial pain – almost as though he found himself out of countenance before the magnitude of the misery spread out before him. . . .

'After this, he went on to talk for a while with all and each, asking questions, listening; very occasionally achieving a smile. The crowd talked, interrupted each other, broke into tears, fell silent from emotion, burst again into words, sobbed, exclaimed . . . everybody wanted to talk it all out at last, and to him, to recount their griefs, to be told by him that everything was now all right, and would continue so . . . the whole of this time, I could not shake off my impression that he was suffering keenly, that his heart was inundated with the pain of not being able to say to each of these persons the things that all wanted to hear. . . .'

To the Poles, who had endured the humiliation, the rigour, the animal ignorance and worse than animal filth, the abominable cynicism, insane monotony and inhuman treadmill, of the Soviet prisons, labour camps and mines, these relief posts organized by the Embassy, with their familiar colours, their cleanliness (whatever their poverty), their Polish periodicals (however few or worn), the Cross above the door, the attempted gardens, the *lightness*, the *Polishness*, were the first balm poured, since what had seemed like eternity itself, into the worst and the most deep-seated of their wounds. . . .

The chief difficulty before the relief workers, then, was first to find the Poles, and after that to maintain contact with them; a colossal enough task at any time, over the huge area of the Union, in the unfathomable deserts, impenetrable taiga and inaccessible hinterlands of river and ocean, over which they had been scattered, and now further complicated by the presence of enemy armies inside Soviet territory, by the fact of Soviet armies in retreat everywhere and the tremendous strain put on the railway and transport system throughout the Union. In the early weeks, and indeed generally until as late as the end of November, genuine co-operation in the Embassy task was shown by the N.K.V.D. To what degree this cooperation was effectual varied a great deal throughout the Union, with the varying degrees of goodwill, intelligence and actual means at the disposal of local authorities in the various Republics. It varied also, even in these early days, with the political ebb and flow in Moscow. Indeed, the actual news of the Pact itself, of Polish–Soviet alliance and of the Polish 'amnesty' (as it was commonly though inaccurately called) reached the Russian authorities themselves in the various settlements at widely divergent intervals of time; and reached the Poles themselves still later. In some it was communicated to them at once. In others, it was concealed during periods of varying lengths. In a few, it was successfully concealed well into 1942, and in at least one (the walled prison of Magnitogorsk), until 1943. In some, after the news had been passed on, the prisoners were immediately released. In others, release was delayed interminably. In some, transport was put at their disposal; in others, it was refused. In still others, it was genuinely not possible to provide it. But without exception, every Polish citizen who waited for formal release received, and at every subsequent stage of his odyssey on Soviet soil was expected to produce, a document as follows:

'This is to certify that the holder of this present, the citizen X., born
. . . being a Polish citizen, has been included in the amnesty declared in
the decree of the Council of People's Commissars sitting on the 12th of
August 1941, and is entitled in consequence to take up residence anywhere
within the territory of the Soviet Union, with the exception of the frontier
zone and régime towns of the first and second categories. The citizen X.,
of his own free will has chosen as his place of residence . . . Valid for a
period of three months.'

The name of the precise place in which the citizen of his own free will
had elected to reside was inserted by hand, and had very often never
before been so much as heard of by the citizen concerned. It happened
also, of course, that he or she had in fact expressed some preference for
one place or another, but it did not very often happen that this was the
place eventually named on the permit; but it could be so and sometimes
was. There was, too, the general inability of local Soviet authorities
everywhere to believe that the whole thing was true, and that prisoners
once condemned to penal institutions, and in particular to lagier, were
seriously going to be released and allowed to move about in the
community. For months after the first prisoners had already tasted
freedom, very many of those who were eventually to be released were still
turning out with the work columns at dawn and returning after a fourteen-
and sixteen-hour day with the same columns at night; possibly to the
sounds of an orchestra.

Meanwhile, however, the gigantic trek which had now begun, all across
the territory of the Union, and heading towards the Volga, the Army and
the Embassy at Kuibyshev, presented a problem in relief with which
neither the Polish Embassy, nor even the N.K.V.D. itself, with all the
resources at its command, had effective means of coming to grips.

Hundreds of thousands of persons travelled by rail, by water, in carts,
on foot, in one another's arms and on one another's backs; and all were
headed in one direction. Of all these persons not one was adequately, or
anything like adequately, equipped for the shortest journey. All were
undernourished, ragged, wretchedly clad, physically and mentally
exhausted. All were possessed, and obsessed, with the notion of getting
somewhere; on principle, to the south, the way others had gone, to *their
own people*, to green food and to a sun which warms yet does not strike;
but, in fact, so long as they were moving, it scarcely mattered, in their
revulsion of feeling, whither they might be bound. The great thing, the
indispensable thing, was to move and to keep moving; to leave behind
the region, wherever it was, in which their captivity was spent.[4] Very
many of these people were carriers of disease. Enormous numbers of them
were children; and for the most part orphans. There were also many

In considering this great trek it is important to keep in mind the conditions in the institutions and camps everywhere out of which all these people poured. It is not surprising that the epidemics raging through the trains on which these people travelled were so serious and so uncontrollable that the Soviet authorities were forced to place whole trains in quarantine, to forbid such trains to stop in stations, to close down whole evacuation points, etc. These methods, while ostensibly solving some part of a given problem at a given moment in a given place, far from doing anything to clear up the general situation, simply made it much worse. The conditions of the deportations, with their epidemics, loss of life, monstrous suffering, privation and disease of all kinds, were now being reproduced in reverse, and on a still more gigantic scale.

Very many, in their first joy and in their panic fear of being left behind (and in their mistrust of the infinite procrastinations, shelvings and evasions of the Soviet bureaucratic system) had not waited for their legal safe-conducts, the tickets-of-leave and the permits to enter, to go or to stay, to work, to travel, to buy bread, etc. without which nobody at all can move in Soviet Russia; and had simply put their bundles on their backs (if they still had a bundle), made what provision they could, trusted in Heaven and joined the trek.

All these persons, for these reasons, were in danger every minute of the day and night of being taken off the trains as runaways, and as having broken about a dozen laws. Others who were anxious to get off, to find work or to buy food or to receive instructions for themselves or their families, could not do so for the same reasons. In the clearing stations and evacuation centres into which passengers were herded the death-rate rose higher and higher each day. A single example of one of these trains may serve for innumerable others. It is taken from a statement made by a young girl, Anna I., who, with others, arrived back at Vologda, through which they had been taken as convicts in 1940. The small, provincial, completely primitive town was crowded like London before the Great Plague.

'More and more Poles kept arriving every day. The town was crowded beyond capacity and getting more crowded all the time. In the bread queues only the strongest could stand up long enough to get any bread, and even for them there was never enough. There were no medical post, no medicines, no help of any kind. People were again dropping down where they stood, from hunger and exhaustion. The only precaution against epidemics was that great packing cases were set out in the streets for the corpses. These cases leaned against the walls and five corpses could be packed into them at a time. When the cases were full they were taken away somewhere outside the town by horses. Nobody much troubled where. Even relatives seldom asked where a body had been taken or what had become of it. There was nothing they could do and it was all past caring. All that we felt now was a frightful sensation of panic. At the posiolek we had left death behind us, and now here it was in Vologda again out stalking for us. All we cared for was once more to get away.'

When a train at last came, they hurled themselves on to it. Eight persons were left behind, standing in a bread queue. Never mind. Only to get away. To move on. To move faster. Further. Away from the past. Away from the known. The unknown can only be better. Or, at least, if it is worse, it will not be this. Rigid with a single purpose, their eyes set straight in front of them, tens of thousands of persons, without money, provisions or even a destination, turning their backs on the huddle of huts, the barracks and the N.K.V.D. surveillance which at least had kept them together, had provided them with some kind of shelter, had made them somebody's business, if only for the exploitation of their toil, ran for the sake of running, like the Malay in the strange sickness that sends him running amok. And, as they ran, they were pursued and everywhere overtaken by pestilence, exhaustion, hunger, insanity and death. To say that they died like flies would be to say too little. They died like human beings; the children, especially, died. Even in places where such things were available at all nothing like enough coffins could be got ready for the burying of them. Of those who survived, thousands lived night and day in the streets, hiding in, sleeping on, and eating refuse. In the small town of Guzar, thirty and more were buried daily. In this same town, twelve doctors and seventy sanitary workers were buried with those they fought so hopelessly to save. In the single town of Kagan, in the month of December alone, 280 children were buried by a single priest.

These Soviet towns, which have never yet been able to provide (by Western standards) the smallest decencies of life for their own populations, simply did not possess the machinery for coping, had they had the best will in the world, with this new problem from outside. The Poles, for their part, feared nothing as they feared being washed back again to the unscratched steppe, the kolkhozy, the mines and the unending abysses of space which are taiga and tundra. Life on a refuse-heap with some kind of hope, or illusion, that some time within a week or a month (or possibly on this very day) a train might leave for somewhere, was infinitely preferable to the slow extinction, the intolerable isolation, of kolkhozy and steppe. At the thought that a train might leave and they themselves not be on it large numbers of people, after two and a half years of sublime fortitude and faith, simply went out of their minds. In the towns, these hordes of Poles were inevitably mistrusted and disliked. First of all on principle, as foreigners; in the Soviet Union all foreigners are spies. Further, they were ex-convicts; they were lousy, destitute, full of disease and in want of food and shelter; and food and shelter are the two things (shelter includes clothing) which the citizen of the Soviet Union has an unremitting, competitive and, in the main, hopeless struggle to get hold of for himself. Further, the whole notion of this extraordinary assembly of reprieved prisoners was in itself so unlikely that wherever possible it was much safer to have nothing at all to do with them. Whoever heard, in the Soviet Union, of amnesties which really resulted in anybody being let off?

The hordes of immigrants lived, lay, ate, slept and died on the railway stations, in the streets and in the queues for food; alternately beseeching the N.K.V.D. for permits to stay, for food-cards and work, or for transport with which they might move further on. The N.K.V.D. partly helped them and partly hindered, promising transport, sometimes even finding it; promising permits to stay if work was found first, and simultaneously making the permit to work dependent on the previous possession of the permit to stay; sometimes, concentrating them in one place, at other times breaking them up. On the whole, if they could, they flung them out, but meantime, while they were getting this done, a new lot, or the old lot back, had always taken up the same places on the rubbish-heaps and in the queues; and the diseases, problems, doubts and queries associated with these foreigners ran like wildfire through the overcrowded dwellings and the insanitary streets. The injunctions sent out by the Polish Embassy to wait, to be patient a little longer, to avoid panic and confusion, were either disregarded – and though these injunctions were wise and even utterly necessary they could not, humanly, have been other than disregarded – or never arrived.

A particular concern of the Polish Embassy and its delegates after the Amnesty was for the children of Polish origin in Soviet orphanages, trade schools, etc. A witness described the condition of Polish children in Soviet institutions.

'Very many Polish children were scattered about in children's homes, orphanages and crèches. If they were six years of age or more, they were able to remember a former life, and they knew they were Polish and clung desperately to everything that was Polish too. Others, younger than this, many of whom were only now learning to speak, spoke only in Russian already. Their parents were dead. The children neither knew their own names nor possessed documents of any kind. The orphanage workers knew no more of them than that they were "children of Poles". And of how many was not even this known! How many figured purely as Soviet citizens! At this period I was constantly among these children in Buchar and saw very much; yet being myself without any kind of a roof over my head, there was very little that I could do. The delegation helped as and how they could, but they too had almost no stores and no power. In Buchar, Polish children and Soviet children were treated absolutely alike; that is, both were permanently ravenous. Probably, however, they were yet better off materially than they would have been with us, for they did at least get food of a kind every day. . . . a nurse assured me, in the absurd way in which all these persons do make assurances, that they received soup, bliny, gruel with plenty of fats and fruit mushes every day – nevertheless, passing very much time every day at the bedside of one boy, I saw for myself that none of the children ever had anything but thin gruel and black bread. The children themselves said that this was their permanent diet . . . it is true, though, that before the war children in Soviet institutions were much better fed than this.'

About the existence of these children, about their numbers and about the conditions in which they lived, the Soviet authorities were particularly secretive, and up to the last days of the Embassy no real admission of their existence was ever made and no facilities were given and no effectual steps made possible for their rescue.

The children themselves, with that extraordinary precocity and more than adult resolution which colours the whole story of the Polish children on Soviet territory, were the first to convey news of their own existence and whereabouts to the Embassy. Letters, messages, and even telegrams, from these children arrived by a variety of routes and combinations at the Embassy headquarters in Kuibyshev. Large numbers of children escaped and made their way to the army or to other groups of Poles. Older children especially feared being sent to work in Soviet factories, in stone quarries and other places where the work was cruelly in excess of their frail strength; and still more than this they feared being placed in Soviet trade schools. Boys of twelve and fourteen, feeling themselves to be already men, and indeed possessing a far profounder and grimmer knowledge of life's hazards and terrors, with bodies more inured to privations and risk, than very many grown men, believed firmly that if they could once reach their own army they would be admitted to the rank of soldiers and would be allowed to fight for Poland. Boys of these ages and still younger arrived among the soldiers in the south in number as many as four or five a day. With them arrived still younger brothers and sisters whom they had been forced to bring along since there was no parent left alive, or at any rate known to be alive, and there was nobody else to take them in charge. Here is a typical extract from a report made by a woman auxiliary who later reached England:

'After I had myself joined the army, I went backwards and forwards to Fergan, where there was a children's home. From this home we successfully evacuated two children (a girl and a boy) whose mother had been removed to hospital with typhus and three other children; a girl whose mother had died and whose father was with the army and a brother and sister who were orphans. At the news of the army being on the move, many children fled from this and other institutions, ready to risk anything rather than to remain behind on Soviet territory. These children anxiously gave details of many others still inside Soviet institutions, too little or too weak to set out to us on foot. In one institution a boy of twelve had remained who might himself have accomplished the journey, but who refused to leave his little sister aged four who could not possibly have attempted it. This little sister already spoke Russian only; another reason for which the big brother of twelve could not bring himself to leave her, but sent word only of how he was fixed, and begged for help. His mother, the children said, when dying, had charged him never to leave his sister alone, and laid it upon him with her last breath somehow to bring her up as a Pole. This boy's prayer for help reached us at the moment when our unit was leaving.'

The story of civilians in the Soviet Union – of whom the overwhelming majority were of course women and children – is one of great hopes, constantly shifting policy, promise without performance, though of some performance too, concealed motives and fundamentally unchanged programme. . . . From the first days to the last, the Embassy could be certain of two things and of two only: of every apparent concession, obtained with infinite difficulty, turning in its execution to something else and of its own part in any transaction being tricked out as something it had never been. From the first days to the last of the Polish Embassy on Soviet soil, a tenacious, morose, and increasingly fatal tug-of-war was engaged between, on the one side, the group of Poles charged with the desperate task of bringing some degree of relief, security and consolation into the mutilated lives of over a million of their compatriots and, on the other, the N.K.V.D. who, in point of fact, now as before, presided inexorably over the destinies of all these human beings. Once again, inevitably, it was the N.K.V.D. who were able to hang on longest and pull hardest, whilst the Poles were all the time losing ground.

Whole volumes could be filled with an account of these relief undertakings of the Embassy, and the subject still be hardly touched. A first indispensable condition was to obtain from the L.K.S.Z.[5] the same privilege, of purchase of a minimum per person of essential goods, as is granted to Soviet hospitals, orphanages, hostels, etc. This privilege again, so essential to the plan, was at no time either wholly conferred or wholly withheld. Many Polish institutions benefited from it, either intermittently or consistently. Others never enjoyed it at all.

In December 1941 approval was given to the establishment of infant schools in districts inhabited by Polish citizens in order to 'bring aid to children deprived of their parents'.

Yet permission to open schools for these children was never fully conceded. In some districts it was point-blank refused, in others tolerated. In still others, local authorities even helped when and where they could. In still others, schools which had been allowed to open were later closed. This discrepancy went on over the whole territory and throughout the whole period, with a rather more marked tendency than not to disapprove of schools and to class the desire to maintain them as having political significance. It was argued that with Russian schools available the Polish children did not require schools of their own. The Polish sentiment, of course, was that they required them very much, if they were not to forget even how to read and write in their own language. The children themselves passionately desired to attend Polish schools; this school being to them, of course, not only a school, but somewhere which could be felt to be their own, somewhere which, in contrast to everything in their lives since they had been forced away from their own country, was bright, clean, familiar and kind. In addition, older children, at least, did desperately regret their own descent into ignorance and illiteracy since 1939. Many of them were painfully aware that already, from moral exhaustion, shock, and physical deprivations of all kinds, their mental powers had become terribly blunted. Mental effort of all kind had become painful, unfamiliar and, to many, even impossible. If they were not now to make their way up out of the abyss into which they had been cast, in future years, however favourable the conditions, it would be entirely beyond their power. On this point, the bitterest regrets were felt. The older children, aware of the years which had been missed, besought, pleaded, urged, wept, and begged for at least pencil and paper; for at least a few old text-books, teachers and a blackboard; for the primitive outline, at least, of the Polish classes in which, had it not been for the war, they would have been moving normally forward, one year at a time.

Of all the tragic pictures presented by that assembly of spectres in the Soviet Union, I know of none more heart-rending than the picture of those stunted and starving children, imploring to be given books and instruction, imploring to be allowed to make up at least the grossest leeway of the time they had lost in the mines, the kolkhozy, and the penal settlements of an alien State which declares on all occasions its protection of and care for defenceless children. I have written with calm of other wrongs; I have attempted to approach with objectivity the starvation, demoralization, enforced labour and terrorization of these unhappy infants. It is impossible for me to write with calm of this further grief, of this supremely moving demand on a society which had robbed them of everything. I am not able, I shall not even try, to forgive a world in which that demand could be, and was and is, refused.

All of these children were devitalized, many blind and deaf from the effects of prolonged starvation; the majority had frost-bitten limbs, scurvy wounds, itch and sores of all kinds. Looking through photographs of these children taken in orphanages and schools, with the army and elsewhere, is like looking through a register of human skeletons. It is almost impossible to believe that a human being could be so thin and yet live. When, later, a small number of these children did leave Soviet territory, months passed before they could be fed on anything like the normal diet of a human animal. Actual physical alteration had taken place in the organs, especially in the digestive tract, making it impossible for the organism which had been living so long on roots, grass and refuse to absorb more normal foods. Post-mortems performed on children who died after evacuation to Persia, India and other places, showed layers of this normal food, especially fats, retained whole in the system, which had simply lost the power of absorbing or making use of them. Very much of the clothing and material for clothing which arrived from abroad, arrived in ruinous condition, having been soaked through many times over in transport and lain for months without being shaken out or dried. The long-awaited, passionately desired food parcels from abroad, when they arrived and were opened, turned for the same reasons to masses of mildew and corruption.

Boots, again, which looked durable and well-made, even of army pattern and studded with nails, were useless against the climate and conditions where the mud, dust and heat simply burnt them up, and to dream even of obtaining such commodities as paste or grease of any kind with which to preserve them was out of the question. In some institutions, clothing for the children was improvised out of blankets cut into roughly shaped jackets and trousers for girls and boys alike; but that left them without any other covering for the cold southern nights. Besides, 'we have immense difficulty in obtaining and in paying the very high prices asked for sewing cotton'.

A few institutions were comparatively better off. In Kagan, for example, much local aid was forthcoming right up to the end. In Bukhara, where 500 children attended a Polish school, the local authorities lent maps and exercise books, and gave a small stock of food. The children here were even able to run their own wall newspaper. In the Palevitsa region two infant schools were unique of their kind, permission to open having been granted only on condition that the Poles would accept the Soviet schoolchildren also. Half of the products in use came from the Polish Embassy and half from the Lespromkhoz. In contrast to such happier examples, in the Molotovska oblast, among others, the N.K.V.D. persistently asserted that there were no Poles there at all and consequently there was no object in organizing Polish relief or schools; yet it was known to the Embassy that in this very district there were 4,901 Poles for certain and possibly more, and that, out of these, 1,536 were children. The Molotovska oblast, unhappily, was by no means an exception, and is cited only as one example out of many.

In the infant schools, the children were at least warmed, fed and cared for, though with immense difficulty and in the most primitive style; but this was in itself so immense an advance on their former state that it was worth making the whole effort to have achieved this alone.

A few Polish books here and there had been smuggled inside a bundle of clothes or food at the time of the deportations. These volumes had been passed from hand to hand in settlements, lagiers and prisons; read, touched, kissed, and copied from, until there was almost nothing of them left. A rare textbook came to light among such volumes. Teachers improvised lessons in arithmetic, geography, nature study, history, etc. The children wrote and drew on doors in the absence of blackboards; knelt on the ground in the absence of forms and desks; instead of paper for their exercises they used the bark of trees and the cardboards and wrappings off the parcels containing clothing and drugs brought in by the Embassy from abroad. On their way to school, they were mobbed and even stoned in many villages. In the mud of autumn and spring and the deep snows of winter, the majority of them would never have reached school at all if some adult or elder child had not struggled along with them on their backs. Almost none of them had anything but rags in which to wrap their feet.

As with the question of schools, so with the equally urgent, and perhaps even more urgent, question of medical aid. The Soviet doctors were not nearly numerous enough to cope with the needs of the situation, and did not possess anything like enough medical supplies. Nevertheless, full permission for medical stations with Polish doctors was never obtained; on the whole, the authorities persistently opposed the plan. On the 10th of September 1942 only, consent was finally obtained for Polish doctors to collaborate officially in the work of certain institutions. The question of consent to travelling dispensaries and medical posts was still left open, and in practice the permission of September the 10th never really came into general effect. The same attitude and procedure was extended to the scheme for workshops of various kinds in which persons definitely unfit for work of other kinds might be trained to do light work of great value to the community, such as repairing footwear, taking care of clothing, carpentering, etc.

In what may be called the first stage of the Embassy plan, i. e. the opening and maintenance of orphanages for completely destitute children, of infant schools, soup kitchens, refuges for the disabled, shelters, mobile ambulatoriums with doctors and dentists, bath-houses, dining-rooms, workshops, etc. from October the 1st to February of 1942, organization went ahead rapidly. In Kazakstan, in particular, the first district of all to be organized, regional and local collaboration was friendly and even active. An orphanage was opened in Kustanaiz, a feeding centre and night refuge in Pavlodar, a school in Irkutsk, a school and other classes in Semipalatinsk, etc. I do not know whether enough has been said to convey even a slight idea of what an achievement all this was.

In the second phase, that is, from February onward, the Embassy set up over the whole territory a network of delegates, each of whom was charged first with representing the Poles of his own district and with distributing that proportion of Embassy relief, in money or kind, which could be got through to the district; and later with the organization and surveillance of Embassy institutions as they were established in the district. These delegates played a very great part in the plans for relief. What contact it was possible to establish and maintain between Poles throughout the Union, was established and maintained through these persons, men and women. Their record of achievements is indeed high. To find, and then to obtain possession of, premises of any kind for their institutions, was a problem at least as complicated as that of obtaining food and fuel with which to keep them going once the premises had been found. The cost of putting such a place to rights – even relying entirely on the volunteer labour of any able-bodied Poles there were – and of obtaining a few planks or (almost out of the question, this) a handful of nails to do it with was very often in excess of all the funds at the disposal of the organizers for the entire scheme. The cost of fuel permanently surpassed the funds at the disposal of anybody, nor was there often any to be had anyhow, at any price, official or otherwise. The same insoluble problems recur all the time in the files of all relief workers reporting from all over the Union. The following extracts have been chosen as characteristic of all:

'. . . We have organized a so-called brigade to deal with the problem of fuel. The fuel itself consists of every kind of wild plant which can be cut down in the steppe. The majority of these plants are covered with thorns. We have no wood and no coal. The stuff had first to be scythed, then stacked, then carted to the spot. The brigade consists each time of two to do the scything, two to do the stacking and piling on the cart, and one to do the actual carting. The horse is hired from the kolkhoz. The cost of keeping this brigade going amounts to 4,000 roubles, hire and feeding of the horse, 1,900 roubles.' 7 December 1942. Shaulderski, South Kazakhstan.

'. . . To give you a working idea of the economic problems we have to solve here, the best thing will be simply to describe the geographical layout of the settlement itself (Leninzdol). The settlement is in a deep ravine, surrounded by mountains, fifty kilometres from Dzabal-Abad. A rapidly flowing river, without a bridge anywhere, divides us from the neighbouring region of Bazar-Kurganski and in autumn and spring cuts us off entirely from the rest of the world. To establish communication with us at any time, the only way is to get across this river, which comes pouring down from the heights with great violence and rapidity. This position creates an infinity of difficulties in the way of our supply of food and fuel.' 4 December 1942.

From a larger orphanage in Majun-Kun, consisting of five little rooms or cells in the outbuildings of a kolkhoz plus a tiny storeroom, a clothes cupboard, another sort of recess-room used as a larder, and a passage: 'We have divided our rooms into (1) a dormitory for boys, (2) a dormitory for girls, (3) classroom plus dining-room, (4) office plus larder plus staff-room, (5) kitchen. The floors are earthen, the walls very wet, there is no glass in the window; in a word, the whole interior is that of a decayed byre and not of an educational establishment with possibilities of hygiene and suitable conditions for child-welfare. We possess twelve little beds. Whatever we do, we cannot possibly fit so many (sixty) children into or on to so few beds, and the majority sleep on the ground on mats made from reeds. The classroom-dining-room is also a dormitory at night, and, when we have to, we also use it as a laundry. The kolkhoz has no wash-house of its own, and it is now too cold for the women to stand and wash in the passage. We cook for the children in this passage, in a cauldron which is nothing like large enough; and we have so few utensils of every kind that the children have to eat by rota. The worst of all is the absolute impossibility of effecting any kind of isolation. Children arrive from the kolkhozy full of infections, especially itch, and there is no means of disinfecting them. The kolkhoz bath-house is not working, and we ourselves have no disinfectants of any kind, and in the event of an epidemic would be altogether helpless. Everything in our conditions would be favourable to the rapid spread of such a disaster.' 19 December 1942.

With all this, the setting up of a system of delegates, so advanced the possibilities of organization that by the 30th of March 1942 there existed twenty-four orphanages sheltering 2,135 children, thirty-five infant schools for 870 children, sixty-eight feeding centres providing meals for 3,117 persons, twelve refuges sheltering 800 invalids, ten schools, twenty-five organized classes, fifteen travelling medical posts disposing of sixty-eight doctors and fifty-seven medical orderlies, eleven 'hospitals' containing 745 beds, and thirteen night refuges.

During April, May and June this work of rehabilitation was greatly expanded. By June the 30th, throughout Kazakstan, the oblasts of Novo-Sibirsk and Altaisk, the whole of the south and the Republic of Komi, there existed 129 institutions caring for 6,012 children, thirty invalid homes, twenty-one feeding centres serving 3,570 persons, 115 other food kitchens, etc. As well as this, independently of the Embassy, in the territory in the south, the army maintained under its own care 4,632 children, chiefly orphans. . . .

However, there was soon to be a change for the worse.

It was now alleged that the concession of purchase of food and other essential goods at state prices had been intended strictly for the use of orphans in the legal sense of the word. The privilege was now either withdrawn or subject to sharp restrictions. Then in July, without warning, all the Embassy delegations were liquidated, the delegates themselves were arrested and the acts and documents of the delegations confiscated.[6] Throughout Kazakstan, where an enormous number of Poles were still concentrated, the relief organizations also – infant schools, orphanages, medical stations, etc. were closed down. Embassy property, including clothing, footwear, medical supplies, etc., was in places confiscated or put under seals.

This action, with the evacuation of the army, was a darkening of the scene and a foreshadowing of what was to come which in fact extinguished all practical Polish hopes in Soviet territory. From now on, though the scene for the final act was not yet, the pace became almost furious. One terrible event followed another, until after the second army evacuation in August only a vast mass of unarmed and increasingly helpless women, children, and civilians were left behind. Very large numbers of Polish citizens remained in or were returning to prison. Others were being incorporated in the Red Army, or posted to labour battalions or to Soviet factories.

Editors' Notes

1. General Sikorski, an important military figure in the Polish–Soviet War of 1919–20 and the Prime Minister in the coalition government of 1923–4, had opposed Piłsudski's dictatorship after the May coup in 1926. He became head of the Polish government-in-exile, established in France on 30 September 1939, and later transferred to London after the French capitulation to Nazi Germany.

He was killed on 4 July 1943 when his plane crashed into the sea off Gibraltar.

2. A town on the Volga to which many of the departments of the Soviet government were transferred in late 1941 in face of the advance of the German army. The Polish embassy was located there. (See Map 2, pages 34–5 above.)

3. Professor Stanisław Kot, the Polish ambassador to the USSR.

4. After his evacuation from the Soviet Union to Persia one Polish officer, who had, by a miracle, escaped the fate of so many of his friends and brother officers at the mass execution in Katyn, expressed his revulsion as follows: 'There were rumours that Russia was advancing and was going to capture Persia. We told ourselves that if Russia were to do this, we would set out to walk over the desert to Africa, to the jungle, anywhere but not into Russian hands' (editors' transcripts).

5. LKSZ, acronym for Lespromkhoz, a Soviet supply organization.

6. Vyshinsky (Deputy Commissar for Foreign Affairs) gave as the reason for this action: 'because all the delegations had engaged in hostile activity and espionage instead of welfare . . . Unable to give any proofs, Vyshinsky took refuge behind a cloak of mystery', (postscript in Stanisław Kot (1963) *Conversations with the Kremlin and dispatches from Russia*, Oxford: Oxford University Press, p. 271).

Afterword

The people of Poland suffered intensely during the Second World War, irrespective of social class and ethnicity. The Nazis and the Soviet authorities were equally blameworthy, although Nazi atrocities received more publicity in the immediate post-war years. When Zajdlerowa's account of Polish experiences at the hands of the Russians was published it rang true, as reviewers commented. But was it expressing only a partial truth, did it exaggerate or distort, was its emotion designed to shape opinion before all the facts were available and a calm judgement could be made? Was the publication designed to speed the hardening of western opinion against their great wartime ally? The publication of so many accounts of the Soviet system of penal camps and prisons since 1946 have assuredly confirmed Zajdlerowa's testimony.

Nevertheless, there have been attempts, if not to exculpate the Soviets, at least to show them in a relatively favourable light in comparison with the Nazis. Needless to say, such apologia have not generally originated with the Poles. Interviews with survivors of deportations to both Germany and the Soviet Union have revealed that there is no disposition to place the perpetrators of death and terror in some sort of hierarchy with the Nazis at the top and the Soviets further down. These survivors are not prepared to accept that there is any distinction, from the viewpoint of the sufferers, between the destroyers of a national group and the eliminators of a social and political category. They cannot accept that there was any qualitative difference between camps in Germany and in the Soviet Union. All were death camps, and though life was prolonged in the Soviet Union, death's progress was inexorable, as Solzhenitsyn, who should know, has argued:

> The main thing is: avoid *general-assignment work*. Avoid it from the day you arrive. If you land in *general-assignment work* that first day, then you are lost, and this time for keeps . . . that it is in the main and basic work performed in any given camp. Eighty per cent of the prisoners work at it, and they all die off. All . . . The only ones who *survive* in camps are those who try at any price not to be put on general-assignment work. From the first day.[1]

Similarly there was no hope of release in either system. The Poles believed

171

fervently that they would get out, but they were in an exceptional position. The Russian prisoners had no expectations at all of release or survival, and were amazed when Poles were let out after the amnesty. If, by some chance, you survived your eight years, the NKVD would slap a repeat sentence on you. Death came fast or lingeringly, but it assuredly came. To assert, as Levi does, that death was not expressly sought in the Soviet camp system is a partial truth.[2] Re-education and labour were other aims, but it was self-deception or misunderstanding on the prisoners' part not to accept that an eight-year sentence was tantamount to a sentence of execution. It is widely accepted that the camps were an ugly stain on Soviet socialism. But while socialism and camps are not generally regarded as indivisible, the same cannot be said about Nazism and camps. Neither can it be said about Stalinism and camps. Gross has used the term 'spoiler state' to describe the Soviet Union, and quotes Stalin's maxim that 'the State under communism wages war on society', commenting that the Stalinist system 'predicated a massive extermination of its subjects', comparable to 'wars between sovereign states'.[3]

Hence, while the Nazis eliminated or enslaved enemies of the Aryan race and those who obstructed the achievement of Nazi strategic objectives, the Soviets liquidated or enslaved enemies of the people or party and those who stood in the way of *their* strategic goals. General Anders, who had suffered in Soviet prisons, was outspokenly anti-Soviet and shocked Churchill when he burst out in conversation: 'There was no justice and honour in Russia, and there was not a single man in that country whose word could be trusted.'[4] His commander-in-chief and Prime Minister, General Sikorski, a man of careful judgement, given to sober assessment of the facts and politically aware, could not refrain, again in conversation with Churchill, from venting his indignation and anguish at the treatment of his fellow Poles in the Soviet Union, referring to 'the unbelievable brutality and refinement in the tortures inflicted by the Bolsheviks on many Poles', and 'the monstrously barbarian methods of the Russians' which were beyond all belief.[5]

Such sentiments, based on evidence independent of Polish sources and which corroborate the subject matter of *The Dark Side of the Moon*, could also have reached Churchill through official British channels:

When the Red Army marched into Poland . . . mass arrests and transportation to prisons and penal servitude in Russia commenced at once. . . . Nobody will suppose that the arrest and deportation of . . . Polish subjects by the N.K.V.D. . . . was a haphazard affair, and that they just grabbed anybody without plan. It had behind it a very definite plan, and the classes involved are themselves an indication of the policy adopted by the Russian Government in Poland. . . . The manner and condition of transportation, and the fate awaiting these people in the most distant and dreaded areas of Siberia and the Far North, can leave no doubt in the mind of anybody in a position to study the subject on the spot, that the aim was that they should not return. A great number have died from lack of food, exhaustion and epidemics. We all know the job it has been recently to recover a mere handful – those evacuated recently to Persia with the first party of troops. The great majority remain for the most part beyond reach of help, due to distances, lack of transport and travel facilities, and the withholding by the Soviet Government of cooperation to Polish Red Cross and Embassy workers. The latter in fact, now – June 1942 – meet with obstruction in their endeavour to reach and help their people. . . .[6]

How was such evidence of Soviet action against Poles, reaching the West from Polish as well as from British sources, interpreted? The Soviet threat to Poland's future was perceived by the London Poles as being even greater than that of the Nazis. The British Foreign Office drew a different distinction between Soviet and Nazi policy towards Poland: 'The Russians are concerned primarily to destroy not a national but a social order'.[7]

In our view there is nothing to be gained by making distinctions, however subtle, between two types of human destruction. Both should be equally abhorred and the victims, in either case, honoured in our remembrance.[8]

The fate of Poles in Russia *was* known in British and American government circles several years before the publication of *The Dark Side of the Moon*. Some of the facts had leaked out in London but Soviet sympathizers on the left of the political spectrum rejected them as the product of Fascist disinformation. Although the Poles were an honoured ally of the British, and Churchill held Sikorski in high esteem, Foreign Office officials tended to think of the Poles as causing difficulties.[9] The record of the Polish government in domestic policy between the wars was not widely admired. Perhaps Keynes's cutting verdict that the Poles' only industry was anti-Semitism had been widely shared in ruling circles in London. Furthermore, there was little support for Polish territorial gains in the Treaty of Riga in 1921.

Nevertheless the cruel experiences of the Poles since 1939 ought to have swung British and American opinion in their favour. That they failed to do so was not mainly attributable to the ineffectiveness of the publicity and propaganda department of the Polish government, although it bore some responsibility. The Poles faced an uphill fight to win public sympathy owing to the appreciation in leading British circles of the importance of the Soviet Union to the success of the war against Hitler. Since the British and the Americans were, in 1942 and 1943, dependent on the Soviet Union, and the Polish government was dependent on the

British and the Americans, there was little the Poles could do to influence public opinion against the USSR, in the matter of the deportations and the camps. Not only would Western opinion be likely to reject the facts in face of a Soviet counter-attack, the truth was that the Western allies put pressure on the Poles not to make their facts public for fear of alienating the Soviet Union and driving her into a separate peace with Germany which could have been disastrous to the Allied cause.

British sentiments towards the Soviet Union had fluctuated in the early war years. The Soviet invasion of Poland's eastern provinces was greeted with understanding in London, but the Soviet attack on Finland on 30 November 1939 brought an abrupt halt to British efforts for a *rapprochement* with the Russians. British public opinion was outraged and the British press denounced the USSR in the sharpest terms. However, following Hitler's attack in the west in May 1940 Churchill looked again to the Soviet Union, despite the frigidity of Anglo–Soviet relations since the Russo–Finnish war. Sir Stafford Cripps, labour politician and warmly pro-Soviet, was appointed British Ambassador in Moscow.[10] Throughout May and June 1941 the British Foreign Office passed to Maisky, the Soviet Ambassador in London, information about the German military build up. When the Nazi attack on the Soviet Union was launched, public opinion became enthusiastic in its support of the Soviet Union as an ally. During the last weeks of 1941 and the first part of 1942 the British press, the BBC and public opinion in general was so enthusiastic about Soviet military efforts that Maisky intervened with the Ministry of Information and directors of the BBC to tone down their descriptions and to emphasize the difficulty of the Soviet Union's position. In December *The Times* carried an advertisement about Mrs Churchill's 'Red Cross Aid to Russia Fund' affirming that the British people welcomed the opportunity 'of showing their individual appreciation of the sacrifice and suffering of the Russians . . .'. Soviet heroism was being praised especially by the Beaverbrook press, which called urgently for a second front to relieve the Soviet ally. This was consistent with Beaverbrook's view, expressed at the time of his visit to Moscow in October 1941 that 'There is today only one military problem – how to help Russia'.[11]

During the same period in the United States, individuals with strong pro-Soviet inclinations had the president's ear. Harry Hopkins in particular argued for a special relationship with the Soviet Union. The American press and public opinion were also becoming pro-Soviet in thought. R. M. Ingersoll, the influential editor of the New York daily *P.M.*, argued for a Soviet sphere of influence in a divided Europe and the large and vocal organization, Russian War Relief Inc., expounded the Soviet Union's right to Poland's eastern territories. The 1942 edition of the *Encyclopaedia Britannica* omitted Poland, simply showing the Soviet Union and Germany separated by the Ribbentrop–Molotov line.[12]

Roosevelt, though, preferred to leave the problem of Polish–Soviet relations in British hands to avoid alienating the five million Polish American supporters of the Democratic Party. The British government followed a policy of appeasement of Stalin; they had little choice in the matter. When Sikorski claimed in March 1942 that he might not be able to prevent publication of a book detailing Soviet treatment of Poles in the camps and prisons if the British recognized Soviet territorial demands in Eastern Europe, Churchill and Eden 'energetically objected to the publication of such documents'. Churchill later had occasion to warn Anders about expressing publicly his virulent criticism of the Soviet Union: 'No good would come of antagonizing the Russians'.[13] Later in the same month Churchill explained to Sikorski why he was in no position to demand anything of Russia; the Allies could claim no military victories and were unable to give Russia any effective assistance, even in war equipment. By contrast Russia had not only suffered grave losses in men, equipment and territory but had inflicted a punishing blow on German military strength by destroying a quarter of German military manpower. Ready to make concessions to Russia when she was suffering defeats in order to deflect her from making a separate peace, the Allies were in no position to resist Soviet territorial claims in Eastern Europe when the military balance swung in her favour.

Nor was it possible for them to come out openly in support of Polish criticism of Russian treatment of the deported Poles. On his return from the Casablanca Conference in January 1943 Roosevelt told the Polish Ambassador in Washington that the moment was unfavourable for diplomatic intervention in Moscow because the Russians were 'in a phase of considerable success'. He advised the Polish government 'to keep their shirts on'. The Poles gained no support from the Allies when they protested about the forcible imposition of Soviet citizenship on Poles in the Soviet Union. Neither was there to be any 'strong intervention on behalf of Poland in Moscow' on the question of Poland's claims for her original eastern boundaries.[14] When Stalin's claim to the Curzon line was made public for the first time on 1 March 1943 there was such a vociferous debate on the future of Poland in the Western media that the British government decided to place curbs on the press in case it upset Allied unity. The battle for the Polish eastern provinces was fought out in the public domain where Polish interests were submerged in an anti-Polish, pro-Soviet environment.[15]

Soviet propaganda put the Poles on the defensive, attacking the Polish government-in-exile and the Polish émigré press for 'plotting to tear the

Ukraine apart' and challenging the right of the Polish government to represent Poland. Wanda Wasilewska accused the Polish government in *Izvestia* of being controlled by Hitlerite elements, the leaders of Anders' army of being anti-Semitic and the Poles of harbouring imperialistic ambitions towards Soviet territory.[16]

The firmest evidence that the Poles had lost the battle for Western minds is revealed in two episodes where the Soviet Union was placed on the defensive and still managed to emerge relatively unscathed. The first of these concerned Henryk Erlich and Viktor Alter, two Polish Jews who were prominent leaders of the Bund, taken into Soviet captivity after the Soviet invasion of Poland. The case should be examined in the context of accusations of anti-Semitism against the Polish government and army made in the Western press. Sikorski had issued an order to the Polish army on 5 August 1940 strictly forbidding any unfriendliness towards soldiers of the Jewish faith 'through contemptuous remarks or anything humiliating to human dignity'. All such offences were to be severely punished and the order was to be read on parade to all soldiers. Sikorski also included Jews in his government and the wife of one member of the first National Council was the prime minister's private secretary.[17]

When Polish relief agencies were established in the Soviet Union after the Polish–Soviet agreement of 31 July 1941, most Polish welfare officials treated Jews without discrimination and thousands of Polish Jews, for example Menachim Begin, the future prime minister of Israel, owed their lives to the Polish welfare system. In fact, Jewish Poles on the whole fared better than Christian Poles because a large number were located in urban centres and had easier contact with relief agencies, whereas Christian Poles tended to be settled in the countryside and were more isolated.[18]

Soviet officials prevented the departure of many Jewish Poles in the evacuations. The Soviet authorities blamed the decision on Polish officials, but their refusal to permit Jews to claim Polish citizenship and their reluctance to allow harmful reports of the deportations and imprisonments to reach the West gave them an inducement to place responsibility on the Poles.

The case of Erlich and Alter highlights the strength of pro-Soviet sentiments in the West and weakens the charge of anti-Semitism directed against the Poles. On their release from prison in the Soviet Union they became involved in the debate about the status of Jewish Poles and were opposed to the formation of separate Jewish units in the Polish Army as advocated by Zionists and extreme right-wingers. They expressed loyalty to the Polish government and asked to be represented in the National Council. Their loyalty and influence meant that on 4

December 1941 they were re-arrested as German spies. Before their arrest they had sent messages, embarrassing to the Soviet Union, to their contacts in the West.[19]

There were widespread protests in the West when news broke of their second arrest. Many prominent personalities, among them Eleanor Roosevelt, Wendell Willkie, William Green, the president of the American Federation of Labor, and other labour leaders protested against their imprisonment and interceded on their behalf. In reply to a further telegram to Molotov on 27 January 1943, the Soviet government issued a statement towards the end of February announcing Erlich's and Alter's executions in the previous December. This generated enormous indignation in the United States, particularly in the labour and socialist movements, which issued a statement rejecting as absurd and slanderous the Soviet accusation that Erlich and Alter were advocating a separate peace with Nazi Germany. Yet despite the injustice, the protesters were determined to prevent the incident dividing the Allies. A mass meeting of trade unionists in New York on 30 March 1943, while scornfully rejecting the charges against Erlich and Alter, resolved that it would not allow the incident to weaken the Allied cause. 'Neither can or will the terrible judgment and execution of our two friends . . . diminish our admiration for the heroic, indeed superhuman, achievements of the Russian people . . . against Nazism and aggression and for freedom'. In short, the protests against the executions were not to be allowed to affect the unity of the Allies in the war against Hitler. Soon, however, the event was forgotten. It became apparent that this act of totalitarian brutality would not affect the pro-Soviet sympathies rapidly gaining ground in the United States.[20]

The second episode concerned the missing Polish army officers who had been a constant concern of the Polish government-in-exile since the re-establishment of Polish–Soviet relations. Numerous inquiries of the Soviet government failed to elicit any credible information about their whereabouts or movements after they were taken from the three camps where they had been held since being deported from Poland. Then, on 13 April 1943, Berlin radio announced the discovery of the bodies of about 10,000 Polish officers buried in mass graves in the Smolensk area. According to the broadcast, German troops had been taken by locals to a place called Kosogory at the northern end of Katyń wood, an area occupied by the Germans since 14 July 1941. Here 'the Bolsheviks had perpetrated secretly mass executions'.[21]

The Soviet Information Bureau in London alleged that the German statement was a fabrication by 'Goebbels' slanderers'. The Polish Cabinet met and, in view of the gravity of the charge, decided to seek an explanation from the Soviet embassy in London and to ask the International Red Cross to investigate. In the absence of General Sikorski, General Kukiel issued a detailed account of the Polish–Soviet communications concerning the missing Polish officers. His statement ended with the words:

> We have become accustomed to the lies of German propaganda and we understand the purpose behind its latest revelations. In view however of the abundant and detailed German information concerning the discovery . . . and the categorical statement they [the missing Polish officers] were murdered by Soviet authorities in the Spring of 1940, the necessity has arisen that the mass graves discovered should be investigated and the facts alleged verified.[22]

Stalin broke off relations with the Polish government, describing its behaviour towards the USSR as completely abnormal and expressing resentment that the Sikorski Government failed to counter the 'infamous fascist slander against the USSR'. So far from backing the reasonable Polish requests, western press and public opinion showed scant sympathy for the Polish government. In an American paper, Stalin was compared to 'plain speaking' Andrew Jackson.[23] Western news media gave full coverage to lengthy *Tass* invectives but failed to mention the Polish case. Unsurprisingly, the *Daily Worker* in London accused the Poles of being in direct contact with the Germans, but Low's cartoon in the *Evening Standard* (Goebbels driving a wedge in British–Russian–American unity aided by Sikorski) must have presented the Polish government with dismal evidence of how far public opinion had deserted them. A. J. Cummings in the *News Chronicle* reinforced this conclusion when he charged that 'the Poles are inveterate propagandists and always have been. What they seem now to forget is that their liberation can come about only through the exertions and sacrifices of the Russians with whom they are constantly picking dangerous quarrels'. A TUC resolution of 30 April 1943 implied the Polish government was fascist.[24]

Churchill urged reconciliation on Stalin, unsuccessfully. He hoped to obtain Russian concessions on the further evacuation of Poles by persuading Sikorski to withdraw entirely 'from the position he has been forced by his public opinion to adopt'. Churchill was concerned to limit the damage to the Polish position; of all British ministers, he was most sympathetic and admiring of the Poles' valour and courage and their contributions to the Allied cause. But in the face of this atrocity, which at the very least deserved investigation, Churchill undertook to persuade Sikorski to back down and to free himself from his militant constituency. The Poles had held their tongues for a long time, under British pressure not to alienate Stalin. It would have been intolerable to have kept silent on an issue which had concerned them deeply for three years. Their response was moderate. Churchill was trying to assist the Polish position *vis-à-vis* the Soviet Union, but his well meant appeasement came too late to prevent Stalin's wrath being directed at the Polish government.[25] As a result of the break in diplomatic relations, the Poles in Russia were isolated from their government, and the Poles in the West lost much of their remaining support in public opinion. In this context we can better appreciate Zajdlerowa's determination to lay before the public the treatment of her compatriots by the Soviet Union between 1939 and 1943; to constitute, in short, 'a record and a memorial'.

Editors' Notes

1. Alexander I. Solzhenitsyn (1973–4) *The Gulag Archipelago*, New York: Harper and Row, Part II, p. 564.
2. Primo Levi (1957) 'Afterword: The Author's Answers to His Readers' Questions', in *If This is a Man. The Truce*, London: Abacus, pp. 391–2.
3. See Jan T. Gross (1989) *Revolution from Abroad: The Soviet Conquest of Poland's Western Ukraine and Western Belorussia*, Princeton: Princeton University Press, pp. 225–40. See also the excellent review article of this important book by Anna Bramwell in *The Times Higher Education Supplement*, 13 January, 1989; see also note 9, page 41, for an additional interpretation of Stalinist economic policy in Poland, 1939–41.
4. *Documents on Polish–Soviet Relations*, p. 422.
5. *Ibid*, p. 299 and see note 4, page 37.
6. Report from Lt. Col. L. R. Hulls (British Liaison Officer to General Anders' GHQ) to H.E. The (British) Ambassador, Kuibyshev, 18 June 1942. PRO, FO 371/31088, XC/7 011475. See also note 37, page 43.
7. Minutes on the report produced by the Polish Ministry for Foreign Affairs in May 1941, "L'Occupation Allemande et Sovietique de la Pologne", PRO, FO 371, 26724, C4932. Also referred to in J. Coutouvidis and J. Reynolds (1986) *Poland 1939–47*, Leicester: The University Press, p. 109.
8. Nicholas Bethel (1972) *The War Hitler Won: September, 1939*, London: Allen Lane, p. 347.
9. See minutes of 18 January 1940 by F. K. Roberts and R. Makins on Letter from Prince Radziwill in Warsaw, PRO, FO 371/26723, C278.
10. See also notes 51 and 55, page 44.
11. *The Times*, 10 December 1941; see also PISM, PRM 73/1, 23 April 1942.
12. R. E. Sherwood (1948) *The White House Papers of Harry L. Hopkins*, London: Eyre and Spottiswoode, I, pp. 395–6.
13. *Documents on Polish–Soviet Relations*, pp. 299, 422.
14. *Ibid*, p. 427; see also Churchill's letter to Roosevelt, 1 March 1942, in W. S. Churchill (1951) *The Second World War. The Hinge of Fate*, London: Cassell,

IV, p. 293; Jan Ciechanowski (1947) *Defeat in Victory*, New York: Doubleday, pp. 151–2, 156.

15. *Documents on Polish–Soviet Relations*, p. 501. See also article by Alexander Korneychuk in *Radianska Ukraina*, 19 February 1943, reprinted in *New York Times*, 21 February 1943.

16. *Izvestia*, 28 March 1943. Wanda Wasilewska was a leading spirit behind the Polish Communist paper *New Horizons* published in Lwów in 1939 after the Soviet invasion. She became a leader of the Union of Polish Patriots founded in the Soviet Union, 1 March, 1943 and married Korneychuk (see note 15 above), Deputy Commissar for Foreign Affairs.

17. Within the Polish National Council (a substitute, in exile, for a parliament) Herman Lieberman and Ignacy Schwarzbart were Jews. It was the latter who in June 1942 informed the FO of genocide of Jews in Poland (see PRO, FO 371/31097 C11658). Lieberman served in Sikorski's government from 3 September 1941 until his death on 21 October 1941. He was Minister of Justice. His wife was Sikorski's private secretary.

18. See PISM, PRM 71, Memorandum from Ciechanowski to Sumner Welles, 17 July 1942 and PISM, PRM 74/3, 9 May 1942, a letter from Jewish citizens expressing thanks to the Polish government.

19. See *Foreign Relations of the United States, Diplomatic Papers, 1942*, Washington, DC: Government Printing Office, 1961, III, p. 172.

20. See the pamphlet (1943) *The Case of Henryk Erlich and Victor Alter*, foreword by Camille Huysmans, London: Liberty Publications; and Isabelle Tombs (1988) 'Erlich and Alter, "The Sacco and Vanzetti of the USSR". An Episode in the Wartime History of International Socialism', *Journal of Contemporary History*, vol. 23, no. 4, October, pp. 531–50.

21. *Documents on Polish–Soviet Relations*, pp. 523–4. Of a number of studies concerning Katyn, the best is by J. K. Zawodny (1967) *Death in the Forest, the Story of the Katyn Massacre*, London: Macmillan. See note 36 on page 43. The father of our interviewee quoted in the Acknowledgements (page x) is listed in A. Mosżyński (1974) *Lista Katynska (the Katyn List)*, London: Gryf, p. 31. See also J. Coutouvidis and J. Reynolds, *Poland 1939–47*, p. 327, note 26. *The Times*, 8 March 1989, reported 'Poland accused the Soviet Union for the first time yesterday of having committed the massacres of more than 4,000 Polish officers at Katyń forest . . .'

22. *Documents on Polish–Soviet Relations*, p. 525. See also *Christian Science Monitor*, 30 April 1943.

23. *Evening Standard*, 29 April 1943; *News Chronicle*, 27 April 1943; *Daily Herald*, 30 April 1943. Jackson, President of the United States, 1829–37, was renowned for his humble origins, directness and identification with the interests of the common man.

24. See *Daily Herald*, 30 April 1943.

25. *Documents on Polish–Soviet Relations*, p. 535.

Bibliography

The following selection of articles, books and collections of documents, published in English, are suggested to readers who may wish to pursue the theme of *The Dark Side of the Moon* at greater depth. References to material published in Polish and to specific files in archives held in London (Archives of the Polish Underground Study Trust, APUST – Polish Institute and Sikorski Museum, PISM – Public Record Office, PRO) are contained in the notes to the Introduction (pages 37–46) and Afterword (pages 179–80).

Anon (1946) *The Dark Side of the Moon*, London: Faber and Faber.

Conquest, Robert (1968) *The Great Terror*, London: Macmillan.

Coutouvidis, John (1986) 'T. S. Eliot's preface to *The Dark Side of the Moon*: His model of society in the light of Polish experience', *Text and Context. A Journal of Interdisciplinary Studies*, I, no. 1, autumn.

Coutouvidis, John and Reynolds, Jaime (1986) *Poland, 1939–1947*, Leicester: Leicester University Press.

Coutouvidis, John, Garlicki, Andrzej and Reynolds, Jaime (1990) 'Poland', in Salter, S. and Stevenson, J. (eds) *Working Class and Politics in Europe and America, 1929–45*, London: Longman.

Documents on Polish Soviet Relations (1961) edited by the General Sikorski Historical Institute, renamed PISM, vol. 1, 1939–42, London: Heinemann.

Feis, Herbert (1967) *Churchill, Roosevelt, Stalin: the War They Waged and the Peace They Sought*, Princeton: Princeton University Press.

Grudzińska-Gross, Irena and Gross, Jan Tomasz (1981) *War Through Children's Eyes. The Soviet Occupation of Poland and the Deportations, 1939–41*, Stanford: Hoover Institution Press.

Gross, Jan T. (1988) *Revolution from Abroad. The Soviet Conquest of Poland's Western Ukraine and Western Belorussia*, Princeton: Princeton University Press.

Herling, Gustav (1987) *A World Apart*, (1951) reprinted Oxford: Oxford University Press.

Kennan, George (1958) *Siberia and the Exile System*, vols 1 and 2 (1891); reprinted in one volume, Chicago: University of Chicago Press.

Koestler, Arthur (1964) *The Yogi and the Commissar* (1945), reprinted London: Jonathan Cape.

Kot, Stanisław (1963) *Conversations with the Kremlin and Dispatches from Russia*, London: Oxford University Press.

Kusnierz, Bronisław (1949) *Stalin and the Poles: An Indictment of the Soviet Leaders*, London: Hollis and Carter.

Solzhenitsyn, Alexander Isayevich (1973–4) *The Gulag Archipelago*, parts I and II, New York: Harper and Row.

Tombs, Isabella (1988) 'Erlich and Alter, "The Sacco and Vanzetti of the USSR": An episode in the wartime history of international socialism', *Journal of Contemporary History*, vol. 23, no. 4, October.

Umiastowski, Roman, *Russia and the Polish Republic, 1918–1941*, London: Aquafondata, n.d.

United States (1951–2) *Hearings before the Select Committee to Conduct an Investigation of the Facts, Evidence and Circumstances of the Katyn Forest Massacre*, 82 Congr. 1 and 2 Sess. House Select Committee, Washington Government Printing Office.

Zawodny, Janusz (1971) *Death in the Forest: The Story of the Katyn Forest Massacre*, London: Macmillan.

Anon (Zoë Zajdlerowa) (1940) *My Name is Million: The experiences of an Englishwoman in Poland*, London: Faber.